THE STUDENT ACTOR'S HANDBOOK

Theatre Games and Exercises

Louis John Dezseran
University of Minnesota, Minneapolis

Mayfield Publishing Company

For all the game players, especially
Cathy, Mickey, Susan, and Patti.

First edition 1975

Library of Congress Catalog Card Number: 75-270
International Standard Book Number: 0-87484-324-3

Manufactured in the United States of America
Mayfield Publishing Company
285 Hamilton Avenue, Palo Alto, California 94301

This book was set in Illumna by Applied Typographic Systems and was printed and bound by the George Banta Company. Sponsoring editor was C. Lansing Hays, Carole Norton supervised editing, and Liselotte Hofmann was manuscript editor. Michelle Hogan supervised production, and the book and cover were designed by Nancy Sears. Text illustrations by Nancy Lawton, and cover photo by Dennis Anderson.

CONTENTS

PREFACE

This is more than a textbook. It is a book of games, a supportive guide designed primarily for the serious student of acting. Even if you are such a student, this book alone will not teach you acting—no book, no person can teach anyone that. The aim here is less audacious and more practical: to complement and extend your studies by showing you how to play theatre games. These games, or exercises, can truly help you to let go, to concentrate, and to communicate not only your own thoughts and feelings but those of the character you are playing.

You can play some of these games by yourself, some with a partner, some with a group. And while all of them can be done outside your class if you are in a scheduled course of study, many of them will work equally well in class. Be careful not to approach the games in a forced or erratic manner. It has been said that "in calmness, there should be activity; in activity there should be calmness." Try to do the exercises with this in mind, harmonizing them with your studies, making them serious fun, not frantic pursuits. Be willing and open. Let the games lead you to combine imagination and technique in such a way that your audience, as well as you, can derive pleasure from your performance.

Of course, working actors, too, can apply and develop these games to enrich their art; and teachers may find the book a resource for ideas and for illustrative exercises.

Practitioners of theatre games comprise a long list of teacher-professionals: William Ball, Alan Fletcher, and Edward Hastings of the American Conservatory Theatre, San Francisco; Charles Werner Moore of Brandeis University;

Hal J. Todd of San Jose State University; Dugal MacArthur of Temple University; Lewis Palter and Robert Benedetti of the California Institute of the Arts Valencia; Richard Brown of the University of California, Riverside; Mamako Yoneyama and Carlo Mazzone-Clementi, internationally famous mimes, who now operate their own schools and theatres; Robert Moulton and Wesley Balk of the University of Minnesota; Mary Corrigan of Florida State University; and Ken Ruta of the Minnesota Theatre Company. I am grateful to have been a student or a colleague of these teachers and performers during the past fifteen years. This book is a composite of my experience with the games techniques and with improvisations under their guidance.

It is possible that several of these teacher-professionals no longer use the games that are attributed to them, or that they have modified them to some extent. Each game is presented in the text as closely as possible to the way it was introduced to me in my acting studies. The games offered here are the ones that have helped the greater number of students to appreciate and explore the craft of acting.

I wish to thank all the actors, directors, mimes, and teachers who have allowed me to use or adapt their ideas in this text. Of course, many of the games and techniques included here have been handed down through generations by a legion of professionals and teachers, some of whom practiced their craft perhaps as long as two hundred years ago. To trace the originators of many of these exercises would probably be impossible and would serve no purpose anyway. It is far more important that those of us in the theatre share our thoughts as we explore what works for us in our performing.

INTRODUCTION

If you have ever gone onstage in front of an audience, you know that special quiver, that sensation just below your belt that says, "It's up to you to make this production work." If you are lucky, you are more excited than nervous. Perhaps you can rest on some of the techniques you learned in your early training days. Perhaps you can assure yourself that your coach and your director have prepared you well. You may be kidding yourself, but as long as the production clicks, you can retain your old confidence. However, if your performance should be a little "off" this time, if some of your old techniques fail, or if the work you did in reshearsal with such zest and appeal seems suddenly stale and lifeless, it may be time to re-examine the creative foundation that you've built your technique on. Somehow you're going to have to find a way to relax and trust yourself. Of course, there are no proven formulas for success in any art form, and that knowledge is no solace to you now.

The answer to your problems is as close as the nearest actor onstage with you. Ask yourself: Did I really listen to the last words he spoke? Do I know why the playwright wrote this scene for at least two actors to perform, instead of simply writing a soliloquy or a narrative? What do I need from every other actor who happens to be onstage with me right now? Once you know what you need from your co-performers onstage, you can plot a logical plan of action to fill your need. If you are truly talking to your fellow actors onstage, sharing an experience with them, and playing with them, you must be on the right track.

All animals need to play and human beings are no exception.[1] You may have to retrain yourself to play, to have fun. No matter how real any moment appears onstage, you are still pretending. The better the performer you are, the more successful you are at giving the audience the impression that something is actually happening up there onstage. In order to satisfy your audience's need to play, you yourself must learn how to play with your fellow artists and with your own sense of imaginative realities.

An acting coach or a director must be a vicarious animal. His function is to promote and guide a spirit of creativity within a group of heterogeneous people. Such a responsibility can be tenuous, frustrating, and deeply rewarding at the same time. He must encourage his actors to play together and to trust him, one another, and themselves. It is a tricky job. Some members of his group may have to be whipped into activity; some may freeze if their director merely looks at them; others may need to exhibit themselves constantly. If you have become a lonely virtuoso, whether it be in high school, in college, in your community, or in the professional world you may have to accept the fact that you will have to unlearn some bad habits before you can begin to play with your colleagues freely or to put an emotional claim on them, so to speak, with simplicity and economy.

Words like "honesty" and "sincerity" are so loaded with social implications that they are often worthless in referring to the craft of acting. Try to create a concrete vocabulary. Criticism can be constructive only if cogent terms are used to describe the efficiency with which you communicate the dramatic conflict that you begin to experience while rehearsing with the other actors in a specific scene. The coach, the director, and you, the performer, must construct both a vocabulary and a technique that promote the act of "playing" in clear and tangible terms.

Since the word "playing" is the handmaiden of the word "games," the expression "theatre games" makes delightful sense. The type of creativity encouraged by the theatre-games process itself accounts for its success; for example, actors with a wide range of experience can participate in the improvisations inherent in the games method. Games themselves present approximately the same responsibilities that you will encounter in public performance. Constructive criticism can easily be applied to the success of each game. The observers and participants share the self-satisfying feeling that something spontaneous and alive is taking place. Perhaps the most significant aspect of theatre games is that you will learn to teach yourself by creating a situation similar to the one in which your character finds himself.

During the last decade, actor training has undergone a phenomenal historical development: exercises have replaced purely didactic lessons as the basic method of instruction in both conservatories and universities. Viola Spolin is the acknowledged progenitor of the movement toward the improvisational instruction called theatre games.[2] The technique of theatre games is as old as Thespis and the ritual dances of ancient man that anthropologists label "sympathetic magic."[3] Spolin's work formalizes what might be considered a return to the most basic dramatic instruction: the re-formation of the actual creative process inherent in life itself—play.

Constantin Stanislavski used improvisational methods both as part of his daily classroom instruction and as rehearsal technique in as specialized a field of performance as opera.[4] Theatres such as the American Conservatory Theatre (ACT) of San Francisco have approached theatre games with such exuberance that improvisation has become a way of life for the performers.

Everyone who uses the games technique seems to have his own opinion about the method of application as well as the end-result of improvisation. Working on verse drama with a group of young professionals, Stanislavski employed a technique he called "rough sketching."[5] He defined the characterizations and circumstances for his actors and then gave them objectives to play that were similar to the objectives of the roles in the structured play. He repeated the improvisations, refining as he progressed, until his actors spoke words similar to the ones the playwright had selected.

In another experiment, Stanislavski attempted to create a situation that would provide a young actress with an emotional response that jibed with the nature of the character she was playing. Her job was to play a lost blind child. Stanislavski turned off all the lights in the theatre, hid himself, and commanded the young girl to find him in the dark. As she reached her peak of emotional confusion, the girl automatically began to speak her character's lines, echoing the playwright's intent.[6] Of course, Stanislavski was not burdened with the necessity of fitting his rehearsals into a union time schedule.

While working on the Actors Studio production of Chekhov's *The Three Sisters,* Geraldine Page was surprised that Lee Strasberg did not "stop and improvise little scenes" as he usually did in class.[7] Evidently Strasberg expected his professionals to do improvisations as homework; he preferred to concentrate his entire five-week rehearsal period on the script and on polishing the production. Nevertheless, Strasberg himself advocates animal or object studies, such as emulating a cat or a table, for type-cast actors who are limited by their overriding concern with having a marketable stage or film "personality."[8]

In his book on acting, Sir Tyrone Guthrie tended to dismiss improvisation: "I cannot see of what use this is to an actor."[9] Guthrie did concede that professional actors and their director might use improvisational exercises to search out the meaning of a difficult scene, but he simply refused to believe that any actors could improvise dialogue that might carry the weight and form supplied by the playwright.

Paul Sills, Viola Spolin's son, who is famous for his work with the Compass and the Second City, shares Guthrie's skepticism about dialogue exercises when a formal play is being rehearsed. Sills believes that the only result of such exercises is that the actors reciting "ideas they've received before," negates any aesthetic growth because the improvisation degenerates into an exercise in memorization with no spontaneous interaction between the actors. For Sills, improvisation is an end in itself, or in his own words, "an attempt to find the art in confrontations between groups of people and in their living together within the theatre form—which includes the audience sitting and witnessing."[10]

In his work at the Old Vic School (1946–1952), Michel St. Denis treated improvisation as a separate training aspect, like stage movement, although St. Denis did feel that in improvisation his young students could "experience the very fact of acting . . . in complete silence without the hindrance or the help of a written text."[11] He stripped his students to near nakedness so that they would have to deal candidly with their own bodies and those of their peers; and he asked them to use mimetic expression, instead of speech, props, or setting, to explore the structure of the theatre itself. When his students had advanced far enough to compose scenarios based on classic themes, St. Denis added masks to their improvisations so that they would focus on their total physical communication rather than rely solely on their facial expressions. Like Guthrie and Sills, St. Denis was not aiming at a structured play as the result of this training, but rather at an exploration of techniques and styles of period movement.

Robert Lewis, cofounder of the Actors Studio in 1947, employed a similar method of examining the components of style. He asked his students to study a period painting, then assume the pose, then add props, costumes, and music, and finally, choose a pertinent piece of poetry or possibly a dramatic scene (if there was more than one person in the painting). By stressing that the student always use the playwright's words, Lewis hoped that the text and study process would help the student "incorporate the elements that are going to be necessary" to play a role in a Molière or Shakespeare play.[12]

Perhaps the theatre craftsmen who are the most comfortable in using the games technique are the actors themselves. Geraldine Page has admitted that she not only believes that improvisation is the key to explore the "links that aren't immediately observable," but that she actually does "adore it in performance."[13] Michael Redgrave agrees that improvisation "is part of the stock-in-trade of the actor's craft," and adds that "new inflections, new business can be invented or refined or altered, within the framework of the production, long after the fiftieth performance."[14]

The teacher and the legitimate professional in theatre have a host of fine examples from which to choose in selecting a method for the implementation of improvisational techniques. Obviously, there is no set formula, or even an accepted norm. Whether you are an actor, a director, or a teacher, you have the right to experiment to determine what will work for you. Perhaps you believe, as Viola Spolin does, that your "constant concern . . . is to keep a moving, living reality for ourselves, not to labor compulsively for an end-result."[15] If this is your credo, take up Constantin Stanislavski's challenge to go beyond copying by improvising upon what has already been done in the field.

You as the performer, the director, or the coach must gain the respect and trust of the individuals with whom you are working so that no one will feel the need to hide behind what has usually worked for him in the past.

Neither a director nor a coach has the time to coddle an individual or the right to assume a mystical attitude. All attention should be channeled into the formulation of a friendly, creative atmosphere devoid of pretensions and inhibitions—an atmosphere in which any experience can be a "lock in," a moment of perception from which you may gain many insights that are true about yourself, your role, or your craft. If you are a defensive actor, bent on protecting what a god-like someone passed on to you as encouragement years ago, you are denying yourself the opportunity to learn from a new situation. Patience is usually the answer, whether you are the performer or the coach. Even if only a few members of a group find an acting exercise successful, the exercise is still worth doing.

As an actor you have the right to expect your coach to treat you as an individual; to point out where you carry physical and vocal tensions; to suggest ways in which you may learn to deal with these tensions; to help you in the development of a personal set of creative "jump-offs" and inspirations that will work for you in performance; and to assist you in selecting the most successful audition material. You should also expect your coach to be ruthlessly honest, regardless of feelings that may be hurt. You are in the business of amalgamating a personal aesthetic of performance that may help you all of your artistically productive life. And you must realize that a classroom, by its very nature, imposes artificial conditions. You are dealing with the most critical audience you will ever encounter; even the most unwilling Tuesday night house will give you more response than a classroom full of your fellow students.

The games in this book can be applied in several ways: a student as well as a director or coach may use the exercises to tackle specific problems, to refresh a sluggish rehearsal or performance, to re-examine the efficiency and the clarity of the performance of a specific piece of business, or to supplement current teaching or learning by using the schedule of exercises in the order in which they appear (rather like a long-range syllabus of study). Your aspiration should not be to make a headlong dash to finish all the suggested exercises so that you can consider yourself "trained." The exercises and improvisations are intended as complementary material to sound teaching or as partner physicalizations to the acting texts cited in various chapters.

The third chapter offers a series of sensitivity exercises that have precedence in community, school, and professional use. Such exercises are aimed more at interpersonal relations among a study group than at the craft of acting itself, though, in a larger sense, the creation of a productive ensemble among the members of a group studying an art form or working on a play is paramount to getting the job off on the right foot. The initial exercises in this text are designed to help you prepare your body (your instrument) and your mind for a discipline that demands relaxation, confidence, openness, and receptivity, as well as public performance and an organic approach to dramatic material. You must learn to deal with yourself and your environment with simplicity and awareness before hurtling yourself into the task of dealing with another actor onstage; otherwise you may develop a habit of pushing for results too quickly, thereby belittling both yourself and your craft. You must learn how to be able to surprise yourself before you can appreciate the audacity that is needed to surprise your fellow actors in rehearsal and your audience in performance.

Eventually, you will penetrate the study of characterization by finding a means of going beyond yourself through the acceptance of an assumed human identity; or at least you will learn how to give your audience the impression that you are going through an experience in which you must make the logical choices for the character you represent. Finally, you must step even further into this social transformation by experimenting with a foreign time and space, perhaps even a social etiquette and style of movement remarkably different from your own. The term "style acting" in reference to this experimentation can be somewhat bewildering, misleading, or even frightening, for it prompts you to remember that there is a present-day audience watching you, and that you must play a "real human being"—one with identifiable wants and needs, likes and dislikes, emotions and conflicts with which your audience can sympathize or possibly empathize. Regardless of your role, you must discover how to perform with clarity, warmth, and beauty.

chapter 1
CONSTRUCTING A BASIC WORKOUT

When you sense that you are not tuned into the business of the day, a workout session is called for. You may be reluctant to begin improvising and working in class because you feel that your "creative juices" are stopped up—or because you're just plain embarrassed. Nevertheless, whether you are working with a partner, with a group, or alone, try to construct a set of basic exercises to promote an aura of creativity. Once you let yourself trust your exercises, you may find that they will serve to limber you up emotionally for years to come, whether you're in class, in rehearsal, or preparing for an audition or even a performance. Though it may take time to create your warm-up, it should never take longer than ten minutes to do your exercises either by yourself or with your classmates; otherwise the warm-up ceases to be a stimulus for creativity and actually saps the juices needed for the energy of performance itself.

A good workout should have several features:

1. You should enjoy the exercises, supplying imaginative motivations and images, and possibly altering the images occasionally to keep the workout period both fresh and stimulating.
2. Your workout should incorporate physical, emotional, and mental stimuli, just as any structured scene or drama would.[1]
3. Your workout should help you determine where you have specific tensions that day so that you can teach yourself to deal with them,

often using tension to find release. For example, try gritting or clenching the teeth and then slowly relaxing the jaw from the front to the back hinges (just in front of the ear lobes).

4. Your workout should encourage actors studying together to work together. Don't hesitate to ask for an emotional response from a partner. Eventually, the members of your study group will experience a mutual enjoyment that will ease the tension of performance.
5. In order to leave you in an energetic mood for class work, your workout should run from mild exertion to relaxation and back to mild exertion.

Try the following exercises and select the ones that work best for you.[2] Perform them in the order in which they are given so that you progressively loosen your entire body. If you skip around you may find yourself tightening an area that you had previously begun to relax.

THE HUMAN CLOCK

procedure Try to simulate a clock. Remember that *you* are the *clock*, not its mirror image. Use your right arm as the minute hand, your left arm as the second hand, and your left leg as the hour hand. Reach out diagonally as far as you can. Try to find five minutes, thirty-five seconds past five o'clock. Keep your second hand moving all the time if possible. Vary the times of the day as quickly as you can without causing yourself undue strain or utter confusion. Because you are standing up, certain times will be anatomically impossible unless you use alternate limbs to represent the hands on the clock. Try performing forty-five minutes,

The human clock

5:05:35 **8:45:15** **8:45:15 with limb functions altered**

fifteen seconds past eight, using various parts of your body until you are comfortable. See if you can move your head in imitation of a cuckoo in a cuckoo clock when you come to an hour.

THE PUPPETEER

procedure Bend over from your hips and relax. Flex your knees if your body seems to be straining. Wag your head; let it go back and forth, up and down, as if it had its own free will. You are a puppet. There is a string attached to every joint in your body, including your fingers, and to every vertebra in your back. The puppeteer slowly lifts your controls until you are stretched fully upward. Just as slowly, he now releases the strings in succession, isolating and relaxing your puppet body as he progresses from the fingers to the hands, the wrists, the forearms, the elbows, the biceps, the shoulders, the wings, and the pectorals (alternating sides of the body with each isolation—right-hand fingers, left-hand fingers; right hand, left hand; right wrist, left wrist; and so on). Now the puppeteer slowly releases your head, then your neck, the myriad strings up and down your spine, and finally your right hip, left hip, right thigh, left thigh, until your whole body seems to have collapsed into a moderately deep knee-bend. Then the succession is reversed and you are lifted back up to a vertical stretch again.

DOG-TIRED

Begin with ten or twelve relaxed, swinging toe-touches. Then lie on your back with your knees bent and your feet flat on the floor. Tilt your pelvis up toward the knees one or two inches until the small of the back rests completely on the floor. Now inhale. Maintain a feeling of relaxation in the stomach, and pant like a dog, keeping the throat open and relaxed as if yawning. Stop if the exercise hurts in any way or if the throat feels parched. Maintain the kinesthetic yawn in the throat and keep your pelvis tilted upward. Then, like an exhausted dog, yawn up five quiet "arf's"—"arf, arf, arf, arf, arf"—slowly letting the pelvis sink back as the breath runs out.

Repeat the exercise, this time saying "yes."

Now tilt your pelvis up again and fill the lungs as fully as possible; when the lungs seem totally expanded, try to gasp in even more air, spreading the lower small of the back as widely as possible over the floor. Alternate this with the "arf" or "yes" several more times until you relax enough to find the "arf" vibrating all the way down your torso to your crotch. Be sure that you are looking directly up into the air perpendicular to the floor, so that there is no tension involved with holding your head in a particular position too far back or too far down. Make sure there is no tension in your abdomen. Finally, rise and see if, while standing up, you can duplicate the sensations you felt while lying down as you try the panting and the "arf" or "yes." At first, you may find this difficult, especially if you are working with another actor. You can see each other now that you are standing up, and you may feel a social restriction to pull in your belly.

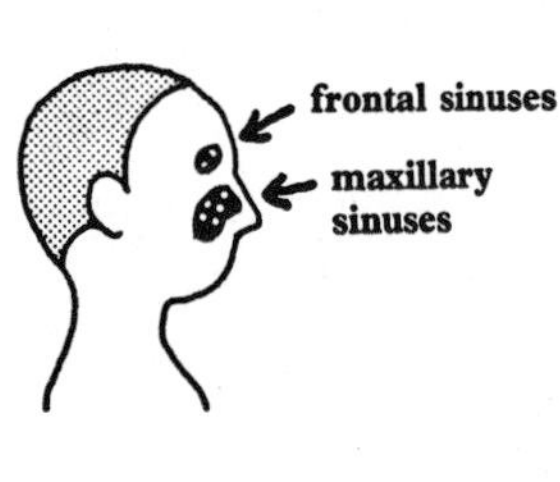

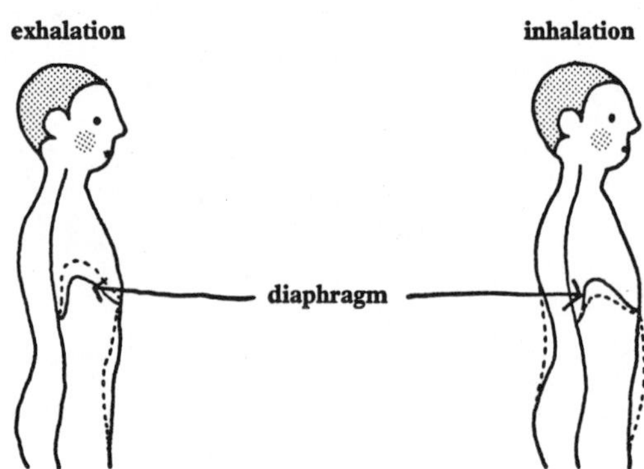

IMAGE SHAPING

Think of yourself as a raw egg slowly cooking in a frying pan.[3] Begin with a light tension in your pelvis and gradually spread the tension outward to the finger tips, the toe tips, and the top of the head. Consciously isolate every area as the tension diffuses. Finally, the entire body will be slightly taut. Begin to ease the tension slowly from the tips of the fingers and toes back to the stomach. Now feel the heat around you, solidifying the egg from the edges inward until the egg is a solid mass. Feel the fat sputtering on the crinkling outer edges of your egg-body. Try to maintain a warm feeling in the center pelvic area, and shift the image from the egg to being yourself at the beach with the sun streaming over you. Yawn up a sound that epitomizes the feeling of summer relaxation and warmth.

When you feel a sexual attraction toward someone, or when you have "butterflies in your stomach," you know that your emotional center lies in your pelvic area. Try to imagine that a pipe extends up through the center of your body from your pelvis to your mouth. The pipe is wide and flexible and is used to funnel up the sensory images stored in the pelvic area. The mental or "head" image will shape a word as it connects with the sensory storage area in the pelvis; then the emotion or feeling will draw your breath up and out.

Imagine first that it is winter. It is very cold, and your entire body feels like contracting. Be sure your throat muscles remain unconstricted. Yawn up a sound that epitomizes the cold and the usual traffic problems of winter. Try to imagine yourself lost in the snow; run through all the sensory images that go with this experience, and then, without tightening the center pipe, try to yawn up a sound that expresses what you are feeling. Suddenly it is spring; you are in a field of daffodils (the contrast may be like the similar moment in the movie *Dr. Zhivago*). Go through the sensory images and yawn up the new sound. Substitute a new set of images each time you do the workout until you discover images that work for you.[4]

VOCAL ISOLATIONS

It is fairly important to do these isolations in order.[5] A handy way to retain the sequence is to remember that air will hit and enter each of the areas in this exercise in succession when you inhale through your mouth.

Phase 1

The motor boat

procedure Purse the lips with a gentle tension as if about to kiss and blow a steady stream of air through the lips, just as a horse blows flies away from his mouth. The sound should be similar to that of a motor boat.

Phase 2

Lip isolation

procedure Lift and flutter one lip at a time, being careful to keep all the other muscles of the face relaxed. The best way to find the position for the lower lip is to say "Why?" soundlessly, using only the lower lip. Now put a finger on your chin to be sure that the jaw is still relaxed and that only the lip is doing the work, and actually say "Why?" as if you mean it. If you are working in a group, focus on a partner. Now give yourself a reason to sneer at your partner and isolate the upper lip into a curl as you say "sheet" or "chic." Try to aim the word from the center of the mouth rather than from only one side of it. Spray the person you have selected with the sound.

Phase 3

Karate chop

procedure Tense all the muscles of the face into a knot (try to isolate the throat so that it stays loose). Increase the tension and raise your *right* hand over your head. When your face feels tight as a drum, find a cry or yell like "aaaiiiiihhhaa!" and chop the air with your hand as you release the facial tension. Try not to let the tension of the chop invade your shoulders.

Phase 4

Jaw wagging

procedure Place your fingers at the base of your ear lobes and bring the tips of the fingers foward over the hinges of the jaw. Check yourself by chewing to see if the muscles bulge just under your fingers. Massage the area gently in a circle on both sides, working down the jaw bone from the hinge to the chin. Now draw the fingers straight down over the area, stroking the face into a relaxed, open-mouthed, jaw-hanging position. Yawn out the word "yaw" several times. Lean the head over and say "yaw," shaking the head gently from side to side. If the jaw is truly free, you will hear it popping at the side hinges. Now repeat the preceding exercise—the Karate Chop—with the *left* hand.

Phase 5

The bellows

This exercise is meant to stimulate the soft palate, the little projection that vibrates at the rear roof of the mouth. (The motion might be compared to that of canaries flying in and out of Felix the Cat's mouth.) Remember that you should control your breath by using the lower abdominal and intercostal areas—not the upper lungs. If your shoulders seem to be heaving, try to rethink the center of your breathing down through your umbilicus as you might do if you were meditating yoga style. Individual members of a group may find it best to do this exercise at their own speed, since it is quite easy to overdo the rhythm and dry the throat from evaporation.

procedure Make the sounds "Kah-keeh-kouh" (kä-kē-kō), on both the inhalation and the exhalation in a series of short breaths. Keep the imaginary pipe in the center of your body free and open, and avoid tension anywhere. Put a finger under the nostrils to be sure that some warm air is coming out, otherwise the sounds will be nasal and tense as a result of holding the soft palate or the adenoids tightly. You should feel the little soft palate flexing back and forth.

Phase 6

Tongue semaphores

Improper exercise with the tongue can cause tensions in other areas. The tongue is delicate and the exercise is not a delicatessen contest; it is neither necessary nor desirable to put as much tongue on the counter as is humanly possible. The idea is to sensitize the tip while relaxing the tongue at its roots.

procedure Hold the tongue firmly between two or three fingers and pull it gently outward until it feels stretched but not taut. While holding it out, count to twenty, trying to say every number as well as you can. Gradually release the finger pressure completely, but keep the tongue extended, just as though you were holding it, and count to twenty again. Now put the tongue back into the mouth and salivate, moistening the inner mouth and tongue.

variation Try a new set of images. Pretend you are making a horror movie. You are frozen in a state of suspended animation, and you know you are about to be buried alive by people who don't realize you are still living. You can move only your tongue. Try signaling with the tongue as far on either side as you can see with your peripheral vision, attempting to contact either real or imaginary people in the room. These people are a burial detail. Remember that the roots of the tongue should be relaxed and free; only the tip is working. The tip may slide back and forth horizontally using the lower lip as a track. Vary the exercise with vertical movement, trying to touch the tip of the nose and then the tip of the chin. Use the image of Tantalus, from Greek mythology: standing in water that recedes as he tries to drink, and with fruit suspended above him that recedes as he reaches for it, he is doomed to hunger and thirst forever. Tomorrow, try a new image. Sensual images work well with this set of muscles as long as you keep your thoughts to yourself.

Phase 7
The nasal workout

procedure Alternately block one nostril with a finger and take a series of short, jet-like inhalations up into the other nostril, wakening the sinuses (be sure to keep the shoulders relaxed). Do this once on each side. Now place the index finger and the center finger of each hand together over the maxillary sinuses, stroking down the bridge of the nose to where the cheekbone joins the side of the nose. Massage lightly in a circle, yawn, and hum the nasal continuants "m," "n," and "ŋ(ng)." Go on massaging and say "man," "one," and "singing." Enjoy the nasal sounds, and prolong them with a hum as you say the words. Now massage the frontal sinuses by placing the same two fingers of each hand over the inner half of each eyebrow. Again, rub lightly in a circle and repeat the sounds and then the words, enjoying the vibration of the nasal consonants.[6]

Phase 8
Drop-overs

This exercise is an amalgamation of the preceding ones, and needs the initial isolation exercises in order to be fully sensed and appreciated.

procedure Begin with the idea of a simple toe-toucher, but flex the knees slightly to avoid tension as you go down. Go from your vertical highest to your bent-over lowest (bending only from the *hips*) without causing undue strain. Naturally, some persons will be able to go farther up and down than others. In order to incorporate the vocal elements, the idea is to yawn up a relaxed "ah," using your lowest comfortable pitch while in an upright position, but modulating to your highest comfortable pitch as you bend over; therefore, the lower you bend the higher the sound you make.[7] Use only the tones within your natural range. Stop yourself if you feel you are shifting into a falsetto or straining for a low tone. Try to synchronize the sound with the movement, so that you do both together. In other words, you are in the middle of your natural range as you reach the middle of your drop-over. Check to be sure that your head and spine are free of tension at all times.

Vocalizing on a drop-over

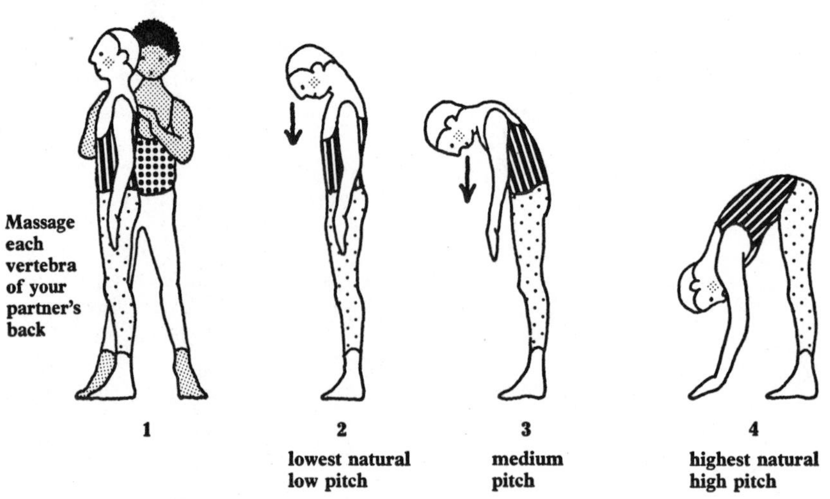

The head should be the first part of the body to drop over as you lean forward and the last part to come up as you stand up again. Try to imagine that each vertebra of the spine is attached to a string, just as in the Puppeteer Exercise, and that one vertebra after another falls into place as the body shifts. Imagine that the puppeteer has dozens of strings attached to your spinal vertebra. He lifts the lower first ten, so you rise up slightly. Then he drops the strings and you bounce over freely again with your head dangling. Repeat the exercise, going higher each time until you are halfway up; but no higher, or fear will replace freedom. If you are working with a partner, the two of you may check the freedom in each other's neck vertebrae. Take turns doing this. Gently take your partner's forehead in your hand, lift his head, and then let it drop easily. Remember that a head weighs at least twenty pounds. Be aware that your partner may try to help you by moving his head in the direction in which he anticipates you are going to move it. Opposing your guiding motion and anticipating any of your motions are equally wrong. Merely let the head wag and bounce gently.

When you are satisfied that you have mastered this technique of relaxation, start doing the same exercise by rising from your lowest low to your highest high. This time, begin the sound by yawning up the "ah" from your highest pitch (without strain) to your lowest pitch as you return to a vertical position. Be extremely careful to avoid strain. Always stay within your own natural range.

You may want to do this drop-over-and-return exercise two or three times daily. Gradually, you will find a way to economize with the sound produced as you come to the break in your voice so your tone will stay clear throughout the vocalizing, whether rising or falling. If you carry body tension in your shoulders and neck, the minute you begin to perform, your partner should be able to see how you tense your shoulders and how erratic and tight your arm motions become. Everyone carries his tension in a different area. Recognizing where the tension exists is the first step in finding a way to free the problem spot. Usually, you can train yourself to make a habit of tensing and then relaxing the area before a performance.

Phase 9

Back rubs

procedure Pair off with a partner who seems about your own size and weight. Watch your partner do the last exercise and tell him where he seems to be straining. When he has done the first half of the drop-over, check his head and neck. Lift his head gently upward and let it fall easily. Vary the position and each direction of lift and drop until you are sure that the head and neck areas are free. Avoid sudden movements or rough handling that may tense and frighten your partner.

After your partner straightens up, begin rubbing his back, starting at the base of the skull—that is, under the medulla, where the skull joins the spine. Massage gently in a circle on and around each vertebra as you work your way down the entire spine to the tail bone.[8] Work back up the spine again to the base of the skull. Now massage out along the collarbones and back again, and finally, move down the spine to the wing areas. Use the heel of your hand and work out slowly, in a circular fashion, massaging toward the armpit while holding your partner gently with the other hand to maintain his balance. Step around to the side of your partner so that you face his profile, and place your fingers at the base of his skull.

Ask your partner to do the drop-over exercise again. This time help him to appreciate each of his vertebrae in action by working down the spine and massaging as he bends over. The process should be slow and gentle, and you must be careful to synchronize the spinal rub-down with your partner's breathing so that it is possible for the partner to do each phase of the drop-over with a single slow breath. Try varying the sound used from "ah" to "eeh" or "oh' (from ä to ē or ō).

Phase 10

Elevators

procedure Pretend that you are in an elevator with your arms full of Christmas presents. The button you must press is in the center of the panel in front of you, and you can use only your elbows—first one, then the other. As you lean over to press the button, breathe in deeply so that the side you stretch is filled with air. Return to an upright position; then use the other elbow, breathing in fully again. Repeat the exercise ten times, and begin the day's work.[9]

chapter 2
EXPLORING BODY CULTURE FOR RELAXATION

Body tension is the major obstacle every young actor must overcome. You may not even be aware of your tension, or the way in which it manifests itself, but it is there. Perhaps when you write you grip your pencil more tightly than you need to; perhaps you tend to force your body to straighten up and square-off when your parents are near you; perhaps, if you are male, you are prone to tighten your biceps in order to impress someone.

The rigors of performance tend to emphasize these emotional pressure points, so that an audience becomes acutely aware of your tension. In fact, the audience will tend to center tension in the same places that you have tightened yourself. An audence re-creates whatever an actor does onstage, which is why an audience walks away refreshed from a performance in which everything seems to happen easily. Conversely, a whole audience can develop a sore throat while listening to you if you are straining and producing a scratchy sound. Try to learn where you center your tension so that you can eliminate it. Any tension is bad tension.

You may tend to "push" onstage for a variety of reasons: the auditorium may be deceptively large and you may feel inadequate to fill the space; the role may call for emotion to which you are not ready to surrender freely, easily, and confidently; or someone you want to impress may be in the audience. Unfortunately, tension will rob you of the ability to act and react freely just when you want to be most successful. For example, if you are playing a role in which you must give the impression of crying, the worst thing you can do is tighten your mind and body into a desire to produce real tears. Tears may come if your emotions are free, but they will never come if you set yourself up for such conscious end-results.

Tension prohibits any freedom in acting or reacting. Tension is the result of "set," a programmed series of responses. Prejudiced people are usually tense because they have constructed opinions about their fellow human beings without really knowing them. You may be guilty of a similar "set" if you consciously strive for an end-result, for an external picture or attitude that you want to impress upon the audience. Relaxation is imperative; it is a way of life. You must learn to relax before you can learn to act.

PHYSICAL TYPES

Typing yourself

procedure Walk freely around your work space or rehearsal area. It is not necessary to "perform" the walk as a character; just walk as naturally and relaxedly as possible. Define your walk in terms of a body metaphor. In other words, develop a set of adjectives that describe your movement, such as "light-footed," "lead-footed." Be honest and objective about yourself. Now consider where you carry your tension—in the shoulders, the calves, the hips, the knees, etc. How do these tensions affect your work and your everyday life? If you are working with someone else, make these decisions together so that you begin to care about your collective growth as artists, not just your personal progress.

decisions Do you seem to be moving with a vertical alignment, or do you lean backward or forward? Do many of the characters you play wind up having this same posture? Does posture influence your life attitude? In other words, if you lean forward constantly, putting tension on your toes, are you inclined to be so over-aggressive that you cease to listen to your partner in scenes? (If you were heavy at one time, you may tend to lean back, rocking on your heels to balance what may once have been a potbelly. If you have a habit of leaning back, do you find that your scenes peter out instead of building and accelerating to a climax?)

variation Kneel down as if you were in church, or simply walk to a chair and sit; then rise, walk around, and sit again. Try to maintain an aura of fun and relaxation while you analyze your movement, rather than being "picky" and supercritical with yourself. If you are working with someone else, ask him if *your* movement makes *him* feel tension anywhere.

Body metaphors[1]

Take a look at the following list of expressions. Try to associate a different postural attitude with each word or phrase. You may be able to identify yourself with some of these metaphors. If so, you will have an idea of where you carry your tension as a personality. Be objective about the character you are playing in a scene. Perhaps such metaphors can conjure up a mental picture of an external aspect of your character that you can use in rehearsal. Create your own list of metaphors; there are hundreds of possibilities.

head in the clouds
head in the sand
hot-headed
talk over his head
hair-raising
save face
two-faced
poker face
highbrow
sweat of your brow
browbeat
hawk-eyed
catch your eye
see through him
nose out of joint
talk down your nose
keep your nose clean
big mouth
bad mouth
foot in his mouth
tight-lipped
stiff upper lip
sink your teeth into
skin of your teeth
tongue-tied
back-handed compliment
tight-fisted
palm off
itching palms
put a finger on
slip through your fingers
under your thumb
in a pinch
knuckle under
tail between your legs
watery knees
drag your feet
both feet on the ground

eat your words
cheeky
turn the other cheek
bend your ear
wet behind the ears
lump in your throat
pain in the neck
shoulder a burden
get it off your chest
bleeding heart
sinking heart
lots of gall
vent your spleen
lily-livered
butterflies in your stomach
get off her back
monkey on his back
shove it up your ass
kick in the pants
ants in your pants
open arms
twist his arm
elbow your way
limp-wristed
heavy-handed
give him a hand
sit on it
about to break
fall in love
sucker
get a kick out of
itching to do it
kiss off
piss off
keep in touch
fight tooth and nail
treading water
hang loose

underfoot
cold-blooded
bloody disposition
feel it in your bones
thin-skinned
skinny as a rail
fat as a hog/house
soft as a baby
gnarled as an oak
straight as a rod
sitting high and dry
sitting tight
uptight
pressed for time
pushover
pusher
blow-hard
blowing in the wind
blow your mind
rise above it
wallowing in it
put down roots
walk a straight line
walk a fine line

TENSING UP TO FIND RELEASE

Phase 1
The whole body

procedure Lie on your back on the floor in your work space. Perform this series of images with concentration.

You are the neck muscles of a performer who is about to do the first scene of his life. Put your arms at your sides and begin a tiny tension in your buttocks. Your scene is the next one up! Let the tension spread into the whole pelvis. You might forget your lines! The tension is going to permeate your body until your entire body is rigid. You can feel it creeping upward and downward at the same time. It invades your chest and breast now, as well as your thighs; however, your arms, feet, and neck are still relaxed—but they know it's coming- Now your collarbones, your upper arms, your knees are tense. Your scene will be up in two more minutes! The tension is invading your elbows and calves and neck. Oh, God, what do I say after he says, "Then what happened, Pinkerton?" Now the tension is vibrating into your hands, turning them to fists, and into your feet until they become claws, and your face looks like an astronaut's at blast-off! Your whole body is locked in tension. You dare not move or speak. Wait, oh! Class is over and the leader will see your scene tomorrow. Slow relief! The tension leaves your face, then your hands and feet, and gradually retraces its path back to your stomach and pelvis. Now your upper arms and calves are loosening. Your collarbones and chest are surrendering the rigidity; so are your knees and thighs. Finally, your stomach and pelvis relax, but your buttocks are still tight. Why? That's right, you'll have to go through another sleepless night worrying about that scene, and you'll have to suffer all that tension again. Do something about it! Get in touch with your partner. Rehearse the scene again so you feel confident; and this time, go over the lines two hours before class instead of mouthing them while the other members of the group do their scenes. Involve yourself in their scenes and you won't be so nervous about your own.

You have to put yourself back together now. Stay there like a puddle on the floor. You are a Betty Crocker cake mix, with all the necessary ingredients added. Blissfully you lie in the baking pan. You are happy because you are going to be of service after waiting on the shelf so long at that grocery store. This family is going to eat you and enjoy you, and you will attain Nirvana. You are being lifted, and you glide back and forth in the pan as you are carried to the oven. You are set down, the oven door is opened, and you are put on the top rack. Feel that delicious warmth around you. It makes you relax and expand and diffuse. Feel your back and thighs and your buttocks spreading across the floor until you seem completely widened out. Take a deep breath, and when you feel you have absorbed as much air as you can, breathe in still more deeply, sending the air down into your lower back and swelling yourself even more. Keep breathing deeply; the air is soft and warm and luscious and now your baking powder is making you stretch out. You are growing upward; your whole body is expanding and getting more and more solid as you bake. Relax your breathing now, but feel that your breath still begins down as deep as your pelvis and thighs. Feel the Crisco spatter around your edges, making your corners nice and crispy, solidifying you. You are just about done, but your belly is still nice and soft. The oven door is opened and you are gently lifted out. A toothpick is inserted in your bellybutton to see if you're done. It tickles. Sure enough, the toothpick comes out without any of you on it. You're done! You are taken out of the oven—which was getting just a bit hot—and allowed to become comfortably cool.

Phase 2

Areas of the body

procedure

The shoulders and upper arms If you feel that your shoulders seem to crawl up around your ears when you perform, try this. Sit on a chair that permits you to grab the sides of the seat in the areas where your thighs join your pelvis. Relax there for a moment. Take the sides of the chair in your hands and bend your arms at the elbows, extending the elbows directly out from your sides like wings. Keep your elbows out perpendicular to your body and grip the chair, pulling the sides of the chair up as you force your shoulders down. Keep pulling until you feel as though your shoulders have joined your buttocks! Now slowly use the trunk of your body to grow upward through yourself between your arms. Feel your *whole head* and neck lift upward as you gently bring your spine into a supported vertical line from your anus to the top of your head. Look directly forward, not up or down. Find a spot at exactly eye level across the room. Grow upward until you feel you are fully lengthened along your spine; now let the tension go out of your elbows. Slowly, the tension drips away from the entire arm, and the arms relax, dangling at your sides.

decisions Exactly where did you feel the most tension? Do you carry one shoulder higher than the other? Do you write so much that your body bends to accommodate your writing arm? When you were in sports, did you develop one side of your body more than the other?—for example, did you throw the discus with only one arm? Instead of lifting one shoulder to meet the other, can you learn to relax them both so that they will stay on one level? Tell yourself that if you don't take the time to do this now, you will carry this tension into every role you play, and finally probably develop spinal arthritis. Do the exercise twice a day, and always do it once before performing a scene.

procedure ***The neck*** If you feel that you usually try to punctuate everything you say by bobbing your head "yes," you may be placing undue tension on the top vertebrae of your spine because you do not trust the playwright's words to be emphatic enough. In the long run, you will appear smaller and weaker unless you learn to relax this area.

Sit in a good straight-backed chair with your arms resting at your sides or on your lap. Find a spot across the room that seems to be just about at your eye level, but not higher or lower. Without tensing, let your back lengthen into a supported verticality. Feel your *entire head* rising in relation to that spot across the room. Where your head goes your body must obviously follow (which is no news to you if you ever took tumbling). Do not strain. When you feel you are at your lengthened peak without stress, relax your shoulders completely and let your spine, from your shoulders up, begin to relax. Support your back from your tail bone up to your shoulders as you let your neck and your head drop slowly forward. Now you are going to allow your head to roll around very slowly. You are not going to *make* it roll around. Your head should feel like a wind sock on the end of a pole. Using your hips and pelvis, tilt your body to the right, letting the mere weight of the head roll the head to the right. As the head drifts over the right shoulder, slowly tilt backward until the head rolls back. Relax and loosen the jaw—the mouth may fall open. Slowly tilt left, then forward, until you have made a complete circle. Repeat the same action going counter-clockwise. Do this several times.

decisions Does your neck seem to catch anywhere in particular? Can you remember falling on that spot, or did someone ever hit you there? Are you so tall or so short that you crane your neck to talk to people? Do you feel your emotions come up to your neck when you get frustrated or angry? Do you trap them there? Do you secretly hold onto your tension, or do you ease it by going to other people when you're down? Do you construct real objectives that require a partner when you act, or do you water down your needs and try to take care of them yourself? Do you do this in life?

variation Stand up and let your body relax as though you were going to do some toe-touchers. Flex your knees and lean into a drop-over. Let your arms and your head dangle. Your spine is a centipede with a hundred little feet standing inside of you. The centipede starts to lift up from the small of your back way down at your tail bone. Only ten of his feet take hold and lift you, so only the bottom tenth of your spine straightens up. Then he slowly lets go and your arms and head dangle again, slowly, always slowly. Beginning at your tail bone, the centipede now leisurely takes hold with twenty of his tiny feet, so that the bottom fifth of your spine is lifted up, and then once again he slowly lets go. Again your head and arms dangle. The centipede keeps repeating the process until finally, using ten of his feet at a time, he manages to stand up, fully and relaxedly. Your head is now securely—but not stiffly—supported on your neck.

decisions Were you successful in separating your spine into ten distinct areas? Did you find any special kinks along the way?

The pelvis and thighs

procedure If you seem to lead with your hips and pelvis when you perform, as Yul Brynner does purposely in the film *The Ten Commandments*, you may be locking your legs with tension or freezing your pelvic movement. Occasionally, actors and actresses will do this to look manly or sexy. Sometimes improper training in winter sports or water skiing can result in tension in these areas. Unfortunately, postural tension only draws attention to what you may be trying to hide.

Tense the area completely, and then systematically let go, draining the tension away. Lean slightly forward and rise up on your toes, then let yourself back down slowly, touching the floor with the ball of the foot before the heel. Grip the floor with your toes and rise up again. Repeat the movement twenty-five times. Do some jumping-jacks before you start a scene, or even a rehearsal. Stomp a few times, being careful to stomp directly *under* you, not to either side. Keep your feet as far apart as the width of your pelvis, and stomp again. Grip the floor with your toes, rise up on them, then settle slowly down, using the whole foot. Bounce lightly again, but keep your toes on the floor at all times. Focus on a point directly in front of you at eye level. Think: "My back will lengthen and widen as my whole head moves forward and up, aligning my body with my legs."

decisions Do you feel in contact with the floor? Do you feel you can trust your legs to hold you up?

variation Lie down with your knees bent, and press the small of your back into the floor by rolling your pelvis up slightly. Put a tiny amount of pressure on your toes and the balls of your feet, and roll the pelvis up slightly again. Release it, and exhale. Roll it up and inhale deeply. Release and exhale. Look up at a point on the ceiling directly above you, roll up the pelvis as you inhale fully, then release as you exhale again. Have a friend hand you a chair as you lie there in that position. Take the chair by the back legs, balance it, and bring it back over your head. Now balance the chair and move it down over your pelvis, keeping your back and head on the floor the whole time. Bring the chair back over you and move it slowly from side to side. What must your body do to compensate for the weight of the chair? Can you relate this to what you are doing to your body by unbalancing your posture? Relate the kinesthetic feeling of the chair over you to the feeling of being over yourself. Roll over on your side and stand up as effortlessly as possible.

Phase 3

Memorizing lines

procedure If you find yourself tensing up when you try to learn a scene, perhaps the following method will ease you into memorizing. Put a clean rug or mat on your floor at home and lie down with your knees up and feet propped against the wall, or with your calves resting on a chair. Try to keep as much of your back, including the small of your back, as flat on the floor as possible. If you lie perpendicular to the wall, you can use it to prop up your feet. Look *directly* above you at a point on the ceiling. Try to feel that you are looking at a point that is exactly perpendicular to the floor at eye level. Have a friend check to see that you are looking directly upward. Relax and get the kinesthetic feeling of how your head feels in this position. You should be able to find this position again on your own.

Now go over your lines, or memorize them, in this relaxed position. If you have an emotional part, speak that part to the ceiling. Imagine that the person you're speaking to is up on the ceiling, and contact him up there. Keep your head and neck relaxed. Feel the emotion begin down deep in your pelvis. Feel it as it extends upward and expands, widening and widening as it moves along through your body until it passes easily through your throat and up to the ceiling. Feel how hard the floor is under you and how hard the ceiling over you must be from taking all that tension away from you. Spatter your tension across the ceiling. See your script up there over you and spit your lines up at it without tensing your neck. Breathe deeply for each phrase and splash it across the ceiling. Enjoy it! Give that ceiling all the tension of your role. After you have gone over the script several times in this manner, roll over on your side and try to get up using the least amount of tension possible.

When you are standing up straight, repeat the procedure, this time splashing the wall in front of you with the tension as you drain it out of yourself. See if you can recapture the same relaxed support that you had on the floor. Try to relax into this new habit of letting the words do the work for you. Trust the playwright and trust your breathing. If you find your head wagging when you are either on the floor or standing up, relax and begin again.

TAKING A BALLOON RIDE INTO RELAXATION

procedure Lie on your back with your knees up, legs together. If you are more comfortable with your legs out flat, go ahead and straighten them. Now picture a balloon, a big one fifteen feet in diameter, way up above you, perhaps sixty feet up. It is attractive, your favorite color, and it is indestructible because there is no rigidity to it—it will adapt itself to anything. It seems to be dancing in the breeze, wafting softly back and forth. You want to join it, and it beckons you. Slowly it settles down toward you, forty, twenty, ten feet, until it rests on your body from your chest to your pelvis. It is so warm and light that you want to play with it. Relax your arms and use your pelvis and chest to roll it back and forth. It's huge, but soft and warm and fun. You want to be part of it. It seems to be absorbing you. You are now part of its outer skin, and it caresses you, warms you, protects you. Slowly it lifts you up, higher and higher, without fear, and it takes you from the work space into the warm sunlight. You've left your tensions on the hard floor and joined the happy balloon as it sails into the sky.

Take an aerial tour of the city or countryside, describing the sights as you float along in your balloon. After about five minutes of flying, turn the balloon around and bring it back to the work space. It slowly, gently settles right back onto the floor in the same place from which it began its journey. The balloon gradually separates from your skin, and you can play with it again, rolling it over your body. Slowly it ascends, but hovers so close above you that you can call it down again whenever you feel tension and need relief.

extension

Roll over on your side and find a way of getting to your feet with a minimum amount of tension and effort. When you are standing erect, try to find the same spinal adjustment that you had while lying on the floor. See your balloon across the room hovering over the floor directly at eye level. Bring the balloon toward you and let it envelop your head, lifting you gently, not pulling you. Walk across the room and try to think of your whole head rising upward and taking you forward as you move along with your head in the balloon. Glide with alertness; do not become a zombie! Try to go up and down some steps, letting your head float in the balloon as it carries you up and down. Visualize the balloon moving along in front of and with you as you move.

decisions

If you have access to a full-length mirror put a chair in front of the mirror and try to sit and stand naturally. Where are you putting tension? Do you see your muscles "set"? Do you recognize a pattern of muscular attack that your body succumbs to when you sit or when you begin to stand? Do you tense your shoulders when you stand? Can shoulders really help you stand?

extension 2

Sit forward on the chair, allowing your spine to lengthen as you let your head go up and forward. Say to yourself, "My back to lengthen and widen, my whole head to go forward and up." Reach for your balloon; let it envelop your head. Look at yourself with your balloon. Repeat the phrase and let yourself relax into standing. Did you see any tension of muscles that cannot possibly aid you in standing up? Sit and try it again, this time using your thighs and hips to raise your weight. There should be no movement in your upper torso. Once again, try to sit and stand without putting any tension into any area that cannot aid you in moving either up or down.

decisions

Any person who is studying or practicing theatre as an actor deals with his emotions constantly; therefore, he should take some time out of every day to relax. This does not mean watching television while guzzling beer. Television is a distraction that prevents you from coming to grips with your personal tensions; it is a means of hiding from yourself by watching someone else. An actor must learn to "fall" into basic artistic choices by getting out of the way of his own self. The desire for immediate results is the bane of most young actors.

Read the short second chapter, "Dressing a Character," in Constantin Stanislavski's *Building a Character.* Why was Tortsov so congratulatory to Kostya? Was he the first or the last out of the dressing room? Why was Tortsov so critical of the other actors? Did the other actors have any inner sense of the externals they had chosen?[2]

Do you like to set your blocking in the first few rehearsals? Does this give you a sense of relaxation, knowing that you have a framework? Do you allow yourself to change later in rehearsal, or do you generally feel that your first choice is right? Be careful not to trap yourself with early choices of end-results.

When you are dealing with an emotional scene, you must expect that there will be some tension present. Can you separate your tension as an actor from the tension of the character you are playing? Does your personal tension make you feel as though you're doing something emotional? Are you controlling the character, or are his tensions controlling you? Do you trust the other actor to pull off his half of the scene, or do you feel that you must provide all the "drama"? Are you allowing yourself to play your objective by placing emotional claims on your partner in the scene, or are you selfishly keeping all the tension locked up in yourself? Have you tried to give your partner your tension by forcing him to make a decision?

In your next scene, refuse to keep any tension yourself. If it is an emotional scene, hand the tension over to your partner and force him to deal with it. If he is a decent actor, he will hand you the tension right back, because he understands that reciprocating the tension is the only way to build the scene dramatically. Hand it right back to him! Have you ever been bored watching a scene even though the two particular performers in it were very emotional and tense? Were these actors predictable? Why was this? Were they sharing any emotions, or were they just hammering at each other? Were they indicating their emotions and reactions in grand style? Were they listening to each other? Was either of them at all cognizant of how vulnerable his character might have been? Have you ever seen a play in which the performers seemed to be proclaiming, "I want to show the audience how powerful I am and how much I can suffer"? The next time you see a play, ask yourself afterwards what the actors wanted from one another in the play as it *was* performed, not as it *might have been* performed. Were the actors sharing the tension and the emotions, or were they selfish? A tender little scene can be just as thunderingly dramatic in its own way as a death scene from a great tragedy.

DEALING WITH UNNECESSARY TENSION[3]

Phase 1

Maintaining postural balance

procedure Have someone help you with this exercise. Sit in a comfortable straight-backed chair and find a point directly in front of you upon which to focus. The point should be at exactly eye level. Imagine that the balloon you used in the last exercise is floating on that point. Now ask a friend to assist you by following this procedure:

Massage your partner's shoulders along the collarbones toward the spine. Use moderate thumb and finger pressure, massaging in a circle, encouraging him to relax his shoulder muscles. When your partner has surrendered his shoulder tension, you may concentrate more on the center of his back along the spine. Continue the circular massage along the top three spinal vertebrae to the point where the spine joins the skull.

Observe the angle of your partner's head. Place your fingers at the very rear of his jawbone on both sides of the head and gently stroke backward and upward under the ear, giving his *whole* head a gentle upward and forward encouragement.

Ask your partner to think, "My back to lengthen and widen, my whole head to go forward and up." Tell him to avoid all tension, and above all, to avoid doing anything that will "help" you guide his head into alignment. If you feel he is trying to lift his head consciously and muscularly, tell him to relax; and begin the entire process again. If he remains comfortably passive though alert, start to rotate his head at the top vertebrae by placing your fingers gently but firmly under his ears and along the base of the skull. You may wish to keep a finger or two on the rear of the jawbone. Avoid all poking or forcing as you help him rotate his head into its own natural alignment. Maintain the light rotation until in profile a line connecting the temple at eye level and the top of the ear could form the crossbar of a perfect "H"—an "H" comparable to that shaped by the stance of an archer with his drawn bow and arrow. Your partner should appear to be looking straight ahead, and his head should be in a comfortable, supported, vertical position.

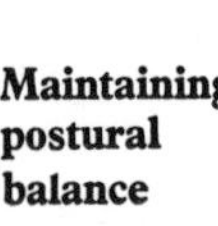

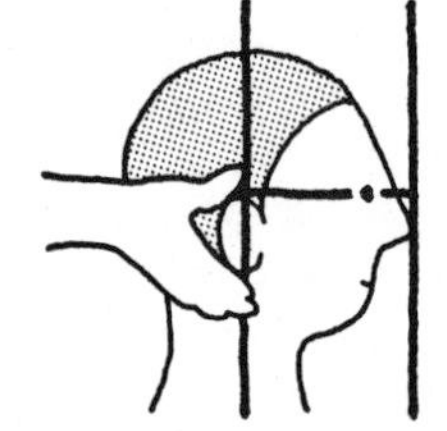

Maintaining postural balance

During the rotation process, your partner may seem to get slightly taller. This should occur not because he has pushed for "results," but rather because he has relaxed enough to get out of the way of his own upward growth, (it may take constant relaxing and massaging for short daily periods over several days for this to happen). In actuality, this lengthening is realized by your suggesting an upward direction to his head, and by your prohibiting a downward pull of the neck and the upper thoracic muscles.

decisions When your partner is helping you, are you thinking of your *whole* head going up, or is just the front or the back of your head going up. Are you really concentrating on the spot you have chosen in front of you, or are you concentrating on concentrating? Are you comfortable? Do you feel tensions anywhere? Tell that spot to let go. Are you trying to help your partner by pushing upward from your tail bone? The correct lengthening will occur only when you give up "trying." Do you seem to be in line?—in other words, do the right and left sides of your body seem to balance each other?

Phase 2
Experimenting with balance

Repeat the whole process. This time you are going to stand when you feel ready. You are going to avoid "setting" the *upper* part of your body, which can't really help you stand anyway. Ask your partner to place his fingers gently at the base of your skull and at the rear of your jawbone. Think the phrase, "My back to lengthen and widen, my whole head to go forward and up." Concentrate on your balloon, and let it rise with you when you feel ready to stand. As you rise, your partner should keep his fingers at the base of your skull. Neither of you should push. Your partner will be able to sense whether or not you are rigid anywhere; he will know when your entire body is relaxing upward.

Get into some physical positions that are common to your daily life, such as typing, key-punch operating, standing and lecturing, writing on a blackboard, kneeling, scrubbing, peeling potatoes, playing a pinball machine. Have your partner watch you pantomime these activities. Do you find yourself exerting a tension in any part of your body that does not help you to accomplish your task? Where do you place this "set"?

Try some old-age character walks or Period Theatre movements and bows. Walk across the room and sit down, trying to give the appearance of old age. Is there unnecessary pressure and tension in your movements? Redo the same old-age character walk, using your balloon and keeping your head in alignment. Do you feel you've "lost" anything that was good the first time you tried the walk? If so, try to recapture the first walk, maintaining a relaxed alignment of your head, neck, and shoulders.

Choose an audition piece, a monologue, or a soliloquy from Shakespeare. Perform it, first sitting, then standing up, and finally as you would for an audience. Are you falling back into an unnecessary "set" when you rise to perform?

Try singing several bars of a song. Are you exerting any specific pressures in areas that you don't tense up when you normally speak? Do you feel that you cannot sing? Everyone can carry a beat, even if he cannot always distinguish a pitch. Being able to sing is largely a matter of your conception of yourself and where you carry your tension.

decisions You can help yourself avoid classroom tensions by making negative words taboo in your criticism of scenes, speeches, and singing. Words like "avoid," "never," "no," and "don't" only freeze an actor's creative juices and encourage him to stick with what he knows will work for him. Try to find new ways to see a character, an emotion, or an interpretation of a role. Decide what was good, as well as what was inefficient, about each piece of work. Try to make this positive and fresh outlook part of your daily life.

EXAMINING BODY TENSIONS IN A MIMETIC LIFE CYCLE[4]

ANIMAL	*baby*	*egocentric*	OCTUPUS
VEGETABLE	*adolescent*	*expansive*	SEED TO PLANT
MINERAL	*adult*	*contained*	IRON
SPIRITUAL	*death*	*formless*	SMOKE

The age of a character is inextricably bound to the type of energy he exerts and consumes. As a character grows older, he does not necessarily exert less energy; he actually transforms his energy so that it operates in different directions and in different ways—that is, physical energy may be changed into mental energy. However, a character may be just as wasteful with his mental energy as he is with his physical energy. The element of tension is what separates people into definite physical categories.

Phase 1

procedure Lie on your back on the floor and let your muscles sink into the floor. You are a baby. Your bum is getting wetter and wetter; you are hungry; you are thirsty; your throat is parched; you can't fall asleep; you are cold; you feel helpless; you need warmth, food, cuddling. Slowly allow yourself to experiment with all the above physical sensations. Flash them through your consciousness like subliminal advertising. Give in to them.

decisions Where was your tension most obvious? Did you feel that you were expending a great deal of physical energy? How much mental energy did you expend? In what direction did your energy move when you found yourself giving in to gesture and other movement? Did you find yourself reaching out and drawing back in? Since you had no words or vocabulary, did you find yourself using gestures like octopus tentacles? Were your gestures shouting "ME! ME!"? What types of characters do this in their adult lives? When you work on a script, do you find yourself in early rehearsals pointing to yourself when you say such pronouns as "I," "me," and "my"? Perhaps you can justify some of these moves by saying that "I" is in contrast to "you," but isn't it easier to let the words do the work of the gesture? When you really need a gesture, do you find that you have worn out the effectiveness of gesticulation because you've already been acting like a windmill? What kind of characters in plays move like babies? Look at the role of Ajax in *Tiger at the Gates* by Jean Giraudoux.

Phase 2

procedure Relax into a fetal position on your knees. You are a seed growing into a plant. Start a tiny vibration in your pelvis. Reach out your roots. Grow downward as well as upward. Force your body through the dirt above you until you reach the air. Respond to the sun and rain. Grow up through the hole you have made. Follow the sun in the sky. Feel the difference between the earth and the air. Branch out. Grow buds and let them change into fruit. Remember that you must be fertilized by the other plants around you, so you must relate to your neighbor. Let the fruit weigh you down.[5]

decisions Did your center of tension change as you grew from a seed to a young plant? Could you feel physical shifting into mental energy as you grew buds and related to your neighbor? Did you feel staid and developed when you had produced the fruit? Were the bulk of your gestures expansive, moving outward from your very center? At what point were you the most ungainly and vulnerable? Can you relate shooting up out of the ground and blossoming into flower with adolescent acne? What is the significance of the phrase "feeling your oats"? What types of characters remain awkwardly expansive in their adulthood? Such tension may create a "pushing" personality. Where do such people carry their tension? Happy in Arthur Miller's *Death of a Salesman* may be this type of person.

Phase 3

procedure You are a robot. Try doing a simple task, such as taking off or putting on your shoes, or perhaps moving furniture to another section of the room. You are an automaton; therefore, you need to expand only the barest amount of physical energy to complete your task. Feel the capability in your machine-like muscles, the inevitability of doing the job efficiently and correctly.

decisions Where was your center of tension? How much physical energy did you need to expend? Was your transition to mental energy obvious in your movement? Did you feel any real form of vulnerability? What is the significance of the phrase "solid as a rock"? Of course, not all adults are so capable or solid. This is a figurative exercise. Did you feel hemmed in by the exterior of the robot? Can you understand the inner tension of the adult robot who knows that he is trapped into being mechanical in Karel Capek's *R.U.R.?* Middle age is difficult for young people to play because there are no identifiable movements associated with performing it. It is much easier to be objective about the movements of very old people.

Phase 4

procedure Begin by doing a drop-over and giving up your tension to the floor. Slowly come up, placing one vertebra over another until you are erect. Without leaning back, feel your body continue to unfold upward as though a string inside you were connected to the ceiling, supporting you weightlessly. Draw your balloon to you and let it surround your head, moving you forward and upward until you are floating. Glide along the ceiling of the room, looking into ceiling corners and at overhead lamps.

decisions Do you feel tension at all? Do you feel the need to exert physical energy? If, in tiny snatches, you succeed in leaving your body behind, how much mental (imagination) energy would you say you have to expend? Do you feel that you are floating or gliding? Look at the role of Elvira in Noël Coward's *Blithe Spirit* and of the Ghost in Shakespeare's *Hamlet.* You would probably want to play these roles without giving the impression that you are feeling any physical tension at all.

chapter 3

CREATING AN ENSEMBLE APPROACH WITH OTHER ACTORS

You have a virtual storehouse of facts and inspirations within yourself. You should find a way to tap these areas of your own background that will help you understand the role you are to play; you must learn to be observant about yourself and your relationships with other people. Of course, an actress does not have to become a part-time prostitute to be able to play Anna Christie or Blanche Dubois. In creating the role, the actress must first decide why Anna or Blanche became a prostitute. She should then delve into her own background to determine whether she has had a similar experience, even if the experience is only indirectly related to the emotion that Blanche or Anna feels. For example, an actress who has been overweight at one time may remember a craving for candy that might approximate promiscuity to a degree. Anyone who has been jilted may have stored up some resentment toward members of the opposite sex in general. Your task is to zero in on such past experiences and attitudes so that they can be solidified into specific images that will aid you in rehearsal.

After you have begun to flesh out your role, exploiting your own background, you must use your subjectivity in such a way that you can communicate your emotions to your co-performers and to the audience. If the memory of an experience, such as the death of a parent, is so vivid that the recollection controls you rather than vice versa, or if the recollection is so personal that it traps you into tensions that never really communicate to the audience, the experience should be discarded as a steppingstone. In order for drama to be conflict, one actor must be able to place an emotional claim on another in tangible, aesthetic terms with which an audience can identify. Acting must be "sharing." Never let your private emotions isolate you onstage.

The following exercises are designed to help you appreciate observation; first, observation of yourself, and secondly, observation of the people and the environment around you. The more complicated exercises that appear later in the chapter are aimed at encouraging you to transfer your personal feelings about your past into immediate physicalizations that can be shared with your rehearsal partner. Several of the exercises can be done alone, but they will be more effective if you have a friend with whom you can share the experience.

Try to find a good room to work in. If you and a partner can lie down on the floor and move your arms and legs in spread-eagle fashion without touching each other, the room may be large enough. The best type of room is one that has little traffic and can be easily kept clean. The floor should be smooth and secure. The dimensions of the room should encourage free, expansive movements, and demand at least moderate projection of the voice.

THE "COOKIE"[1]

needs Bring a kerchief or a simple blindfold. Strips of muslin five inches wide and thirty inches long will do.

Phase 1

procedure Ask someone to help you with this exercise, or try it in a rehearsal hall or outdoors with your entire study group. One partner elects to "initiate" the exercise, and the second partner blindfolds himself. Both partners join hands and interlock their fingers like the couplings on a train. If you are the seeing partner, slowly begin to lead your blindfolded partner around the center space. Try to prevent him from bumping into anything. Gradually accelerate the pace until you are both jogging. After you have established your partner's trust in you, stop the exercise. Now repeat it, this time with you as the blindfolded partner.

Phase 2

procedure Join hands in the same way and apply a friendly amount of pressure, looking at each other's face and body. Again decide who will wear the blindfold. If you are the seeing partner, begin by saying "Cookie" to your blind partner. Try to be as personal and as individual as you can in the way you pronounce the word. Now start to lead your blind partner around the room by his fingers, saying "Cookie" at the same time. Gradually let go of your partner's fingers and lead him around the room using only the sound of your own way of saying "Cookie." Slowly accelerate the pace. Do not be overly protective of your partner; you should expect him to find you.

When the acceleration reaches a point of confusion, stop and freeze.

Now try to get as far away from your partner as possible, while he remains in the center of the space. Call out "Cookie" to your partner. If you are working with a study group, wait until all the seeing partners have said "Cookie." Now the blind partners must grope along, trying to find their own seeing partners; however, the blind partners are allowed to use only the sense of touch to identify their seeing partners. When a blind partner reaches his seeing partner and identifies him, he is allowed to remove his blindfold. If there are stragglers who cannot find their original partners, a seeing partner may take the initiative to approach them and ask them to name one specific physical feature of their original seeing partner. Then he may escort the blind partner to any seeing partner bearing such a physical feature. The blind partner must identify his original seeing partner, using, again, only the sense of touch.

decisions Did you discover, in your identification of your seeing partner, that you are not as specific as you think you are? Stragglers who have to name one physical feature of their seeing partner will learn that simply saying "brown hair" is insufficient.

In order to establish confidence between you and your blind partner, try to lead him in a more effective manner by keeping your hands at least one foot apart on a level, horizontal plane. Maintaining this balanced position will encourage your blind partner to put more faith in you. The idea is to foster a warm, relaxed, yet alert and sensitive relationship between you and your partner so that you will trust each other with your emotions. Never toy with your inner feelings. Remember that your emotions and those of your partner are to be respected.

THE "HIT"[2]

needs Several light rubber balls like tennis balls or basketballs will do, though a variety of shapes and sizes is desirable.

Phase 1

procedure Stand anywhere from sixteen to thirty feet away from your partner. Begin with the tennis ball and focus on a part of your partner's body. Your partner should try to receive the stimulus of the spot at which you are aiming. Direct all your attention at this spot, and then gently throw the ball toward it. After the receiver catches the ball, he tells you where he felt you were aiming. Then he becomes the initiator of the stimulus and throws the ball at you.

After five rounds with the tennis ball, put the ball away and try the same exercise in pantomime. If you note a high percentage of error in guessing where the initiator is aiming, return to using the tennis ball periodically.

Phase 2

procedure Try a variation of the exercise, experimenting with time, space, and weight. Remember that your hands must describe the size of the ball, its shape, and its speed; for example, a beach ball takes a wider hand position and travels more slowly than a soccer ball. Do everything in mime. The receiver tries to catch the specific ball at the spot it is aimed at. Verify the target and the type of ball; then choose a new type of ball to throw at your partner in mime.

Phase 3

procedure Pair up emotions with the physical gesture of throwing the ball. Choose very specific emotions and reasons to feel them. For example, recall your frustration at not being able to find a parking place near the rehearsal hall or work space. Take a moment to remember the tensions you felt: the sights, smells, and sounds of traffic around you that added to this frustration. Concentrate on a section of your partner's body with all that frustration. Pantomime throwing an imaginary ball (e.g., tennis ball, baseball, ping-pong ball) at that spot. The receiver should guess where the ball was aimed, what type of ball it was, and what the emotion was.

Phase 4

procedure Dispense with the miming. Focus on your receiver's face from the collar up, aiming all of your concentration at one feature—for example, the protruding part of the skull just above your partner's left eyebrow. When you feel that you have made contact, simply say "Hit," aiming the word at that feature. Check your accuracy. After three rounds, add an emotion to your concentration, just as you did with the imaginary ball. Your receiver should attempt to guess the spot you aimed at and the emotion coupled with your concentration.

purpose Home in on each other while externalizing your emotions. Though each step of the exercise may seem like a bit of extrasensory perception, you will soon develop ways of manifesting your intentions clearly so that your partner, much like an audience, can easily identify, and possibly empathize, with you. The more violent emotions, such as anger, are the easiest to deal with, but as you progress through the exercise, graduate to sadness, despair, or love.

suggestions Never repeat an emotion once you have used it. Prepare a short mimetic action for your partner to watch. The action should be a part of your daily routine, and it should have a beginning, middle, and end in relation to the progression of your attitudes toward the action. If you choose to eat a piece of fruit, there should be a progression of speed and intention as you wash or peel it. Modulate your speed as you take the first bite. As your enjoyment of the piece of fruit reaches a peak, your appetite slackens and the eating becomes routine. Finally, the core or seeds or the remnants of the fruit are thrown away.

The entire exercise will be affected by the extent of your hunger: whether you are "simply dying" to eat something, or whether you are rounding off a full-course dinner and are already stuffed. Your choices—eating, applying cosmetics, brushing your teeth, putting in contact lenses—are generally more successful if there is some immediacy about the action; for example, you might pretend that someone is waiting for you to go on a date. Be specific about the weight of each object you handle.

THE "SENSES"

needs Have on hand one blindfold, three clean teacups, a basin of clean water, and a large hardbound book.

Phase 1
Sight

procedure Try this exercise with a partner in a room full of objects, or if you are working with a study group, ask the members to arrange themselves haphazardly around the space between you and your partner. Pretend you are blind and walk across the room, trying to avoid falling over the objects or the persons in your way. Try to find your partner. After you have crossed the room once *pretending* to be blind, blindfold yourself and repeat the exercise, going back to your original corner of the room. Now remove the blindfold, and repeat the exercise again as you did it the first time. Try to incorporate what you learned the second time, when you were really blind.

decisions In the first walk, did you seem to focus your sight in order to protect yourself from falling? Was your body alert to possible danger, or did you seem too confident that sight would save you at the last minute? Were your hand, knee, and leg positions different on the second and third walks? In the third walk, did you find a way of focusing on a spot in the air to avoid focusing directly on the ground before you? Did you merely step over the objects or step around the persons in your way, or did you examine your space prudently to avoid them? Did you try to "show" your partner how blind you were, rather than simply try to get across the room? Check your answers with your partner.

Phase 2
Sight

procedure Search for an article that was stolen but that you think you may have lost somewhere in the work space. After you have searched for four or five minutes, give up. Give a valuable possession, such as your wallet or credit card, to your partner and leave the room. Your partner hides the article, and then calls you back to look for it.

decisions Were you *really* looking for something the first time? Were there many extraneous gestures, or did you look in logical places? Was your survey staccato or economical and simple? If your head was bobbing up and down, you were probably "showing" your partner that you were searching instead of really searching.

Phase 3
Smell

procedure Sit in a comfortable position and blindfold yourself. Your partner now selects articles made of leather, such as wallets, belts, shoes, or jackets. He holds each article under your nose, being careful not to let it touch your face. Guess the nature of each article by its individual smell, relying on the odor of the specific type of leather or the human odor that would locate the area of the body with which the article comes in contact.

purpose How did you react to the particular body smell of the leather articles? Pantomime smelling a shoe again. Remember that in some structured scenes, you must maintain the first-time illusion of smelling what surrounds you and react to it.

Phase 4
Touch

procedure Blindfold your partner and ask him to stand up with his right hand extended as if welcoming people. Try some individual handshakes—for example, the "hearty" handshake, the "painful presser" handshake, the sensual handshake, the noncommittal handshake— and finally, secretly put your hand in a basin of water and give your partner a limp and wet "dead fish" handshake.

decisions How did your partner react to the different handshakes? What was your reaction as he responded to your hand pressure?

Phase 5
Touch and taste

procedure Put three clean teacups on a chair. Fill only one cup with water. Now ask your partner to go to the opposite side of the room. Pick up a cup at random and drink from it, pretending that it contains liquid even if it is an unfilled cup. Try to fool your partner.

decisions Ask your partner if he believed the speed with which you raised the cup to your lips, your tipping of the cup as if liquid were in it, your swallowing action, your tipping of the cup after it had been partially drained, and your replacement of the cup on the chair.

For a variation, get three pieces of cotton and saturate one of them with household ammonia. Lift each piece of cotton to your nose and sniff it. Try to react as if each piece reeked of the ammonia. Analyze the difference in your reactions.

Phase 6
Sound

procedure Blindfold your partner. Tell him to relax, to count five beats, and then to react as if a very loud explosion had occurred directly behind him. After he has performed this reaction, tell him to begin to count to fifty slowly. While he is counting, slam a heavy book on the floor behind him when he does not expect it. Where did he center his body energy when the book hit the floor?

HAND GEOGRAPHY

procedure Sit down next to your partner and take his hand. Close your eyes and apply a small amount of pressure on his hand. Forget about his identity and try to construct a new person through your sense of touch, using only your partner's hand and your own. Run your fingers along the wrist. Do any bones protrude here? Is the wrist strong and supple or soft and weak? Travel up to the meaty base of the thumb, and squeeze gently. Is there turgor and power here.? What sports, hobbies, or jobs might this person usually engage in? Sneak your fingers up the thumb, over the first joint, and onto the thumbnail. Explore the cuticle and the nail itself. Is this person well-groomed? Does he have a calcium-rich diet? Gently slide your fingers back down the thumb to the palm of the hand. Is it moist or dry, resilient or surrendering, ticklish or insensitive? Slowly work up to the pads at the base of the fingers to ascertain if there are calluses there. Again, decide upon sports, hobbies, occupations. Feel the fingers themselves. Are they long or short? Are there paper cuts or is the skin torn anywhere? Are the cuticles clean? Are the nails long, or short, or jagged? Are the knuckles smooth or chafed? Smell the hand. Does it smell as you expected it to? Are there any identifiable scars or rings? Go back to the wrist. What kind of watch, if any, is he wearing?

Now formulate a personality for the hand, asking yourself these questions:

1. What "type" of person is he?
2. What are his favorite expressions, and what does he say when he gets extremely angry?
3. What is the extent of his education, and which parts of it did he enjoy most?
4. What type of exercise does he indulge in?
5. What is his favorite music? Who are his favorite musicians? Specifically, which composer or group or singer does he like best?
6. What are his favorite foods?
7. What type of clothing does he wear?
8. What is he like when he wakes up in the morning? What is the first thing he says? What are his morning grooming habits?

PASS THE PENNY

procedure Try doing this with a group of fellow students. Everyone gathers in the center of a cleared work space, and a volunteer offers to begin the exercise with a penny. The group mills around the work space. The volunteer tries to pass the penny to another member of the group as secretly as possible, and in turn, this member must pass the penny on to someone else. No one can refuse the penny when it is passed to him; for it is also his job to disguise his acceptance of the penny. No one can have his hands in his pockets or his arms folded. Neither is it fair for members of the group to straggle around the periphery of the space; once a person reaches the outside edge of the group, he should turn around and walk directly through the center of the space again.

Arrange a signal for the group to halt and freeze. The last person to pass the penny remains silent, and the group guesses who has the penny. If the group guesses wrong two or more times or seems very divided in its choice, the current owner of the penny admits he has it; but he gets to keep it.

In the second phase of this exercise, the group uses a nickel. The same rules prevail, except that everyone in the group must stay at least a full foot away from any other member. In addition, each person should act as if he has the nickel, and he may palm someone else making believe that he is passing the nickel. Discuss the "sneaky expression" on the faces of the members who are accused of hiding the nickel.

MASKS OF EMOTION[3]

procedure Try this exercise either with your partner or alone with a mirror. If you are working with a partner, take turns performing the exercise; criticize and improve each other's work. Try to find the most specific way to physicalize the emotion being represented.

Face your partner at a distance of about five feet. Put your hands up in front of your face. Begin with the emotion of "frustration." Try to recapture the last time you were truly frustrated. Concentrate on all the sensory impressions that were present at that time: the sights or colors, smells, tastes, textures of clothing, and so on. Try to associate them with the specific emotion of frustration, heightening the reality of the recall by breathing just as you did at the time. You may find that your evoked frustration causes certain physical tensions that appear in your facial "mask." Hide your face behind your hands; then on the count of three, drop your hands so that your partner may see your mask—or check it in a mirror yourself.

decisions Are you effectively producing the exact emotion called for, or could your mask be mistaken for another emotion as well? Alter one facial feature that will better represent the emotion. For example, looking directly upward while keeping your head perfectly level may help heighten the impression of frustration a bit. However, gazing upward may typify only one of many varieties of frustration!

Try to maintain your facial expression while relaxing your body. Control the mask; don't let its tension control you! Repeat the exercise with such emotions as anger, respect, utter servitude, adoration, lust, self-pity, total despair, elation, and ecstacy.

CIGARETTESMANSHIP[4]

procedure Create five ways to light a cigarette, five ways to hold it, and five ways to extinguish it. Each way must be specific, recognizable, and completely pantomimed with a beginning, middle, and end. Your choices may be representative of a particular character "type" or a novel way of performing the cigarette action. If you are working with a partner, don't allow yourself to repeat his actions. You may, however, adapt his methods or choose to work off him; for example, you might merely lean over and mime lighting your cigarette from his.

decisions Were you specific? Did you reproduce the weight and shape of the package of cigarettes with economy? Was there an attitude toward smoking evident in your manner (either an enjoyment of or a distaste for tobacco) that guided your rhythms?

THE GROWING THREAD[5]

procedure Relax on the floor. Try to keep your action continuous rather than stopping at various stages and forcing yourself to concentrate all over again. Begin the exercise alone, though you may work with a partner after you establish a frame of reference with each other. Use only as much of your body as is necessary to accomplish the task you elect to do.

Select a small task that can be done with a piece of thread, such as threading a needle and sewing on a loose button. Be sure to look down the eye of the needle. Draw the needle carefully out of the back of the cloth, and remember that with every stitch the length of the thread gets shorter. After three to five minutes, imagine that your thread enlarges to the size of string, and choose a new task, such as wrapping a package for mailing. Once again, use only the parts of your body, the amount of action, and the pressure that would be necessary to accomplish this job. After three to five minutes have elapsed again, imagine that your string enlarges to the size of heavy cord or clothesline rope. From this point on, you may work with a partner, but be careful to duplicate each other's sense of weight and pressure. During the next intervals, the imaginary cord increases in size and weight, successively becoming towing rope, thick hemp like that used in fly galleries of older theatres, cable, and, finally, a gigantic ship's anchor cable.

If you begin a tug of war, be sure to maintain sufficient distance between you and your partner; otherwise the rope will give the appearance of being elastic, and the reciprocal action of the tug of war will be lost. Heavy tasks require less arm motion and more of a displacement of the body's center weight around the hips and thighs. Lean into it!

ENSEMBLE PICTURE DEVELOPMENT[6]

procedure The study group sits comfortably on the floor facing one wall of the work space.

Everyone will contribute to the design of an imaginary painting on the wall. Create the colors and subject matter of the paintings and the dimensions of the frame. You are each allowed only one feature at a time, and you must incorporate everyone else's suggestions into your painting. After each member has had a chance to contribute one or two features of the painting (depending on the size of the study group), everyone relaxes and tries to fit all these features together individually and silently until he finds a logicality and a personal meaning for the creation. Title the creation. Develop the central intent of the artist and describe the "story" or "emotion" of the painting together.

decisions The group should discuss which features of the creation were easy to digest into each member's personal view of the painting, and which were hard to assimilate. How do the title, meaning, and story fit in with your personal view of the creation? Although the creation is a group effort in sharing visual realities, you can do this exercise with just one partner, tossing ideas back and forth. Take five or six turns each.

THE CALENDAR

Phase 1
Group rhythm[7]

procedure The study group forms an easy, relaxed circle. The exercise works best with eight to ten people, who will all perform the following steps together. Everyone makes eye contact from person to person, sharing a smile and a feeling of warmth. Each then lowers his right arm in time with his breathing rhythm,

Calendar art opposites

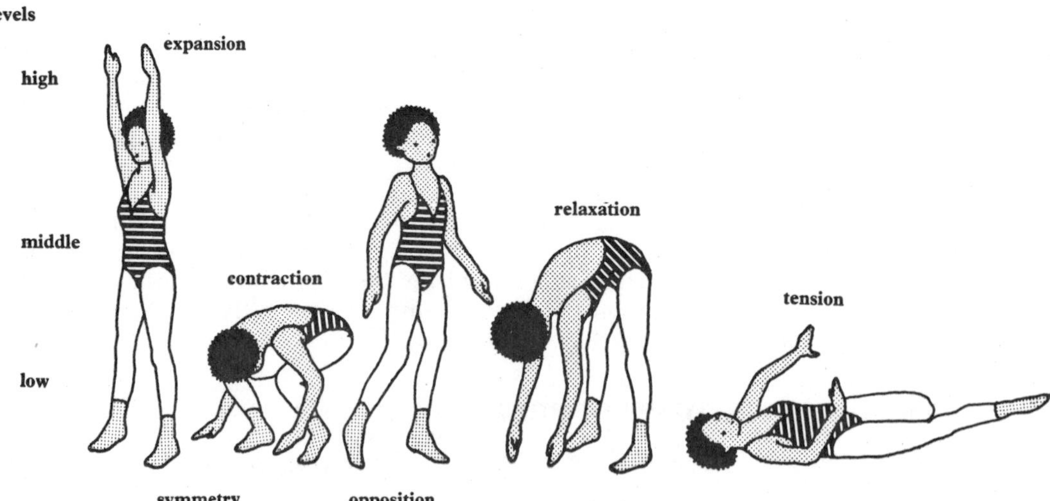

vocalizing the exhalation with an easy "ahhh." After two minutes, everyone slowly synchronizes a mutual rhythm with a friendly-sounding chorus of "ahhh." When all the members have completely tuned in to one another, one member may alter the rhythm, using sound and gesture to demonstrate the change. Each person adapts himself to the new rhythm and maintains its continuum. Anyone may change the rhythm now, but enough time should be allowed for all to accustom themselves to the new rhythm presented before it is changed again. Should two persons begin a new rhythm simultaneously, the majority should choose the stronger rhythm until it overwhelms the opposing rhythm. To be successful, each new rhythm initiated must have its own specific inhalation, exhalation, emotional content, and gesture.

Phase 2

The solitary model[8]

procedure Gather the study group in a large circle around the periphery of the work space. Try this exercise alone in the center of the space. First decide whether you want to move to consecutive months of the year, numbers, or letters. Your objective as the volunteer in the center is to move freely from pose to pose as someone on the periphery calls out each new month, number, or letter.

Each pose should vary as completely as possible from the last pose. The person calling the changes must maintain a moderate speed in order to help you in two ways: too fast a speed will constrict you into a series of self-conscious movements that will result only in your flailing about the circle, and too slow a speed will give you too much time to think and to plan your next moves. Merely responding to your own inner instinct for external physical variation will free you. Planning will trap you into patterns.

Don't associate each new position with a specific emotion, unless it helps free you. No theme is needed. The poses may be totally abstract, or they may be symbolic. You may even vary the speed with which you assume the new pose. The volunteer calling out the changes may help you by varying his speed and varying vocal inflections that suggest emotions, such as anger, fear, warmth, and gentleness.

decisions The opposite of an outward, upward reaching of expansion would be a low crouch of withdrawal. There are many other demonstrable variables, such as physical symmetry, opposition, and diagonal stretching. And there are three major physical levels or planes: you may discover a vertical reaching that could be symbolic of any religious attitude; you may bend your knees into an alert crouch and focus on a point or person on the periphery, using a hunting attitude for a central or horizontal position; or you may lie down on the floor in submission, utilizing the lowest plane physically possible. Use all these variables indiscriminately, skipping from one to the other. Avoid any set pattern. Can you free your body and move in front of a group without worrying about "what people think"? If you feel "tight," try the exercise alone or with just one partner to call out changes of position.

Phase 3

Pose sharing

procedure Repeat the last exercise with two volunteers in the center. A new partner calls out the months, numbers, or letters—for a total of twenty-four. Center volunteers have the same task of trying to vary their positions as completely as possible; but they must also react to their partner's position at the same time, freezing into a new pose as each month, number, or letter is called. Before beginning, the center volunteers may hold hands and establish eye contact in order to gain a physical sense of each other's tensions. They may run their hands up and down each other's arms, experimenting with varying emotions, such as fear, anger, love, lust. The partners then begin the exercise and continue it through twenty-four poses.

decisions As the center volunteers, did you and your partner learn to respond freely to each other without "thinking"? Did you trust each other? Did physical contact aid you in finding real variation? There is a great difference between a forceful grip and a gentle caress.

Try this exercise with a partner when doing structured scene work from a play if you both have lost the knack of really listening to or watching each other. Deal with each other straight-on. Avoid playing emotional scenes to each other's back. That is the lazy actor's way out. Have you seen two actors reach the climax of a scene and turn their backs to each other to "show" the audience what they are going through? Hold your ground and deal with the emotional demands of the script in terms of each other! The ensemble actor must be aware of his own dynamics as well as those of his partner or partners.

suggestions Read Anton Chekhov's *The Three Sisters.* Chekhov creates individual rhythms for each character. These separate rhythms function as part of the whole scene or act. Can you discern a rhythmic difference between Solyony and Tusenback?

Read the "Don Juan in Hell" segment in the third act of George Bernard Shaw's *Man and Superman.* Shaw actually orchestrates the piece. Try to ascertain which orchestral instruments Don Juan, the Devil, the Statue, and Doña Ana might sound like.[9] What would their rhythms and paces be individually, and how would these contribute to the overall effect of the play?

Phase 4

Caption poses

procedure After taking a break, both you and a partner should try to recall silently the last full sentence that each of you spoke during the break. Reconstruct it word by word for yourselves and remember it. You'll both need it again soon.

Once again, begin the Calendar Exercise. Perform it with your partner the same way you did in Phase 3; however, this time, the two of you should maintain a constant flow of movement in relation to each other. Freeze into a position only when an appointed member of your study group says, "Stop!" You may allow yourselves only one tiny movement to justify this position.

Then, taking turns, focus on each other and say the sentence that you each reconstructed earlier. Relate the sentence to the physical position in which you find yourselves. After both of you have said your "lines," resume your movement until you are stopped again in a new pose. You each should then find a new motivation for your line and speak it again.

decisions Did you and your partner watch and listen to each other intently? Did you alter each delivery of your line to suit the new position in which you found yourself and your partner when you were stopped in mid-motion?

BODY SIGNALS[10]

procedure Relax your voice by yawning up and down the scale as you mosey around the work space. Laugh silently with your eyes. Now utilize different sections of your body to manifest enjoyment; for example, laugh with your toes, knees, hips, hands, biceps, shoulders, nose, ears, hair—and now, laugh out loud. Repeat the exercise with a sigh or a hiss such as you might make in response to a villain in a melodrama.

Work with a partner. Alternate doing the exercise and guessing which emotion each of you is performing. How "organic" or complete is the emotion? Train your whole body to laugh or cry so that your audience will be able to identify and empathize with you immediately.

CIRCLES OF LOVE AND ANGER

This exercise in all of its phases can be very dangerous for emotional or volatile people.[11] If you wish to stop, do so at any time. Remember that you are trying to create a believable, controllable emotional response that can be used onstage. Share the experience with your partner. Do not attempt to trap the emotion inside yourself and wallow in it.

Phase 1

Partners in opposition

procedure You and your partner should sit comfortably on the floor and face each other. One of you should choose the emotion of attraction (love); the other, anger (frustration or repugnance—be specific!). You each should then focus on your partner's feet, calves, and knees. Go through a sense memory of the last time you felt the emotion you have chosen. Reconstruct the sights and colors that were around you at that time. Then re-create the smells, the tastes, the sounds; recall the feel of the clothing that you were wearing. Slowly give in to a breath rhythm that seems right for this emotion, relaxing the upper part of your body and breathing deeply down into the abdomen. Flash the sensory images through your mind, and attempt to relate your past experience to your partner.

Start with his feet and slowly let your gaze travel up his body, saving his emotionally charged face for last. Be specific about the individual physical features that you choose to focus on.

When you both reach the point of staring at each other's face, the partner with the emotion of love should allow himself to physicalize his feelings, but the partner using anger should not. Relax, and repeat the exercise, switching the emotions of love and anger.

decisions

Theatrical emotions should exist only for the duration of your scene work. In rehearsal, you may have to supply yourself with fictitious reasons to produce an emotion. Allowing yourself to externalize an internal emotion while using this breathing technique may help you to simulate a real feeling. Center your tensions in your pelvis where you can deal with them more easily. Tensions in such obvious areas of the body as the feet, hands, shoulders, or knees draw attention to themselves. The larger the muscle area, the more capable it is of absorbing tensions in such a way that the audience will not be conscious of them. When you did the exercise, did you find that you began to accept the emotion, even if only for a second? Was your partner "showing" you what "great traumas" he was undergoing, or was he low-keyed?

Phase 2
The circle of opposition

procedure

The members of the study group assemble in a circle (eight in the circle is the maximum) and join hands. Two volunteers sit in the center of the circle. The center volunteers use the emotion of mutual repugnance, creating their own private, fictitious circumstances. Each member of the circle uses the emotion of love, and squeezes the hand of the person on his right as if he were passing a current around the circle. The circle chooses one of the two center volunteers for its affection and completely ignores the other. Working as a unit, the circle manifests its love with wordless sounds. Gradually, the circle accelerates its breath rhythm, ceases the hand-holding, and allows itself to demonstrate its affection physically either by touching the chosen center volunteer or by edging closer to him. The recipient of the circle's affection should remain open to its advances—not close himself off or concentrate on his partner to the exclusion of everything else. He should be able to accept and use the circle's help.

variation

Stop the exercise if the person being ignored becomes increasingly agitated. The exercise should take about ten minutes. If the people in the circle get bored, tell them that all the faith they had placed in the person who had received their affection was not justified, that it had been a lie. They must refocus their love and let it flow toward the other person in the center, building a new faith in him, possibly even humming a tune that they feel he will enjoy—because he knows the circle is with him now. The circle may accelerate its breathing and rhythm and sing louder. Continue this exercise for ten minutes. Encourage the two persons in the center to settle their differences in their minds and change their emotion to love and attraction. Everyone should end the exercise with some form of affection.

decisions If you were working as a member of the circle, were there moments when you felt that you were really sharing with the other members? If you were a center volunteer, did you find one of your partner's particular physical features helped you solidify your feelings of both affection and dislike? Did the ostracized person in the center feel defeated or strengthened by the actions of the circle? Was the person who received the circle's affection able to use it and incorporate the circle into his concentration? Regardless of your function in the game, did you deal with your own body tensions? Did you feel nervous or slightly off-balance after the game was over?

CENTERING YOUR CONTROL WITH A PARTNER

After performing a strenuous emotional exercise, you may want to relax by trying an exercise that will divert your energy and dispel some of the tension. Never toy with, or totally immerse yourself in, your emotions. Stage emotion is the result of sharing a moment with a fellow actor, not the means of removing yourself from the dramatic action onstage. Very often after a strong moment in a play you may have a chance to return to the green room for a cigarette or a cup of coffee. However, your rehearsal had prepared you for that specific moment. In the classroom strong moments occur spontaneously; therefore it may be wise to give yourself a moment to wind down.

procedure Face your partner, standing about two feet away from him. Keep your elbows at your waist and raise your hands, palms up, keeping them parallel and about fourteen to eighteen inches apart. Your partner places his hands directly over yours so that the tips of his fingers are over your wrists. Keep your postures relaxed. Your partner now raises his hands about an inch above yours and gently holds them there. He must keep his hands evenly over yours as he walks as far forward, as far back, and as far to the left and right as he can. He must compensate with his wrists for his body's movement so that he never changes his hand positions. Now he should try to kneel and then rise up on his toes.

If your partner gets off-balance, or if he begins to tilt his hands or touch your hands, either tell him or gently slap his hands. Take turns doing this exercise and develop a point game. Every time one of you fails, it becomes the other's turn to have the top position.

variation Once you have both tried the game, first speed up your movements, then try the game blindfolded. The partner with his hands on top must wear the blindfold. If you are to be the blind partner, attach the blindfold, then place your hands over your partner's. Try to feel the heat emanating from his hands. Lift your own hands one inch; visualize his hands, and again try to feel the heat from them. Repeat the movements that you used in the first phase of the exercise. Begin slowly, focusing your mind on your partner's hands. Every time you make a mistake, your partner is permitted to slap your hands. Try to establish a kinesthetic awareness of your pelvic position in relation to your hand positions.

decisions Can you control your body better moving in a horizontal or a vertical position in relation to your hands? Are you aware of your pelvic center when you are in motion? Were your hands stiff with tension or were you able to relax them as you played the game? A well-balanced body will help to calm a churning mind. This exercise may help you develop trust and confidence in your partner. If you are working with a full group, try to find a different partner every time you do the exercise. Switching around will help you establish artistic trust in all your fellow actors.

THE DEFORMITY DANCE

procedure Both you and your partner choose a strange deformity: a three-pound nose; a huge and distended upper or lower lip; eyelashes over a foot long; eyebrows just as long, none of which can be trimmed because the hair follicles actually have nerves in them; a horn on the forehead; ear lobes over a foot long; a six-pound chin; a tongue extending nine inches from the mouth; wide, fan-like cheeks (gills); a fifty-pound shoulder hunch; eighty-pound buttocks; a two-foot extension from the umbilicus or lower abdomen; fingers or toes over a foot long; legs joined from either the knee up or from the knee down.

Experiment with the affliction. Decide upon the exact size, shape, and weight, as well as your attitude toward the deformity. Be specific about the way it might restrict your current routine and limit your choice of friends and your romantic life. Figure out how you are going to sleep. Find a way to cook and eat a breakfast of bacon, eggs, and toast. Select clothing for a cold, snowy winter day; and decide how you would dress in the summer. Create a character from the deformity. Take the time to make specific decisions, and pantomime them.

Create a party for yourself and your partner. You should both try to be happy, despite your disfigurements. Attempt to dance together, taking each other's affliction seriously. Use a phonograph if one is available. Try an upbeat record, such as Burt Bacharach's "Up, Up, and Away," and follow it with a slow dance.

Should you try this exercise with a study group, don't allow any wallflowers. If your two-foot extension from the umbilicus makes it impossible for you to dance with another malformed person, consider yourself healed. You have become the "god" or "goddess" for the final segment of the exercise. The "Healed God" may roam among the group during the slow dance, observing the individual deformities. After the dance, you, as the "Healed God," have the prerogative of healing one person in the grotesque group. Everyone must try to convince you that his personal affliction is worse than anyone else's. Allow the group ten minutes, then make a decision. (After you select a member of the group to be healed, that person is slowly made whole and your affliction returns.)

decisions Did your partner force you to accept his disability? Accepting your partner's physical characteristics is extremely necessary to create an aura of believability for the audience. In Shakespeare's *Richard III,* if the actor portraying Buckingham finds he cannot accept the logicality of the way the actor Richard uses his crippled arm, the audience will not accept Richard's "suspension of disbelief" either. The entire cast must be able to accept Solyony's loneliness in Chekhov's *The Three Sisters,* as well as the individual physical manifestations of drug addiction in Jack Gelber's *The Connection.* The final segment of the exercise puts the study group into conflict for the first time. Conflict can deter the group from realizing a healthy ensemble if such exercises are introduced too early.[12]

THE BUS[13]

needs Arrange enough chairs or benches in two rows to accommodate all the members of the study group as if they were sitting on a bus. This exercise can also be done with just two persons sitting side by side.

The study group assembles in the chairs and relaxes. A destination and a logical point of departure are agreed upon. Next, each member of the group decides on a specific moment during which he recently experienced a strong emotion. It need not be a tragic moment at all; quite often a happy time will elicit stronger and more creative impulses for this exercise.

procedure Try to recapture the moment as fully as possible, noting the tensions and the breath rhythm suggested by your recall. Flash the various sensory images through your mind. As you settle into your images, ask yourself, "What would I be like if I felt this way all the time? How would my own rhythms and personality alter? Would I look any different? Would my grooming habits be different? What would my favorite foods be, my favorite music, expressions, and ways of relaxing or exercising?" After ten minutes of concentration and decision-making, consciously try to live the alterations you have selected, and interrelate with other members of your group. Your task is simple: remain true to your created character, and try to find out as much as you can about everyone around you. Allow the interaction to continue for fifteen minutes.

decisions Did you try to "perform" the exercise, or did you simply allow it to happen? Which "types" of people are the most observant? Did your choice of emotion restrict your freedom to communicate with others? Where you self-indulgent? Cite all the facts you know about every person around you. Ask your partner how logical and consistent you were in your character choices.

THE BLIND BUS

needs Try this exercise with your partner or with your study group. Simulate the seating on a bus. Everyone performing the exercise must blindfold himself.

procedure Dim the lights so that a bare minimum of visibility is possible. Try to avoid creating "great drama." Simply respond to whatever you and your classmates create. Agree upon a point of departure and a destination. These points should be familiar to everyone performing the exercise. Set up a reason for the journey, such as a concert or seminar.

Begin a sense-memory exercise of the last time you were very cold. As you concentrate on the "cold," flash your sensory impressions through your mind. The bus has gone off the icy road at a point midway to your destination. There was a minor collision, but the only one hurt was your bus driver, who is unconscious and may be near death. The bus seems to have skidded on the ice, broken through a fence or guard rail, and careened into a body of water. In any case, the bus is slowly sinking, and everyone at the front end can feel water seeping into the aisle. The water gets deeper and deeper as the exercise progresses. Try to establish a sinking rate for the bus and the tilt that the bus has taken as it floats. Survival is your objective.

decisions Did you allow the sense-memory work to affect you? Did you establish the cold believably? Did you lift your feet to get away from the water? Did you use the bus furniture, setting up the windows and a fire exit? Were you more preoccupied with your danger and possible death than you were with trying to stay alive? Did the members of the group listen to one another? Did they willingly work together (for example, form a human chain)? Did any specific moments "work" for you? If so, were you involved with doing a real piece of business at the time, such as the act of opening a window? Were you doing this real piece of business with someone else? Was there a spirit of "emotionality" that seemed catchy? Did anyone inspire you with confidence? Real business, even if you must pantomime the action, should help you "lock in," especially if you share the task with someone else. The more little physical tasks you develop when you work on a structured scene, the more real the circumstances and environment will seem to you.

THE STRANDED RAFT

needs Find a prop blanket of double-bed size and either two volleyballs or two basketballs.

procedure Spread out the blanket at one end of the work space. Six to eight volunteers now crowd onto the blanket and either sit or kneel; they represent a shipwrecked party trying to get to safety on a raft. Two other volunteers take the balls and patrol around the blanket; these two are "sharks." All the performers begin with a sense-memory exercise of the last time they were very hungry or thirsty.

The objective of the group on the blanket is to edge itself across the floor to the opposite side of the room. The objective of the sharks is to hit with a ball any hand or foot, arm or leg, etc., that happens to move off the protective blanket. If a member of the group allows any part of his body to budge from the blanket and be hit by a shark, he must react and play the rest of the exercise as if he had been dismembered or bitten by the shark. The group must decide whether to throw the wounded member "overboard" or to absorb him as dead weight in the center of the raft and try to get him back to safety. The group will have to work out its own method of moving the blanket. Once the group has moved away from its initial position, the sharks will have to patrol in a circle opposite each other in order to keep an eye on all the people on the blanket. Allow five minutes for the sense memory, and perhaps fifteen minutes or more for the "raft and sharks" segment of the exercise.

decisions

If you were one of the unfortunates on the blanket, did your hunger or fear seem to permeate your whole body, or did you merely perform with parts of your body? Did you involve yourself with "real" actions that could be accomplished? Did you attempt to put on a virtuoso performance, or did you relax and unaffectedly do real tasks in relation to your partner? If your study group has been able to take this exercise seriously, try moving into the "conflict" exercises in the next chapter.[14]

chapter 4
DEVELOPING AN APPROACH TO CONFLICT

Perhaps you dislike the idea of "conflict." Drama, however, can occur between people only when there is a difference of opinion or a separation of interests.[1] For a play to be effective, the dramatist must create a situation in which the characters are faced with key decisions. If the character you are playing seems to want only to carry on his daily routine, you may be avoiding the potential conflict in your scene. While performing the scene in character, try questioning the validity of following your old routine patterns. Try to impose or create conflict in what seems to be a "quiet" scene.

Examine your attitude toward conflict. Remember that stage life is an acceleration of real life. Stage conflict must be aesthetic, human, performable, and easy for any audience to grasp and appreciate. It must give the illusion that something is happening—a moment is being shared between two people. In this sense, stage conflict requires ultimate give-and-take. Even if you are doing a soliloquy onstage and the argument is within yourself, you cannot perform conflict alone. Every single personal dilemma requires that you take sides with yourself in order to make a decision. The dramatic effect is much like talking to yourself!

The major conflict in a scene is usually easy to discern, although it may not always be earth-shattering. For example, there is conflict in every scene of Thornton Wilder's *Our Town,* but it is a gentle, subtle conflict. The conflict should always involve the other actor onstage with you. In the first scene of

John Osborne's *Look Back in Anger,* Jimmy Porter may be ferociously angry at the world around him, but if you are playing Jimmy you must try to channel his anger into simple, tangible needs in order to share the dramatic action and create conflict with Cliff and Alison, who are onstage with you. You cannot play a generalized attitude onstage if you want the audience to identify with you.

Begin working on a scene simply by reading it several times with your partner. Use as much eye contact as possible. What do you want or need most from each other in this scene? Can you play that "want" or "need"? Will it put both of you into action? Be sure that you each choose a want or need that involves both of you. Restrict yourself to one *major* need or want that you can play from each entrance to each exit in your scene, and then try to find as many ways as you can to fulfill it. Any need or want that carries you from an entrance to an exit is called a French-scene objective. Simplify your work. One need will suffice; it will give you a central purpose to be onstage in that scene. The following exercises are designed to help you experiment with stage conflict.

PERSONAL DILEMMA

procedure Ask your partner to watch you. Choose and perform one of the following three actions: (1) Count the fingers on your hands over and over. (2) Decide whether you want to marry the person of the opposite sex to whom you are closest, or if married, whether you really wish to remain married. (3) Decide whether to run out of the room, hide in a corner, or find a position in the middle of the room.

decisions Did you do more than was required of you? Was all of your action motivated? Were some parts merely a means of "showing" emotion? Ask your partner if you really seemed to be thinking and trying to make a decision? Did you make it "too easy" on yourself? Did you establish a strong emotional claim on yourself? Remember that when you perform you must play what a character "needs" rather than what a character "is."

The first task isn't too difficult as long you supply yourself with a reason to count your fingers, such as numbering the guests at a wedding reception. The third task requires something more—that you construct definite emotional circumstances. At first, the second task seems easy; but remember, you must communicate your mental dilemma clearly to your audience. Repeat the second task, using a set of photographs as props.

THE JUMP EXERCISE[2]

Phase 1

The wants or needs that your character has throughout a play may aptly be referred to as "objectives."[3] To be effective, objectives should be worded in positive terms of "I want," in relation either to the other actor on the stage, the audience, or oneself. The best way to construct an objective is to use a verb that defines the type of action for you, such as "I want to coax (to tease, to compel, to hypnotize, to reason with, to threaten, etc.) him to help me get enough money to provide for an immediate operation for my dying sister." Successful objectives utilize direct or indirect objects. They encourage the solution to an immediate problem, and they put not only you the initiator but also the actor you approach into action.

procedure The study group gathers in a large circle (or you may try the exercise alone with your partner). Each of the performers thinks of an objective that needs another actor to help him perform it. The more life-and-death the matter is, the better. Physicality should be kept at a minimum, and the objectives should not be contingent upon the sex of the other actor because there is no way to control who will approach whom. A member of the group is appointed the "leader." When the leader calls "jump," a volunteer should leave the periphery of the circle and approach another actor with his objective; the latter retaliates with his own objective, beginning a conflict of wills. As soon as two people are actively engaged, everyone else should relax and watch the two performers attempt to solve their dilemma together in the center.

decisions Which performer chose the strongest motivation? Who presented the better case? Did they listen to each other? Was there variety in their respective approaches, or did they merely seem to hammer at each other? Were they illogical? Could they have solved their problems mutually? Remember that the theatre is a place for teamwork, not competition, between actors.

The following suggestions will help you play the Jump Exercise, or any improvisational exercise, more efficiently.[4]

1. Jump immediately into your own objective.
2. Try to use what the other actor gives you rather than ignore it.
3. Adhere to pre-set circumstances, though these may be altered. Accept what your partner says as true, though you may modify it. For example, if your partner says, "I saw you park your car here earlier, and I desperately need a ride to the hospital to see my brother, who had an attack of appendicitis this morning," you may answer, "Oh, no! I just gave my car keys to my roommate to go to the supermarket." It would not be fair to say, "You're wrong. I haven't got a car." In this situation, your partner is protecting himself by setting up certain criteria before attacking. After his first sentence, it is obvious he knows that you have a car, that the car is nearby, and that it is in running condition. You jump in quickly, covering yourself by saying you have lent the keys; then you may add that you have a huge need that he can satisfy—money. He may counter with a statement like "I'm terribly sorry, but I've misplaced my wallet."
4. Listen to your fellow performer. Approach him as your *partner,* not your *opponent.*

5. Resist the impulse to create "great drama."
6. Continue until the leader stops you, or until you have both solved your problems.

Phase 2

Repeat the Jump Exercise, using a new set of objectives.

decisions Did you make the exercise too "easy" on yourselves either by choosing watered-down objectives or by coming to an understanding too soon? Which objectives involved both of you the most? Were you successful in using each other's material? Did either of you seem to be performing for an audience? It isn't always important to feel deep, personal emotions when you perform. In fact, such emotions may isolate you from your partner if you concentrate more on the emotion than on what you need from your fellow worker. Once you find a simple way to communicate with your partner, you will begin to believe in the situation yourself.[5]

YES AND NO OPPOSITION

procedure Do this exercise with a partner. One of you uses only the word "yes," the other only the word "no." Your objective is to get your partner to say your word (without any threat of personal violence or brute force); for example, if your word is "no," begin to unbutton your partner's shirt in order to get him to say "no." The major obstacle is that the "yes" partner can use only the word "yes" to get his partner to say "yes," and the "no" partner is likewise limited to the word "no." Work for at least ten minutes, and then switch words so that if you had "yes" before you must work with "no" now.

decisions Did the exercise degenerate into merely slamming at each other vocally, or were you able to find a variety of ways in which to use your "yes" or "no"? What original devices did you construct to get your partner to say your word?

STRUCTURED CONTRARY OBJECTIVES[6]

needs Place two chairs or a bench in the center of the work space to use when you and your partner need them.

procedure Try performing some of the following structured exercises with your partner. Use the rules for improvisations. If you are working with a study group, send two volunteers out of the room and ask the rest of the group for a relationship between the volunteers and a situation with specific, contrary objectives to put them into action. Call in the volunteers, and whisper to each one his specific secret objective. Announce their relationship and locale out loud

Try substituting a "topic" exercise in which each of you chooses a specific topic or area of concentration. Agree upon a relationship and a locale. In this game, your objective is to get your partner to talk about your own topic as exclusively as possible. You must try to turn the tenor of the conversation so that both you and your partner can discuss your topic logically.

1. Boy and girl on a bus. They have dated steadily for two years and are on their way to see a movie in town.
   His topic: police brutality.
   Her topic: my favorite pet (dog).
2. Two sisters on a double date talking in the powder room of a night club.
   Topics: Cosmetics; and either male chauvinism or gay lib.
3. Boy and girl, steady daters for at least two years, sitting together during Mass in church.
   He: I want to coax her into agreeing to the elopement plans I've set up for tonight.
   She: I want to make him agree that I would have a new and more meaningful life if I became a nun.
4. Two brothers (or sisters) watching television in the living room, with an ill mother in an adjoining room.
   One: I want to force him into assuming support of Mother.
   Two: I want to drink beer and watch the roller derby.
5. Father and daughter visiting together after a long absence, having dinner in a fancy restaurant.
   Father: I want to avoid any troublesome or deep topics by concerning myself and my daughter with the wonderful menu, elegant surroundings, and excellent food.
   Daughter: I want to get Father to allow me to come home and have my baby, though I'm not sure who the father of the baby is.
6. Two sisters in a taxicab.
   One: I want to convince my sister to divorce her husband.
   Two: I want to convince my sister to marry the man she's been secretly dating.
7. Brother and sister in a cemetery while it is raining.
   Brother: I want to get her to help me persuade Father to marry again.
   Sister: I want to get him to help me persuade Father to remain true to the memory of Mother.
8. Father and daughter in the antechamber women's lavatory of a church on her wedding morning.
   Father: I want to convince her to go through with the wedding.
   Daughter: I want to get Father to take me away from here and let me be his little girl again.
9. Mother and son in the same situation as the above.
   Mother: I want to convince him that marrying this girl will mean the end of his career.
   Son: I want to convince her that she has to let me grow up and be a man with my own responsibilities.

10. Two soldiers on a battlefield, stranded two miles in front of their lines with a badly wounded companion.
    One: I want to convince him that we have to leave the wounded guy and cover each other to get back alive.
    Two: I want to force him to help me carry my wounded pal back to our own lines.
11. Two lovers in a bedroom on their last night together.
    She: I want to convince him to go AWOL.
    He: I want to get her to agree that my duty to my country is more important than my feelings toward her.
12. Husband and wife in their lawyer's antechamber.
    He: I want to cajole her into letting me have the child and the color television.
    She: I want to coerce him into agreeing that I should get the child and the color television, but secretly I would trade them both for the Porsche.
13. Husband and wife at the dinner table.
    He: I want to get her to admit that our life together is very romantic, and much more fun because we're alone.
    She: I want to talk him into appreciating how convenient it would be if my mother came to live with us.
14. Husband and wife watching television in the bedroom.
    He: I want her to let me be her baby boy so I won't have any responsibilities.
    She: I want to tempt him to have a baby with me.
15. Husband and wife in a hospital waiting room.
    He: I want to get her to approve signing the papers allowing the doctors to perform an emergency operation on our deformed baby.
    She: I want him to agree that we should withhold our signatures and let the baby die.

decisions Did you follow the general rules for improvisation? Did you defeat your purposes by setting up circumstances that hurt your own argument? For example, if the husband in exercise 13 creates imaginary children at the dinner table, he will destroy the potential for a romantic setting and make his wife's case stronger. Remember that although it is impossible to be perfect in performing these exercises, it is possible to learn how to be more efficient at playing with purposes. Try to create a physical environment around you and your partner, and use the circumstances of that environment to help you play your objective.

THE REUNION

needs For this group objective exercise, which introduces amusing elements of characterization, have a book of short stories on hand (the variety implicit in a book of short stories usually offers more suggestions for the exercise than a novel does).

procedures One member of the group takes the book, opens it at random, and silently reads the first sentence he finds. He passes the book on to the next participant. Each member assumes that the sentence he has read either is *about* his own character or is a comment made *by* his character. Now each participant develops an entire characterization from his particular sentence, choosing an apartment, a car, favorite foods, music, a life rhythm, and a posture that suit this sentence. Everyone has the same objective and situation: this is the five-year reunion of your high school class at a good Italian restaurant in town, and each of you wants to prove in his own way that he has been the most successful since graduation.

decisions Did you allow your character to take on a distinct variation from your own personality? Did you allow your character to influence your choices in playing your objective? Did you find ways to use the periphery, such as the decor of the Italian restaurant and the food or drink to be served?

Phase 1

The wake

needs Arrange a large circle of chairs around a small platform that will represent a coffin in a funeral parlor.

procedure All members of the group take seats in the circle around the coffin, which contains an imaginary dead man. Everyone must choose a family relationship to the deceased (e.g., wife, mother, sister, brother). The kinship each person selects will guide him in playing his objective. Take a few moments to clarify the relationships among all the players.

After you have each established your identity, pass around the same book that you used in the last exercise, and build a new character based on the sentence that you select. You each have the same objective: you want to find a way to prove conclusively that the dead man loved you more than anyone else in the group. Remember to use the periphery of the funeral parlor to aid you in playing your action.

Phase 2

The automobile accident

needs Arrange two rows of chairs at right angles to each other to simulate the waiting room of a hospital emergency ward.

procedure Everyone takes a seat. A young man and a young woman have been critically injured in an automobile accident. The families of both have gathered to hear if their relative is going to pull through. Everyone in the row on the right is related to the young man; everyone in the left row is related to the young woman.

Each person chooses a specific kinship and clarifies this for everyone else in the group. Now, each "relative" builds a personality for himself based on a sentence selected from the book—as in the preceding exercises. Everyone has the same objective: you each want to prove that your relative was innocent (the injured boy or girl, depending upon which side you're sitting on) and that the other family's relative was criminally negligent and responsible for the accident.

DETECTIVE GAMES[7]

needs This exercise works best with eight people. Use a platform to represent a bar, and place several stools, two or more tables, and several chairs nearby. Prepare eight small slips of paper: write the word "police" on two of the slips and the word "spy" on two; leave the remaining four slips blank. On each of the two slips with the word "spy" also write a secret password—a question and an answer—such as "Do you like anchovy pizza?" "Yes, but I'm on the Stillman diet." Fold all eight slips in half (with the words inside).

procedure Sit this one out as you control the game for your study group. Choose an exciting locale or a situation that is likely to stimulate the group's imagination. Suggest that each member of the group go through a sense memory of the keenest moment of his last enjoyable vacation and to concentrate on the sensory impressions. Then ask each person to pretend that he is going off on a similar vacation, and that everyone in the group has come to the airport to fly to his vacation spot. Unfortunately, all planes have been grounded for a specific reason, such as inclement weather or a hijack threat. All the participants have found their way to the airport lounge to wait out the threat of danger. One member is selected to tend bar, another to wait on the tables. The other six participants join in the action by using their sense memory as a stimulus for basic conversation. As the group congregates, hand out the eight pieces of paper to everyone, bartender and waiter or waitress included. Urge each participant to *read* his paper, whether it is blank or not. Everyone disposes of his paper as soon as possible. No participant is allowed to know the identity of any other participant.

The objective of the two spies is to alter the conversation around them in such a way that they can hint at, or easily state, their passwords. The spies must try to recognize each other without giving away their identity to the rest. The objective of the two police is to listen for any unmotivated conversation and arrest whoever they suspect are the spies.

The four "blanks" are free simply to socialize. They may attempt to baffle the police by "playing a role"; however, it is important that they behave as logically as possible within the limits of the exercise. As soon as one of the police is certain he has identified a spy, he makes an arrest, ending the game. But should the spies successfully contact each other and leave the police stumped, you, as the initiator of the game, should wait at least one full minute before stopping the game. After either you or one of the policemen has ended the game, ask these questions of any observers, then direct them at the participants:

1. Who are the police?
2. Did you recognize them?
3. Who are the spies?
4. What was the password topic?
5. Was there any misleading conversation?

decisions Did the eight performers take the time to "get into" their surroundings or did they merely jump in? Who was successful at maintaining the reality of the props? Did any performers really seem to be drinking? Did the participants speak so softly that it was difficult to hear (a habit worth breaking early in group activities)? Can playing the objectives work independently of playing the circumstances? Ideally, objectives and circumstances complement each other to flesh out your dramatic situation; otherwise it is very easy for you to immerse yourself in a mood without playing any needs in relation to your partner onstage with you. By the same token, it is just as easy for you to fall into hammering away at an objective without really considering how logical it would be for your character to do so.

chapter 5
DEVELOPING SPECIFIC TECHNIQUES

Once you have been assigned a role in a play or in a scene chosen for your study group's criticism, you probably begin to look over the role to see what you have to do (you may even count the lines to satisfy your ego). You may discover that you have to cry, laugh, or hit someone onstage. Perhaps you are excited about the dramatic possibilities inherent in such an action, but you may also be frightened by the possibility of failure.

There are few rigid rules for communicating emotion onstage. But there are several efficient methods, and these are described in the following exercises. Find what works for you, and use it. Your director seldom has the time to take you aside and explain how to express a certain emotion. Remember that you will be onstage with another human being. You would be awfully unhappy up there with a self indulgent actor whose crying or laughing left you all alone with egg on your face. Physical or emotional tasks onstage are not feats or end-results in themselves; they are by-products that may develop out of your objectives or out of the sharing of a dramatic moment between fellow actors.

CRYING

procedure Sit in a relaxed position. Try to recall a sad event from your recent past. Go through the recall process sensorily, recreating the keenest moment of your pain by associating it with the smells, tastes, sights, sounds that affected you at that time. Try to center the sensation in your pelvic area, and drop the breath down to this area in a slow, rhythmic manner as you flash the sensory images through your mind.

Yawn and try to maintain the feeling of the yawn in your throat during both inhalation and exhalation. Allow this to go on for a full minute. Begin to vocalize the inhalation softly. Think of your exhalation as your relaxant for the vocalization process. Allow your inhalation to trip gently over the vocal cords, producing a low moan. Permit this to go on for a minute, reminding yourself to keep the feeling of a yawn in your throat. Climax the exercise by accelerating the rhythm and raising the pitch very slowly with each inhalation until you have hit your natural high pitch without strain. Try to find a staccato rhythm of your own over the inhalation. And finally, when exhaling allow vocalization, too, as a slow wail. Peak the cry and let it taper off.

decisions Was the sense memory necessary? Did merely yawning make your eyes water? Did you discover that maintaining the yawn gave you the feeling of having a "lump in your throat"? Consciously try to produce the same sound that you found during the exercise, but use the exhalation rather than the inhalation. Which method requires more tension to produce? Does reconstructing the sound on the exhalation force you to tighten the vocal cords? The theatrical sound for a cry should appear to be "right there" on the inhalation. However, the inhalation may seem to dry out your throat. Try to relax during the inhalation, using the exhalation to ease the throat. Swallow and salivate if you feel dry. And don't try so hard.

The rise in pitch helps create dramatic intensity. What is the difference between a sustained sound and a staccato sound? Try sniffling through your nose at intervals. Does the sniffling make the cry seem more "real"? Is the sniffling infectious to an audience?

Is it necessary to produce real tears? Can tasteful faking do the job? An actor cannot play the objective "I want to cry real tears." Tears may be a by-product of the frustrated objective that you are working for, but concentrating exclusively on tears negates the other actors onstage with you. There are other techniques of crying—looking into a Leeko (a lighting instrument) will certainly produce tears, but it will also damage the retina of your eye. An actor should never consider risking his body or his personal well-being for the "good of the show."

There are dangers in crying onstage. You have to know when crying ends and self-pity begins. An audience will not want to relate to self-pity. Crying can be beautiful onstage, depending on your attitude. If you approach crying as a feat with which to call attention to yourself, you have ceased to play with your fellow actors. A perceptive reviewer will call it "wallowing."

LAUGHING

procedure Try to recall a funny occurrence from your past or a good joke you heard recently. Again, reconstruct the moment when your appreciation of the moment or the joke was at its keenest. Try to remember specific sights (colors), sounds, smells, textures—any sensory images that might aid you in recreating the moment or the joke. Again, locate the feeling in your lower abdominal area and try to keep it there where it can be controlled; don't let it creep up into the upper thorax or chest area. Feel the humor slowly bubbling up through you toward your throat and your mouth. Find a moderately paced breath rhythm that matches the laughter. Flash the best images from the sense recall through your mind and feel the emotion drawing the breath up and out of you from deep down in the pelvis, but don't let it out! Laughter can be sustained by not giving in to it too soon. Peak it slowly in a series of exhalations.

Try to keep the lips sealed, and laugh through the nose on the first exhalation. Press the laugh down inside yourself. Keep it controlled with your intercostal muscles and diaphragm and don't let yourself give in to the laugh. Now allow your lips to open only an eighth of an inch, and gently attack the laugh with the beginning of the second exhalation. Try to avoid wasting breath before you actually vocalize the laugh. Flash the images through your mind again, open your mouth a quarter of an inch, and laugh louder on the third exhalation. Then open your mouth half an inch, and let the sound rise in pitch. Try to visualize the sound leaving you and aim it across the room on your fourth exhalation.

Open your mouth three quarters of an inch and pick up the breath rhythm, attacking the vocalized sound from the beginning of the fifth exhalation. Press the laugh down; don't let it invade your shoulders or neck. Now open your mouth a full inch. Breathe and peak the pitch and volume. Give in to it for at least thirty seconds, maintaining the full sound. Slowly let it subside and press it down. Tell yourself that it wasn't really that funny anyway. Let it dissipate. Keep your eyes front. Let it go. Slowly let yourself dare to look at your partner (or flash the images in your mind again). Look away quickly. Look back at him and begin the laugh again through your nose. Now see how soon you can reach the peak of the laugh, sharing it with your partner as you let it grow in *intensity* (not necessarily in pitch or volume).

decisions What is the value of playing against the emotion? Can you use this same technique with crying? Refusing to give in helps to ennoble crying. Is the laugh better shared or alone? Can you and your partner play the laugh off each other and find a new spark to maintain it? Is the sense-memory work necessary?

Crying may seem effective on inhalation because crying is usually an inwardly directed emotion, whereas laughter is more effective on exhalation because it's an outwardly directed emotion. Can you cry more easily than laugh? Both crying and laughing are forms of relief. Try repeating the exercise; this time laugh at something sad!

Tragedy can exist without tears. Can comedy be effective without laughs?

Can laughter be tragic? Can laughter be ugly? Can laughter be beautiful? What situations do comic characters usually fall into?

variation Perform a character laugh that seems indicative of a specific type of person or emotion. Ask a partner to join you and see how many different laughs you can create. Don't allow yourselves to repeat the same type of laugh more than once. Try to use each other as a stimulus for each new laugh.

decisions Which laughs are particularly effective? Does interaction with your partner help? Which types of laughs seem forced or mechanical? When can a mechanical laugh be used effectively? Are certain "star" personalities associated with certain types of laughs?

RUNNING

procedure Clear the center of the work area. Your partner sits in the center of the work area and you take a position in an offstage corner. Your partner pantomimes any objective that will occupy him. You must choose an objective that has immediacy for him; for example, "Two men are trying to break into our car! Come on, let's call the police and stop them!" Run in and convince your partner to run back out with you.

decisions Was your objective believable? How immediate was your objective? Did your body indicate the strain exerted by running? Ask any observers how long it seemed that you had been running. Did the inclination of your body help express immediacy?

Running with purpose

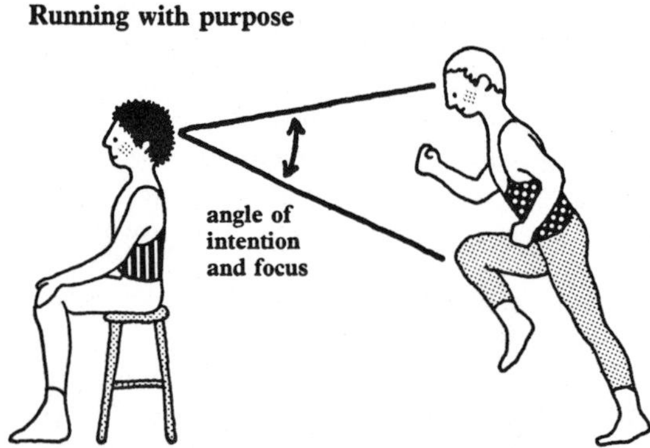

Did you maintain control of your body, or did the situation seem to control you? Did you get off balance? As you ran in, did you slacken your pace as you approached your seated partner or did you overrun, and nearly or actually bump into him? If so, repeat the run and maintain the same speed indicative of your urgency without stumbling over him. Use the same objective, but lessen the inclination of your body as you get near your partner. Finish your approach with a series of shorter, better-controlled steps.

variation Change the objective of the runner by introducing a new set of circumstances, such as "Hurry! Your dog's just been bitten by a snake!" Your seated partner may likewise vary his response to one of less concern. Change the duration of your run to see if you can capture the external impression of having run a one-block sprint as well as a full, exhausting mile. Note the differences in posture as well as in respiration speed. Check your accuracy by really running around the rehearsal hall and back to the work area. You may have only five feet of wing space offstage in a play, but you must still be able to give the audience the impression that you have run a mile as you enter. Look at the physical demands Georges Feydeau makes on his actors in the second act of *A Flea in the Ear.*

WALKING

procedure Simply walk around the work area. Ask your partner to watch you. Ask him if he notices any awkwardness because of stiffness in your joints. If you have had dance training, do traces of it give the effect of "performing a walk?" Are you forcing your shoulders back and up? Do you tend to shuffle? Do you tighten your pelvis to prevent any hip motion? Do you lead with your head, with your pelvis, or with one shoulder? Try some technical walks while walking around a circle: walk on the outsides of your feet (the legs and arms may be like parentheses, or you may look as though you were riding a horse); walk on the insides of the feet (with your knees knocking); walk on the heels (compensating your weight by throwing your arms upward with every step as marathon walkers seem to do); and lastly, perform each step as a fencing lunge (forward and very low).

decisions Do you have a natural and graceful gait? Do you appear to be dancing or clomping your way along? In a proper walk, you can best carry the weight of your body by maintaining the center of your body evenly over both feet. Any singular movement pattern that you have may invade every character you play onstage.

What character types are suggested by walking in a dance-like manner? What types walk awkwardly on the instep, on the outside of the foot, on the heels, or on the toes with the knees knocking? Walking in any of these ways—with the body's center of gravity askew—can suggest a whole new voice or a set of external mannerisms that create a totally new human being. Try shifting your center of weight as you walk in order to produce a psychological gesture as the inspirational basis for an entire character.[1] Deviating from your normal carriage by placing your center of gravity farther forward or backward can make you feel psychologically more on a line and relaxedly in control; on the other hand, it can make you feel slightly out of control. Have you ever seen an actor go "blank," forgetting his lines while doing a scene? He was probably off-balance on one leg or shifting his weight from foot to foot. Physical imbalance can affect mental balance. To find security, relax your weight and distribute it evenly over both feet.

SITTING

Phase 1
Sitting gracefully

procedure Enter the work space and sit on a chair in the center of the area. Ask your partner to watch you carefully. Rise, walk away, and then return to the center of the work area and sit down again; but this time avoid looking directly at the chair you are going to sit on.

decisions When you first sat down, did your partner notice that your body adapted itself to a position or a "set" that seemed to prepare you to sit down? Did this set alter the position of your shoulders? Do you feel that you have to tense any parts of your body besides those directly associated with sitting? Try sitting with your spine relaxed and the upper part of your torso totally at ease.

If you felt tense the second time you sat down, repeat the exercise. This time watch your chair with your peripheral vision until you are in front of it, then turn and feel the edge of the seat with the backs of your calves until you are sure that you are directly in front of the seat. Keeping your torso erect and using only the parts of the body that you *must* use in order to sit down, seat yourself fully on the chair.

variation Use different attitudes while sitting on the chair. For instance, sit with your rear end half off the seat. Then sit on the edge of your seat. Ask your partner if this looks strange from a distance. The nervousness of performance can make an actor feel "at home" sitting on the edge of his chair, but the audience may think he looks unnatural and extremely awkward—or just plain edgy.

Phase 2
Sitting with age

procedure Walk to a chair in the center of the work space and sit down as if you were over seventy years old. Try to demonstrate the ravages of age with your body.

discussion Did your partner believe in your walk? Was the walk convincing onstage? Was it overdone, or were you too subtle? Did you seem to be exerting a lot of energy to be able to do the walk? Aged people seldom strain as they walk and sit down, because they have found the most economical and least painful ways of moving their bodies. Did you take a great deal of time to sit down, or did you seem to sit too quickly? The flesh on old buttocks has begun to fall away. Sitting abruptly can be painful, because the bones where the hip joins the pelvis are more exposed in the elderly. However, it is also true that older people seldom sit down so slowly that they cause great strain in their thighs. Try counterbalancing your weight by bracing yourself by placing one hand on the back of the chair and the other on your knee and settling moderately onto the chair.

KISSING ONSTAGE

Phase 1

needs A partner of the opposite sex.

procedure Ask your partner to stand facing you at a distance of about four feet. Lean toward each other, balancing yourselves with your arms against each other and kiss.

extension 1 Stand two feet away from each other and kiss again. This time, refrain from touching. Now repeat the same exercise one foot apart.

extension 2 Tilt your pelvis slightly forward and repeat the kiss from one foot away. Without using your hands, come close enough to your partner for your bodies to touch, tilt your pelvis toward your partner, and kiss again.

extension 3 Square off your bodies, facing the study group. One of you—the male—tilts his pelvis up against his partner's hips and kisses her by brushing his lips against her cheek. The exercise is repeated, but this time the kiss is made more passionate. Now face each other with your bodies just touching and kiss very slowly, using your arms and your hands. The study group may help you by choreographing your arm movements.

decisions Which of the kisses is most suitable for children's theatre? In each kiss, which partner appeared to be more innocent? What effect does the pelvis tilt generate? When the woman faces the audience and the man presses up against her, their physical relationship may suggest that he is more attracted to her than she is to him.

Slow, rhythmic movements are generally more sensual for an audience to observe than violent movements. Kissing without touching can also be very sensual for the audience because you leave the caressing to the imagination.

It will be necessary to consider which of you will have the lines to carry the scene. Try to keep both of your faces clear of any arm movements so that the speaker can be seen by the audience.

Phase 2

needs Place a couch, a bench, or a platform about eighteen inches high in the center of the work area. Find a partner of the opposite sex.

procedure Sit on the bench with at least a foot between you. Facing straight ahead, lean toward each other, turn your heads, and kiss as you touch shoulders.

extension 1 Change the physical position of your bodies so that your knees touch, but maintain a full foot of distance between your hips, creating a "kissing V," and kiss each other without arm or hand contact.

extension 2 Sit right next to each other with your hips touching. Ask the study group to choreograph your arm movements so that you both look graceful. First the female should have the lines and dominant focus. Redo the choreography to favor the male.

decisions Ask the same questions as in Phase 1. How important are smoothly choreographed arm movements in a serious, romantic scene?

STAGE FALLS

needs Use a good thick gymnasium mat in the work area, or if it's a nice day, find a soft, grassy area outdoors.

procedures Stand in the middle of the mat and go through the following process: decide upon the direction in which you are going to fall and make sure there are no obstructions in the way. Compensate for your weight by tilting your pelvis in the direction of the fall, but tilt the upper torso in the opposite direction—away from the fall. Your body may appear to be curved in the nineteenth-century cliché position for a faint. Perhaps you have seen pictures of Sarah Bernhardt in such a position.

Lift your arms away from the direction of the fall and tilt your head away from it, too. Protect your elbows, knees, and head. Never land on these areas or allow your head to bounce after landing.

Tip the ankles in the direction of the fall, rounding the calves and thighs in a bow-like curve. Relax all joints and muscles. Take a deep, easy breath. Fall gently and slowly, rolling off the ankles to the calves, from the side of the knees and thighs onto the fatty part of the hips and buttocks. When the buttocks and hips have taken nearly all the weight of the body, allow the upper torso to flatten out. When your body has come to rest, let your arms and head relax to the ground. Repeat the entire process, smoothening out the action.

Falling properly

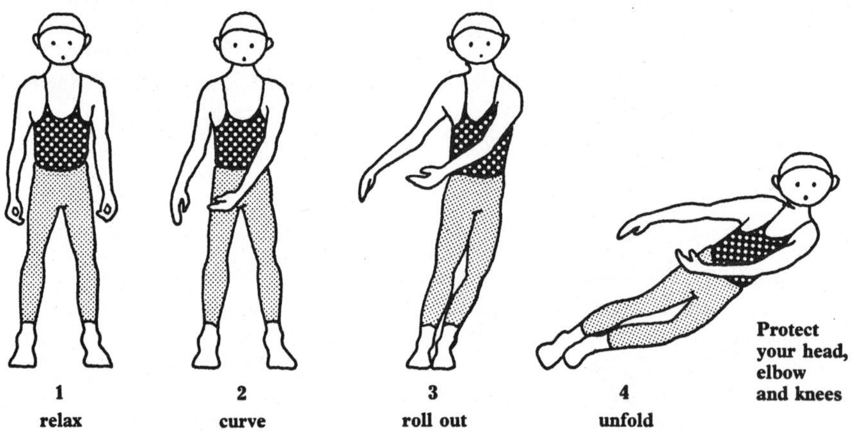

decisions Try to find a real motivation for each stage of the process of falling. Ask your partner if your fall looks real or if it seems mechanical. Are you telegraphing each succeeding step?—that is, are you being so obvious that your partner knows what you're going to do next? Can you achieve a "first time" illusion? Try to alter the motivation for the entire process from a fall to a faint or swoon, then to a shock, to exhaustion, and finally to a deliberate faint such as the one Ann performs in the final act of Shaw's *Man and Superman.*

STAGE VIOLENCE—PUNCHES AND SLAPS

procedure It is not the initiator but the recipient of a punch or a slap who creates the believability for an audience. Reacting to violence onstage takes longer than merely throwing a punch or a slap; therefore the audience has more time to identify with the actor who gets punched. Unless the recipient of stage violence creates the illusion of pain or fear, the punch is ludicrous.

Here are several rules for violence in general: there is never any excuse for anyone to be hurt onstage. Stage violence is pure technique, devoid of real human intention and life motivation. It is *performed* by two actors creating a moment together.

The process of constructing a stage fight is slow. The fight must be choreographed, memorized, constantly practiced, mutually designed, and never altered without rehearsal.

The initiator should practice an open-handed slap so that the fingers of one hand smack across the palm of the other hand. With practice he will find a relaxed slap that avoids bone-on-bone contact.

The initiator swings with his entire body on a fixed, relaxed pivot. He uses as few joints as possible, and never allows himself a wild wind-up that may frighten his partner. He is always sure and direct. He aims only at a *point of focus,* carefully worked out with his partner.

The recipient should get used to focusing on a point behind the initiator so that he will not flinch when he sees the swing coming his way. The recipient must always take the time to plan his fall before working on any other aspect of performing violence. The recipient always falls in the direction of the thrust of the violence.

The hook

procedure Decide whether you or your partner will initiate or receive the punch.

The initiator puts his right hand on his partner's shoulder if the audience is on his left. This way the audience will not be able to see where the punch lands because the initiator makes contact sound *behind* the recipient.

The initiator makes a fist with his left hand and aims at his own right hand. The right hand becomes his point of focus. Now the initiator tries to find a kinesthetic feeling of how high the point of focus on his partner lies. He moves away from the recipient and merely practices aiming at and hitting his own right hand (which would be on his partner's shoulder). As he brings his left fist to his right hand, there should be very little movement in the shoulder or elbow (all joints should remain primed but relaxed). He moves the fist of his left hand toward his right hand, but straightens out his left hand just as it approaches the right hand, which he turns up to meet his left hand, providing a surface for a slap. He slaps the hands together with a solid clap, and immediately re-forms a fist with the left hand and follows through with a punch in the air.

The footwork for the initiator is basically simple. At the start his feet are parallel. As he makes a fist and then begins to connect his hands for the slap, he rises onto the balls of his feet, pivots on his right foot, and swings his left foot around (first to the left and then far to the right) as part of the follow-through, carrying his whole body with it, so that he winds up having made nearly a full semicircle. The body movement in a pivot gives the illusion that the punch has landed with the full force of the initiator's weight. The initiator should practice this technique *alone* several times, until he can hit his right hand easily, making a solid clap without any lack of control.

The recipient's first task is to learn to receive the punch in the direction of the force of the blow. If the initiator is throwing the punch with his left hand, it will look to an audience as if the recipient is taking the punch on the right side of his face. The force of the blow to the right cheek would send the recipient sprawling to his left.

As the recipient sees the punch coming and hears the slap, he rises immediately onto the balls of his feet and pivots on his left foot, swinging his right foot around until he has his back to the initiator. It is very important for the recipient to keep his feet as close to the floor as possible, because both the initiator and the recipient are doing a semicircular pivot and they might kick each other. Once he has his back to the initiator, the recipient falls forward with the momentum of the pivot, using his hands to catch himself in order to avoid landing on his knees or allowing his head to bounce. As soon as he hits the floor, he relaxes onto it. He should practice this fall continually until he is sure of himself. Eventually, he will learn to do his pivot just as the initiator pivots with his punch so that the slap of the punch lands and times out perfectly. The punch should be tried in slow motion first, and faster as both get better acquainted with the method.

variation After you have set this punch with a partner, find a few motivational phrases and build a little scene around the punch. Maintain your control while giving the appearance of arguing. Don't let the argument ruin your physical control.

The uppercut

procedure Once again, decide whether you or your partner will initiate or receive the punch.

The recipient raises and bends both his arms, shielding himself from the attack. He places one arm at the level of his solar plexus and drops the other arm slightly lower and under the first arm. He gently cups his hands, with palms down. The lower hand will become the initiator's target; the upper hand and arm will be used solely to protect himself. The recipient turns his back to the house so that the audience will not be able to see where the blow seems to land.

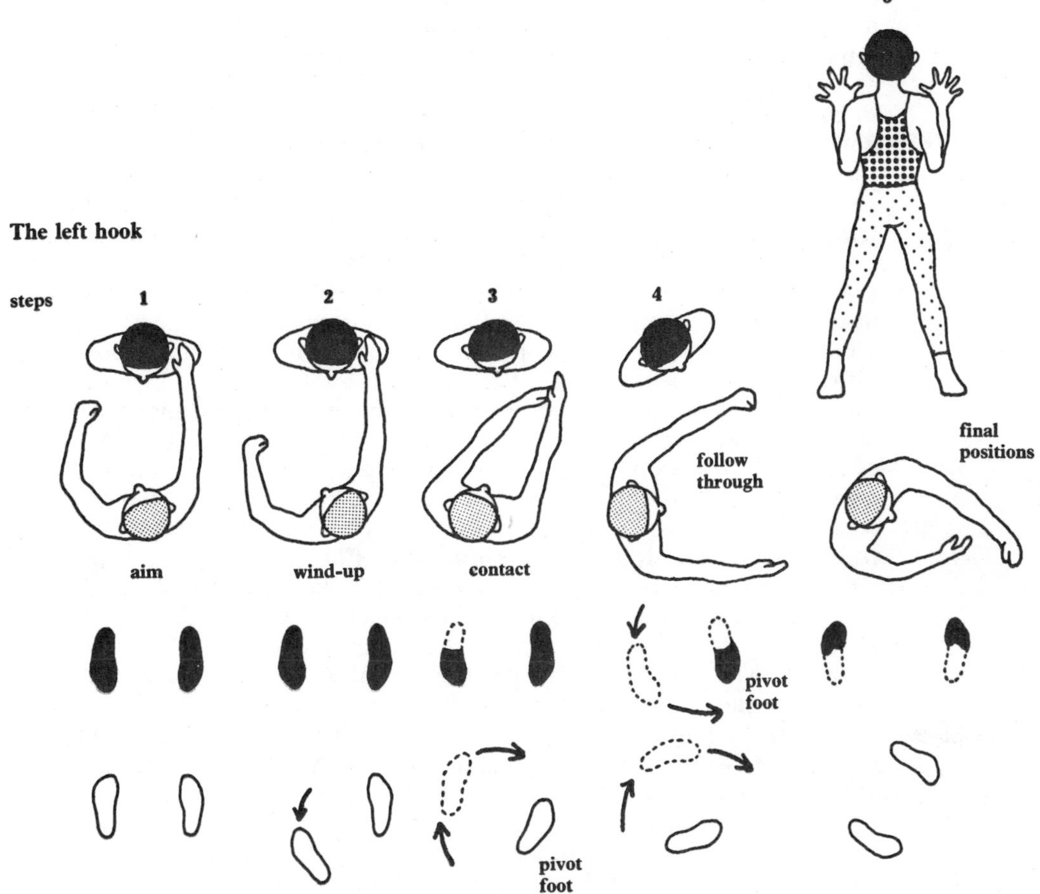

The initiator has the same basic task in regard to hand work as he did with the hook. He begins with a fist, changes the fist to a slap with the open hand relaxed but firm, and ends up with a fist for the follow-through. The point of focus this time, however, is the recipient's lower hand, which he is holding slightly under and in front of his solar plexus. The initiator starts the punch low, sweeping upward. He changes his fist into a slap, and slaps the lower hand of the recipient. He immediately closes his hand into a fist again and continues his motion up into the air. The initiator has no footwork.

After the initiator has the feeling for the point of focus, using the level of the recipient's hand, he should practice hitting his partner's hand several times until both he and the recipient are confident that they will produce a good, resounding slap every time. The recipient must get the kinesthetic feeling of where he has placed his hands in front of his solar plexus for the initiator. This must not vary, or both partners will freeze or flinch. Female recipients attempting the uppercut should keep their hands at the point of focus lower and farther away from their bodies to protect their breasts. Male recipients should place their hands high enough around the chest area so that there is no danger of striking the groin. Both males and females should remember that the recipient's hand that receives the slap will swing upward slightly. It is necessary to keep this hand—and arm—firm but relaxed. Keep the other arm behind this hand in case it does swing upward farther than expected. In effect then, the hand that takes the slap can bounce off the arm protecting the body.

The uppercut makes a greater demand on the recipient than the hook does. He must act with his *back* so that the audience feels that he has received a blow. After checking behind himself, the recipient is ready to choreograph his reception of the punch and the fall. First, he should try to find a natural way to motivate bringing his arms up to protect his body. Perhaps saying "No, no, please!" as he raises his hands toward his solar plexus and turns the bulk of his body away from the audience will help him create an impression that registers as fear with his audience. At the moment of the slap, the recipient relaxes his arms and allows them to rise upward, as if moving with the momentum of the punch. He controls his arms so that he does not hit himself in the face. The recipient rises onto the balls of his feet and pivots in the direction of the punch, keeping his spine relaxed and erect. He completes a semicircular shift of weight that leaves him facing the audience so that he can easily fall on his hands. The recipient should practice the fall several times before attempting to put the entire uppercut procedure together.

decisions

In which positions onstage would the uppercut or hook be more effective? Remember that the spine acts as a unit. Quick, jerky reactions to a punch are not as theatrically effective as a slow, methodical rhythm. Quick actions must be controlled so that you do not strain your neck reacting to the uppercut or sprain an ankle reacting to a hook. Control the action! Never let the tension control you! Very little reality is necessary to *perform* violence onstage. Create short scenes of your own that will culminate with stage violence. An actor must remain relaxed during the build-up to a violent scene. Let the audience do all your tensing.

The Slap

Phase 1

discussion

The real slap Staging violence varies in relation to the type of theatre in which you are working and your distance from the audience. A "fake" slap may be impossible to perform believably for the audience in a tiny theatre. Staging in an arena theatre demands more physical reality than proscenium staging because the audience surrounds the actor. Actors operating on a thrust stage must also be aware that there is an audience on three sides of them. Punches like the uppercut will be quite difficult to throw when an audience either has more than one perspective or is very close to the stage action.

procedure The real slap is used in close circumstances when Realism and Naturalism are the genres chosen by the director. A real slap is similar to a hook for the initiator, except that he actually hits his partner, instead of hitting his own hand. The stage positions remain basically the same as with a hook.

The initiator maintains his body as a unit, swinging as economically as possible. His point of focus is the fleshy part of the recipient's cheek. The initiator touches this area, moves away, and merely repeats the pivoting of his body while keeping his arm firm but relaxed. It is necessary for the initiator to remember that his hand must be relaxed to perform a real slap; in fact, it will be even safer if he remembers to keep his fingers somewhat limp so that when they strike the fleshy part of his partner's face, he will not push his partner's head or force it to turn. The initiator should lock into his entire body the kinesthetic feeling of aiming at his point of focus. He pivots again and again, trying to follow through as if striking the same spot on the recipient's cheek.

The recipient has a simple physical task—to look at the wall or at some point directly behind the initiator. It is extremely important for the recipient to remember to focus on such a spot, or he will flinch as a normal motor response. The initiator, trying to make the slap work, may tense up and possibly hurt the recipient. At the moment of contact and immediately afterward the recipient should react naturally—for instance, bringing up the hand opposite the side of his face that was slapped and rubbing his cheek. He should slowly turn his face in the direction of the blow *after* it has landed; this will give the impression that the slap hurt more than it did.

decisions The fleshy part of the cheek is the center of the cheek itself. Always aim for the fleshy area: striking the recipient with a hand cupped over his ear may rupture his eardrum; striking him too far forward may result in a nosebleed, or a split lip as a result of smacking his lips against his teeth; striking him too low may bruise his throat.

Phase 2

discussion ***The fake slap*** The fake slap can be substituted for the real slap when you are at least ten feet from the audience. Always angle yourself a little in relation to the front row of the audience. Never perform the fake slap, the hook, or the uppercut in profile. It will be too easy for the audience to see that you are not connecting the blow.

procedure The sound of the slap is performed by the recipient, who must time his movements with those of the initiator.

The movements of the initiator are almost exactly the same as those he uses for the real slap; however, he never makes any real contact. He merely slaps through the air in front of the recipient on the same plane as the fleshy part of the recipient's cheek, coming as close to the face as he can without clipping the nose.

The recipient's job is a bit more complex. If he faces the initiator with the left side of his face toward the audience, he will try to simulate the effect of being slapped on that side. To do this, he must raise and bend his left arm and position his left hand near his solar plexus (as he did for the uppercut). As the recipient sees the initiator wind up, he gets ready to use his right hand, which is relaxed on the right side of his body. As the initiator swings, the recipient brings his right hand up and slaps his left hand near his solar plexus, following through right up to his left cheek as if the initiator had slapped him there.

Before putting all the stages of the slap together, it would be best for the recipient to practice the slapping action several times to be sure that he has the hang of it. He must remember to remain relaxed, for if he tenses his arms, he will wind up striking both his hand and his cheek, making a double slap. After he has made the noise, he should slow down the speed with which he allows his right hand to travel from his solar plexus to his left cheek. The slap is fast, but his registering of the pain should be a trifle more gradual. Once again, though, he should slowly turn his head in the direction of the slap in order to give the impression of the force of the blow.

variation Try to find different types of slaps, such as a "haughty" slap, a slap of indignation, a slap of fear, a slap of anger, a slap that seems to lash out from being hurt, a slap typical of the jealous husband/wife, a playful slap, or a slap with definite convinction.

decisions What makes a slap different from a punch? What types of characters choose to slap rather than punch? How do various slaps differ in relation to intent, force, duration, reaction, and wind-up? Are you anticipating the slaps and your reactions? If so, repeat the whole process in slow motion before you try to speed it up.

INNOCENCE (AVOIDING ANTICIPATION)

The Adam and Eve exercise[2]

needs Use neutral masks (expressionless masks that have eye holes and nose holes and very often cover even the mouth), or two paper bags that will fit over the head. If bags are used, cut out two circles in each for the eyes.

procedure Both you and your partner wear a neutral mask or a paper bag over your heads. Lie down side by side in the middle of a cleared work space. Relax! Discover that you are alive and fully formed as an adult. You have just been created. Investigate your entire body and the function of each of your limbs. Motivate everything you do. Try to avoid all pain and tension; pain is sophisticated. Even raising your head to see your feet is problematic at first, for there will be tension in the neck that you would not endure unless there were a reason to see your feet. Eventually curiosity will overcome the discomfort. Discover movement in your own way. Find some reasons to crawl or roll across the work space.

Discover your partner. Explore similarities and dissimilarities in each other. Avoid touching each other with any kind of sexual motivation; just explore and play. Discover planes of verticality together, especially the difficult aspect of balance. Learn from each other.

decisions Why is any type of sexual contact premature? Did you give in to any noticeable movement clichés, such as pointing in the old "me Tarzan, you Jane" tradition? A *motivated* cliché is powerful theatrically because the audience can identify with it immediately. Did any section of the exercise seem to progress a little too quickly? Was there a logical continuum in your movements? Remember that you must discover your hands before your hands can discover anything else. Did you learn to play and to take ideas from each other?

Did you try to do real actions that might accomplish a task, whether or not the task was pure fun? Did either of you isolate yourselves after you had established contact? Were you relating to each other and comparing, or was one partner left alone with egg on his or her face? Were there dead moments late in the exercise that destroyed your rhythm and progression?

discussion Learning to play is the essence of first-time illusion. Consider the Adam and Eve exercise in relation to the preceding exercises in stage techniques. How important is the aura of first-time illusion to the performance of stage externals with your partner? Discuss the techniques of the "star" partner acts: Bud Abbott and Lou Costello, Stan Laurel and Oliver Hardy, Dean Martin and Jerry Lewis, Mary Tyler Moore and Dick Van Dyke, Lucille Ball and Desi Arnaz, Amos and Andy, the Bowery Boys, and others. In setting up a joke, a good straight man creates the humorous situation with the comedian, and both must share the first-time illusion. Hardy occasionally hit Laurel with his hat, just as Abbott sometimes slapped the back of Costello's head. Though stage violence was often used, it was acceptable because no one ever seemed to get hurt. These famous partners had learned how to play with each other, how to surprise each other as well as their audiences, and how to control their physical actions so that no one would get hurt.

chapter 6
USING THE LANGUAGE OF DIRECTION

You should try to familiarize yourself with the basic vocabulary of stage terminology. If your director asks you to "open one quarter right and use your upstage arm for the gesture," you will be very embarrassed if your only answer is "What?" or "Would you show me, please?" The director has every right to expect you to be familiar with stage geography when you come to a "blocking" rehearsal. Most directors, however, will be upset with you if you constantly direct yourself. Your best bet is to take a moderate amount of initiative.

Your basic job is to interpret your own role, not to criticize and analyze all the other characters onstage. You can help your director by concentrating on what your character feels and needs in relation to the other characters, and occasionally you should initiate or suggest movement that seems logical to you. Remember that your director is your third eye. You should be finding ways to play with your fellow performers—leave the basic blocking to your director and try to discover ways to motivate every new piece of stage business in relation to your fellow actors.

Continual awareness that you are performing in front of an audience is part of your craft. You and your partner must share the moments you create with the audience, too; otherwise you are both working in a vacuum. The following exercises are designed to help you appreciate your craft so that you can get the most out of yourself and your partner with grace, skill, clarity, and economy.

RAKING (ANGLING) THE STAGE

procedure Set up whatever rehearsal furniture you have at your disposal—chairs, tables, benches—to simulate a plausible living room or dining area that would be *parallel* to the front row of the audience. Serve a meal and drinks in pantomime, trying to be as cheerful with your partner as possible. Your partner's objective is to break the news that your brother has been killed in a car accident. He must try to tell you the news as gently as possible.

decisions Did you feel hampered by the set? Were you trapped, or forced into a formal pattern of movement? Were you bothered by the fact that the set seemed so rigid and angular? Were you forced to use profile, full-front, or full-back positions?

variation Redress the stage so that the room lies diagonal to the audience. You may use the same furniture relationships, but shift or "rake" everything onstage so it no longer seems parallel to the audience. Survey the set—does it look logical? Remember that couches are usually at right angles with chairs and parallel to coffee tables; however, the entire configuration can be set at an angle to the audience. You will find that when you sit down together one of you will be closer to the audience because of the angle of the set. If you are farther away from the audience you have the "power position." Your partner must "close" himself off from the audience in order to turn and listen to you. When you are done speaking, you should find a logical reason to move toward the audience, giving your partner the power position. The person who moves into the power position "takes stage."

Walk through the set, sit on the chairs, and so on. Can you walk through it comfortably and easily, or does it force you to turn sideways to inch along between couches and coffee tables? Which entrances are the most important? Can these entrances be seen by the entire audience?

Use the new set and try the following improvisation. Your objective is to clean up the apartment with an imaginary dust cloth and vacuum cleaner because Mother is coming home from the hospital. Your partner's objective stems from a clear case of hit-and-run: his car hit a child playing in the street and he drove on; he desperately needs your help in figuring out what to do.

decisions Did the stage create natural power positions during the second improvisation? Did you feel at all hampered by the set? Did you help each other work by using the set, or did you cramp each other into positions that obscured the audience's view?

discussion Nothing in nature exists in a straight line. A curved movement pattern may seem just as direct to an audience, and it is visually more exciting. Classical plays seldom use very much furniture. Does movement in these plays differ from movement in realistic drama? Does the movement make you feel self-conscious? Remember that there must be a real motivation for every move you make.

Some plays require a formal, angular set. Would you call such plays artificial? Even when your blocking reflects formal artificiality, it must still seem human. Compare possible settings for Oscar Wilde's *The Importance of Being Earnest* with those for Edward Albee's *The American Dream.*

The stage manager often writes the stage directions that appear in the acting versions of most plays. Should you follow these directions implicitly, knowing that this blocking was tailored for the first actors who played the roles? Try to find a fresh approach to the scene with your own partner. Look at the floor plans in the last few pages of the acting versions of plays written by Neil Simon. Do the sets seem to be flat and squared-off? Are there interesting suggestions for alcoves? Have you ever taken the time to draw a "thumbnail" floor-plan sketch of the scenes you prepare for group criticism? Do you and your partner take the time to agree upon the surroundings and the particulars necessary to give the effect that you have lived together in the specific house or room that you must create in your scene? Draw a quick little sketch of the set for your next scene and use the set to help you flesh out the role. You may feel more "at home" on the stage than you usually do.

BALANCING THE PROSCENIUM STAGE

needs discussion

Get some furniture for rehearsal and any interesting prop (perhaps an apple).

The proscenium stage has an arch—a huge "picture frame"—separating the audience from the playing platform. Arrange the furniture in the center of the work area in any logical pattern. Divide the work area evenly in half from front to back, and lay a piece of inexpensive masking tape or string along the dividing line. Place the prop exactly in the center of the dividing line. The study group may assemble on one side of the work area.

The front of your set closest to the audience is called "downstage," the rear "upstage." In order for the entire audience to see the stage, early theatre architects knew they had to lift either the back of the stage or the back of the theatre where the audience sat. It was cheaper to lift the stage (this is called "raking" the stage), so the rear of the stage became known as "upstage."

The terms "stage left" and "stage right" refer to the natural left and natural right of the actors up on the stage. The director must make this distinction from his place in the "house" (your left is the director's right!). The director is supposedly more "objective" than the actors about the work being done onstage.

The adjective "deep" means the same thing as extreme; for example, "deep center right" would take you to the edge of the stage on your right, exactly halfway between the audience and the back of the stage. There will probably be a narrow curtain on your right in front of you and behind you. Located both to the right and the left of the playing space, these curtains, called "legs" or "tormentors," hide what is going on offstage in the "wings." Just in front of the tormentors is the "teaser"—the border drapery that determines the height of the stage opening and masks the "fly space" (the area over your head).

There should be two wide curtains across the front of the stage. One is called the "house curtain" because it divides the stage from the house of the theatre, the area in which the audience sits. The curtain in front of the house curtain is called the "asbestos," and is used to protect the audience in case a fire breaks out onstage. If there is any playing space on the stage platform between the house curtain and the audience, this intimate area is called the "apron." The wide curtain across the back of the theatre is usually called a "cyclorama."[1]

procedure You and your partner choose opposite sides of the stage, with the division line and the prop between you. You will take turns. Your partner begins. His job is to find a relationship between himself and the prop that may be demonstrated by a pose. Your job will be to find a relationship between your partner, his side of the stage, and the prop, and then to adopt a position that seems to balance his. Experiment, take your position, and then ask the study group if you have balanced your partner.

decisions If the stage were on a seesaw, would both sides look even? Have you and your partner merely formed symmetrical patterns? This is valid, but it is also the last time that you should allow yourselves the easy way out. What would your partner's objective be in relation to the prop? Is his objective apparent from his position? Has he squared-off with the prop? Is your objective complementary or in opposition to your partner's? Is there any conflict present?

Variation 1
Body positioning

discussion Facing the audience on a proscenium stage is called "full front." Examine the illustrations of physical positions in the figure, and then experiment with these directions: full front; profile right; face down-left one quarter; face up-right three quarters; open to the house one quarter from the last position. Ask your partner to call out different positions.

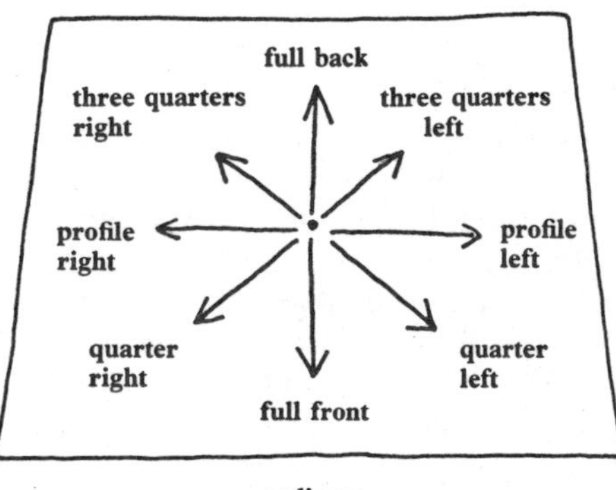

procedures Choose a position in relation to the prop and have your partner balance your pose. Hold your positions and ask the group to decide whether you both seem balanced. Re-balance the focus. Your partner may alter his original pose after considering your position, the prop, and your side of the stage. Repeat the exercise, this time vying for the power position. First, you select a position and freeze; then your partner takes a position opposite you. Ask the study group who has the "dominant focus."

decisions What would your objectives be in the last positions you took? Are you still complementary, or have you found positions that put you into opposition? Which of you should have the focus? Can you balance a person who has taken an upstage position? How important are objectives in relation to stage position? The stage picture is vital to the success of the production because the picture defines the "dominant focus" for the audience.

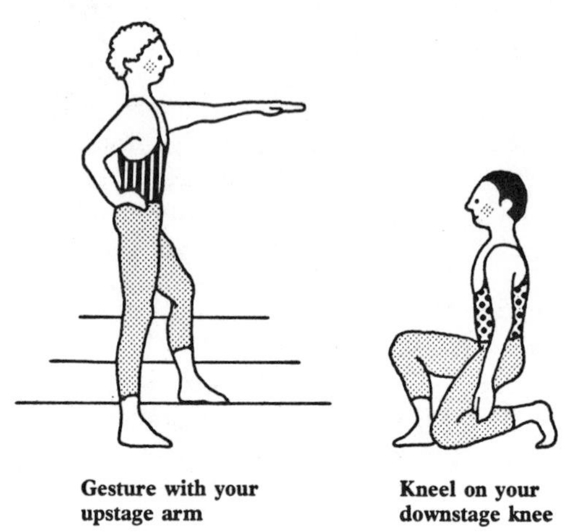

Gesture with your upstage arm

Kneel on your downstage knee

Variation 2
Creating tension

procedure The new task will be to create as much tension for the audience as possible. This time you and your partner should choose more emotional objectives in relation to each other. The study group may suggest ways to alter your choice of position in order to heighten the dramatic tension.

decisions What are your objectives within your apparent positions? Could the group successfully enhance your dramatic tension? Is the tension invading your own body? Keep your body relaxed regardless of your character's inner tension. What did Tomasso Salvini mean by his suggestion that the actor bring the role to a high point, but "let the audience do the screaming"?[2] Do your movements seem too obvious? Even a physically oriented character can produce tension without giving in to obvious externals. Sometimes a brute can provide more tension by being delicate than by being powerful. Always search for a fresh way to play a role.

STEALING THE FOCUS

procedure Find two partners with whom to perform this exercise on a proscenium stage in front of the study group. Using the available furniture in the room, construct a throne room for *Macbeth.* Decide upon a fireplace, rugs, a throne, a long table, and benches. Place these items so that they create a triangle with Macbeth's throne at the apex. Decide which of three roles—Macbeth, the Doctor, the Messenger—each of you will play. The circumstances are these: it is late in the play; most of Macbeth's men have deserted; Lady Macbeth has been ill for several weeks; it is dusk, and everyone in Macbeth's castle expects an attack at any minute. The objectives are these: Macbeth (on his throne) wants to compel the Doctor to diagnose Lady Macbeth's illness as some physical malady that the Doctor can deal with; the Doctor (standing below Macbeth) wants to convince Macbeth that Lady Macbeth's illness is mental and that neither of them can help her; the Messenger wants to tell Macbeth that he *thinks* he has seen Birnam Wood moving toward Dunsinane Castle. After the Doctor and Macbeth have begun their improvisation, the Messenger enters from downstage-right. The Messenger freezes in the shadows, sniffling and waiting to be acknowledged; however, he slowly realizes that he has stepped in dog leavings in his haste to get to Macbeth, and he wants to clean off his shoe without calling attention to himself—the substance is sticky and refuses to come off. The Messenger remains down-right trying to scrape his shoe clean while waiting to be called by Macbeth.

decisions Did Macbeth use the throne as a throne? Was the Doctor conscious of Macbeth's power? Did the Doctor's body illustrate this? Did the Messenger "steal" onstage (move on slowly and quietly so as not to interrupt Macbeth)? Did any of the actors seem to "freeze" onstage, particularly when they had no lines? At what point did your major attention shift to the Messenger? Was the study group still concerned with Macbeth and the Doctor? Was the focus of their attention divided? Was the Messenger moving or doing tiny business during the dialogue between the other actors? An actor in an insignificant role can steal a scene if his action is illogical or unrelated to the dominant needs of the scene. Did the Messenger really seem to believe in the stickiness and odor of the substance? Did Macbeth and the Doctor eventually react to these same stimuli?

PLAYING SOME THEATRICAL NO-NOES

definitions *Crossing.* Moving across the stage to a new position because of some motivation. Crossing is best achieved by moving in a gentle curve, rather than in a straight line. A cross is indicated in a prompt book as an "X."

Covering. Moving into a position between the audience and another actor so that he is blocked from view.

Counter-crossing. Moving slightly to the right or left when another actor is directed to move between you and the audience. This is generally done by stepping in a curve left or right, perhaps in one or two steps. The director should not have to tell you to do this if you find yourself blocked by another actor covering you downstage.

Upstaging. Moving or performing an action to distract the audience from the dominant area of the stage and from the actors who have the lines and are essential to the plot. Upstaging is often done at the rear of the set, "above" the central focus of the scene. You would be guilty of it if, for example, you were cleaning the panchromatic blood off your sword in the back of the crowd gathered in front of Malcolm as he honors Macduff at the end of *Macbeth.*

Downstaging. Carrying out the same type of unrelated movement as in upstaging, but in this case "below" the focal point occupied by the actors with the plot lines. Downstaging is performed right in front of the audience; for example, a jury member adjusting the zipper on his fly during the climactic interrogation between Brady and Drummond in Jerome Lawrence and Robert E. Lee's *Inherit the Wind.* One actor can also downstage other actors by finishing a speech while opening up to the audience and taking a tiny step downstage. In this manner he forces any other central actors to focus down at him. If they need to convince him of something, they will have to alter their positions by moving downstage, too, because they must relate to the actor who moved first. Such a theatrical no-no can also be used in upstaging: merely move slightly upstage at the end of a speech, especially if the actor sharing the scene with you is trapped by a couch and cannot move upstage with you easily; he will be forced to close his body off from the audience, giving you the power position.

Open position and closed position. The position of the actor in relation to the audience. In a completely open position the actor faces full front, turning his pelvis to face the audience. In a fully closed position the actor faces directly upstage, cutting himself off from the house. The actor may think of himself as a clock, facing completely open at six o'clock and fully closed at twelve, in which case facing three o'clock would be called "half left" or "profile left," facing ten-thirty would be called "three-quarters right," and facing four-thirty would be called "one-quarter left," and so on. "Facing" refers to the direction with which the actor's pelvis is aligned when the actor has squared off.

procedure

Clear the center of the work area. Your objective is to perform a Contrary Objective exercise while blocking your partner from the audience by upstaging or downstaging him, or by forcing him to adopt a closed position while he is speaking. Maintain an aura of total plausibility throughout the exercise. Try to use real props and stage furniture honestly.

1. Husband and wife in their neighborhood grocery store.
   He: I want to get her to agree that my mother is a wiser shopper and a better cook than she is.
   She: I want to convince him to let me quit my job and have a baby.
   Circumstances: He has no job and his mother lives with them.

2. Two brothers burglarizing a sporting goods store at night.
   One: I want to coax him into helping me pry open the cash register and the safe.
   Two: I want to convince him that "the wages of sin is death."

decisions Did you handle the set in a believable manner? Were your moves and lines well motivated, or did the exercise degenerate into a frenetic jockeying for position?

variation Ask a third partner to act as a score keeper. Every time you force your partner into an awkward position, the score keeper counts another point for you out loud. Once again, the exercise will be a complete shambles if you and your partner do not try to maintain believability.

PHYSICALIZING A SET AND MARKING A BOOK

Phase 1

Proscenium staging

procedure Read Arthur Miller's *The Crucible* and Tennessee Williams' *A Streetcar Named Desire.* Concentrate on the Proctor-Elizabeth scene at the beginning of Act II in *The Crucible* and the Blanche-Mitch scene at the end of the first act of *Streetcar.* If you have the acting versions, turn to the back of the books and check out the diagrams of the settings for both scenes. If you don't have a stage to work with, decide on which side of the work area the audience would sit. Use the available furniture and create a setting, using the room in your work space as advantageously as possible.

For *The Crucible,* consider these questions:

a. Where is the front door to the cabin? Put the back of a chair there to represent the door area.
b. Where would the bedroom logically lie? Elizabeth must enter from there, because she has been crooning her children to sleep.
c. Where is the dinner table? Can you rake it to the audience?
d. Where is the dry sink? Where would the stove and pantry logically lie? Exactly how does the fireplace-stove function? What pots and ladles are there? Does Elizabeth use a potholder? Upon what does she serve John's meal?
e. What hand props might John have with him? Where would he place his shotgun, and how heavy would it be?
f. Are there any windows in the cabin? If so, where?

decisions Build perspective into your set by gradually aiming the upstage walls in, so that the side walls of the cabin do not seem perpendicular to the audience. Instead of merely setting up a third wall, can you shift the entire cabin diagonally so that it seems as if you are looking at the set on an angle and seeing only two walls? This should build better power positions. Using stage abbreviations, such as "X" for "moves," and letters for stage areas, such as "DSL" for "downstage left," block yourself and your partner as Proctor and Elizabeth into the first two pages of the scene. Mark your books lightly in pencil as you proceed.

Phase 2
Arena staging

procedure Before examining *Streetcar,* alter your work space as if you were working on an arena stage. Consider the doors to your work area and delimit the area in which an audience would sit around you. Use masking tape to mark the boundary. Decide where the aisles might provide exits and entrances from offstage areas for the actors. Use compass directions or the face of a clock to define arena staging: the middle of the work area obviously retains the label "center," but you must now lay out the stage itself in a north-south-east-west arrangement or according to the numbers on a clock. Set up some furniture in the work area in logical patterns for interaction. Repeat the No-No exercises for stealing focus, adapting your moves to arena staging. Is it easier or more difficult to upstage in the arena layout? Usually you will wind up merely blocking part of the audience in the arena, and the rest of the audience will still be able to see your partner.

"Dress' the stage (decide upon the positions for furniture and other props) for *A Streetcar Named Desire.* Consider these questions and then block the scene between Blanche and Mitch at the end of Act I.

a. What would be the best location for the entrance to the Kowalski apartment? Blanche and Mitch have a rather lengthy opening to the scene while fishing for keys and hinting about goodnight kisses. How would the door be represented in arena staging? Would you pantomime the door or use a screen door? Place the door near an aisle.
b. Where would you place the kitchen props? A sink, a small refrigerator, some counter space, a little closet area, at least four chairs, and a table are called for.
c. What could be used to separate the kitchen-living room from the little bedroom? Lay out a piece of tape to indicate the dividing line. Could you use a real bead curtain or just pantomime again? Decide where you would place the bed and a small telephone stand, and mark these areas with tape.
d. Where does Blanche find the liquor and the candle?
e. Where would the fire escape to the second floor be? How can the actors convey a feeling of being closed in, of having people living all around them? Can you use physical means to express this without blocking the audience?

suggestions Here are some pointers on performing on an arena stage:

a. Try to stay at least an arm's length away from the other actors in arena blocking, or, if you must come very close to another actor, try to find a way of motivating a position so that the two of you are on different

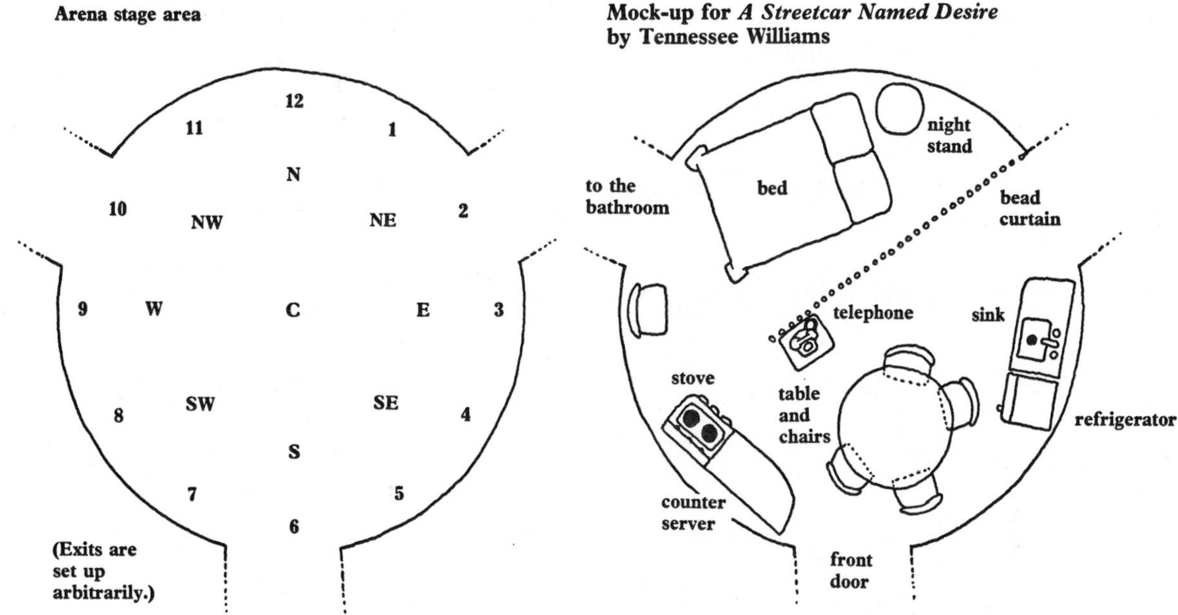

physical planes. For example, one of you might sit while the other stands. Generally try to stay open to the center of the playing area.

b. If you find you must stand and listen for a long time in a scene, try try to find a position with your back to an *aisle* so that you can face in and still not obstruct the view of the members of the audience directly behind you.

c. Cut down your use of gestures unless they are truly indicative of your character's emotion or are directly called for in the script. The audience's proximity to the actors minimizes its aesthetic distance from the action.

GESTURING AS A TECHNIQUE

procedure Choose a task to pantomime for your partner; for example, try to hail a cab on a wet and windy day, or try to stop traffic in order to retrieve a baseball that has accidently rolled into the street. Take your time and be specific. Ask your partner if you made choices that are theatrical, economical, and free from tension, and that elicit immediate understanding and identification.

Try to follow these general rules for gesturing on a proscenium stage:

a. Use your upstage arm for gesturing.

b. Kneel on your downstage knee in order to wind up in a more open position.
c. Control the tension of the character so that the audience doesn't confuse it with the tension of the actor as a performer.
d. Leave yourself somewhere to go physically. Total extension makes an audience self-conscious. Sticking your arm "all the way out" will make you look ridiculous.
e. Use a minimal amount of movement and energy—just enough to do the job.
f. Give yourself a progression of action so that the audience will sense you are accomplishing something. This will necessitate a change of rhythm during a piece of action.

decisions In what instances may you break these general rules? What types of characters are excessive? Can you choose to do an action with an upstage orientation that forces your partner into an even deeper concentration on you? An actor's back can be effective if the actor remembers that emotion is organic. Using only your back, try to communicate what you feel: stand with your back to your partner and see if he can ascertain when you are performing surprise, anger, and fear.

discussion Every gesture you perform must stem from your character's emotional commitment. You should never feel uncomfortable doing a gesture in a role. It isn't wrong for an actress playing Marthy in Eugene O'Neill's *Anna Christie* to wear her father's old coat to a rehearsal or to a class performance of the play if the coat lends credibility to her performance.

suggestions Try pantomiming the following gestures. Ask your partner to criticize your work.

a. Bump into and break a priceless statue at a French museum.
b. Make crêpes for Julia Child and James Beard.
c. You are in your bedroom. Pack a suitcase to escape Mafia racketeers.
d. You have had plastic surgery on your face. The bandages are unwrapped—and you see your new face for the first time.
e. Trail a wounded deer through the snow.
f. Model a bathing suit as a candidate for Miss Universe. Create a runway, and be specific in relation to where the judges are.
g. Bring your prize cow to the judges' stand in an effort to win the State Fair Blue Ribbon.
h. Sneak a look in your Christmas stocking with your parents in the next room.
i. Try to make friends with an angry dog (or try to re-enact Jerry's story about the dog in Edward Albee's *The Zoo Story*).
j. Try to hang a terribly expensive painting on nails that won't stay firmly in the wall.
k. Unwrap a present that you think is what you have hoped for and planned on for a long time. It doesn't turn out to be what you wanted.

l. Create a ritual to bury a dead baby bird that you tried to raise.
m. While washing your hands in the kitchen, you notice that two extremely expensive filet mignons have caught fire in the gas broiler. Rescue the steaks and extinguish the fire.
n. Enter a ruined building and dismantle a bomb powerful enough to destroy the entire city.
o. Try to prevent your dog from going to the bathroom on the steps of the White House. Your dog is a St. Bernard; there is a $100 fine for not curbing your dog, and the guard is only twenty feet away.
p. Try to find your contact lens in the middle of a dance floor at a Polish wedding.
q. You (female) notice that your false eyelashes are coming off, so you duck into the nearest rest room to check them. As you are adjusting one at the mirror, it dawns on you that this is a men's room.
r. Crawl across a battlefield under low fire, trying to get a good shot at the enemy.
s. You come to the front rail of the church for Communion, and as you kneel, you rip open the seat of your pants (skirt). Try as surreptitiously as possible to disguise the rip.
t. You are at a penny arcade. After putting a dime in the slot, you use the electric rifle to shoot at the mechanical bear. You miss twice. On the third try you hit the bear, and it really dies. Brokenhearted, you leave. (Alternate ending: you wound the bear and it climbs out of the machine and chases you out of the arcade.)
u. You are slowly freezing to death. You gather a few sticks in the snow and try to light them, but they won't catch. Eventually your fingers will no longer work, and you drift into sleep.
v. You are injured in an automobile accident late at night. You are alone. You limp over to two phone booths. After you've made it to the first one, you search frantically for a dime; when you finally find one, you discover the phone is out of order. You try to reach the next booth and faint on the way.

chapter 7
EXPERIMENTING IN REHEARSAL

When you begin working on a structured scene for class criticism, try not to "freeze in" (set) your blocking or to choose your externals until you and your partner have met several times to explore the emotional needs in the scene. Select a few games to play with each other, and search for the heart of the scene for yourselves. Try to maintain the spontaneous feeling of improvisation every time you work on the scene. Keep it alive. The classroom is the place for failure, audacity, and expansion. The study group will enjoy your scene only if you enjoy sharing the dramatic moments with your partner. Working too quickly for end-results will lock you into unproductive patterns. Classroom scene study is an examination of the creative process at work. If you feel that you *must* achieve perfection in your scenes, your attitude will be harmful both to you and to your study group.

The following exercises can be used in rehearsal as well as during class meetings and group criticism. These games should not only help you center your energy on your objectives, but should also get you out of the way of yourself so that you may share your natural impulses freely with your partner.

Decide together which games would be good for your specific scene. The choice of the right game can be illuminating and enjoyable. The choice of the wrong game is not necessarily destructive, but it can very often bewilder you. Two people working on a game together may be expending energy and thinking that they are getting somewhere, when in actuality they are merely exercising for the sake of exercising. To be profitable, the game should parallel your French-scene objective; in other words, if the game encourages you to act out what you want and need from your partner, it is worth trying. Using the game, do the scene; then drop the game and see if the scene has new life. While playing the game you may discover some moments that you want to keep for public performance.

AIR KISSING

Air kissing can be used if you are doing a romantic scene or one in which you and your partner are very critical of each other. If your first-time illusion becomes predictable or flat, the air-kissing game may help you enliven your sharing process.

procedure Simply punctuate each line with a kiss in the air. Direct the kiss at the eyes or lips of your partner. Explore your partner's face with each kiss, and try to make the kiss operate as part of the dialogue. Try to accompany the air kissing with a sense memory of real emotion, whether it be a genuine affection for someone else or a somewhat contemptuous attitude. Use the kiss as you would a prop—experiment and play with each kiss.

decisions Did the kiss enhance the expression of your emotion, or did you merely kiss into the air? Was your kiss focused or was it diffused? Did the simple physical act of air kissing lead you into any real emotion? Did you discover any new line readings? This game will work as well for scenes by Tennessee Williams, Clifford Odets, Oscar Wilde, and Noël Coward as it will for scenes by Shakespeare.

ONE-UPMANSHIP

This game is most effective when used in a scene in which two characters are trying to outdo each other; for example, check the final scene of the first act of Murray Shisgal's *Luv* in which Ellen and Harry compete to see who had the more cruel childhood, or the challenge scene between Eddie and Marco in Arthur Miller's *A View From the Bridge.* Interrogation scenes, like those in Sidney Kingsley's *Darkness at Noon* and Jerome Lawrence and Robert E. Lee's *Inherit the Wind,* also lend themselves to this type of game.

procedure Ask two friends to watch your scene and function as score keepers for you. Each of you chooses a score keeper to be on your side. Whenever you advance your scene objective in the slightest way, through words or gestures, you must lick a finger and stroke the air as if to add to your score. The score keepers count the score aloud, pitting you against each other. The score keepers are instrumental to the game, for they are also conscious of their respective actor's objective. If a score keeper sees his actor make a point, but his actor does not realize that he has truly scored a point or that he *might* have done so at this time, the score keeper subtracts a point from his actor's score. In this way, each score keeper is really siding with his actor's opponent. Continue the game as long as it stays fresh.

decisions Were you conscious of any conflict that you had not encountered in the scene? Did you *play* with each other, or did you merely battle? Did you score real points, or did you become so enamored of the game that you began to score points for everything? Were the score keepers' reasons for subtracting points valid? There is a danger in this game of playing the objective exclusive of the circumstances. You must remain true to your character, rather than just to yourself, as you play the game. Of course, the players on each side must agree on their objective for the game to be effective.

TOUCH OF FIRE

This game can be used when you are doing a scene in which your characters are saying devastating things to each other, but you know that you and your partner are taking the easy way out and just letting yourselves say the words. Examine the scenes between Mary and James Tyrone in Eugene O'Neill's *A Long Day's Journey into Night*, or the scene between Ismene and Antigone in Jean Anouilh's *Antigone.* In both instances, the touch of fire belongs to the performer who drives the scene—the actor playing James and the actress playing Ismene. They both have the same basic objective: I want to convince her that her conduct is destructive and profitless.

procedure The performer with the touch of fire must keep in physical contact with the other performer in the scene at all times without resorting to any physical violence. Merely touching, caressing, holding is fine if it advances your beat objective at the moment. The recipient (Mary or Antigone) must find a way to avoid physical contact within the context of the script. Naturally Mary doesn't want James to see her eyes, or he'll realize she's back on morphine, so she may involve herself with her sewing box. Antigone tries to divert Ismene by talking about Ismene's beauty, so she may try to comb Ismene's hair. The recipient must react to any prolonged touch from his partner as if he were being burned by a hot iron. Try to take the game seriously. The further you go into the scene, the hotter the touch of fire becomes.

decisions Was there any real progression in the game, or did the touching merely result in little chases around the work space? Physicalizing the burns should help the recipient find a truer adjustment to the insults and the painful statements in the scene.

THE BOX

This exercise may be used in conjunction with or as a substitute for the Touch of Fire exercise. Its primary aim is to force two actors to listen and react to each other. You will need a four by five- or six-foot box without a lid, such as a small theatre platform turned upside-down. Any method of physically trapping two actors into a small area may be substituted.

procedure Step into the box and place a chair or two between you and your partner. Once again, it is one actor's objective to try to contact the other actor physically. Both of you may use the chairs to your own advantage as long as you don't endanger each other physically. Simply play a game of tag inside the box. Neither of you is allowed to leave the box until the scene is over. Use the words of the scene as accompaniment to playing the objective, so that the exercise does not degenerate into merely a game of tag.

decisions Did you find a variety of ways to contact each other or did you resort to sheer force? Were either of you "tricky"? Did your cleverness invade your words as well as your physical movement?

THE WALL

This game is at its best in scenes in which one character needs another character to help him but the other either is involved with his own dilemma or is consciously trying to avoid him. Look at the Proctor-Elizabeth scene at the beginning of the second act of Arthur Miller's *The Crucible.* John tries to win Elizabeth's affection, but she is unable to forgive either him or herself for John's earlier behavior with Abigail. The game requires a heap of furniture—rehearsal chairs and tables—amassed in the center of the floor.

procedure You and your partner take positions on opposite sides of the work space with all the furniture between you. The actor who wants to isolate himself must build an impregnable wall of furniture around himself. The actor who drives the scene tries to establish contact by moving the furniture out of the way, but the isolationist keeps putting other pieces of furniture up to secure his bastion. The more skillfully the isolationist balances one rehearsal chair or table on top of another, the longer it will take the driver to tear down the wall. Avoid any violent moves that could result in physical injury. When you go back to doing the scene without the game, the isolationist should find ways to busy himself with real physical chores that would enable him to avoid his partner logically.

discussion Did the driver of the scene take advantage of the other actor with any physical threat? Did the exertion of building the wall aid the isolationist in finding new line readings? The addition of real actions and real prop orientation (even if the props are pantomimed) should help you take the scene seriously.

THE INNER DIALOGUE[1]

Using the Inner Dialogue Method in a scene is especially helpful if you find you are cloudy about your motivation, or if you feel you're "marking" the action because you don't seem to have an emotional claim on your partner.

procedure Vocalize not only your written lines but also your inner motivations or beats (units) out loud. In other words, vocalize all your thoughts. For example, the actors playing Iago and Roderigo in the first scene of Shakespeare's *Othello* might actually vocalize all the following lines (the actor's thoughts are italicized):

Roderigo *I want to push him away from me.* (He pushes Iago.) *I want to force him to explain how he knew about Desdemona and Othello and why he never told me about their elopement.*
Tush, never tell me! I take it much unkindly
That thou, Iago, . . .
I want to shame him about the way he has taken my cash, and see his reaction when I tell him that he'll never sucker money out of me again.
. . . who hast had my purse
As if the strings were thine, shouldst know of this.

Iago *I want to keep his money on tap. I want to get him tipsy enough to believe me and arouse Brabantio in the middle of the night.*
'Sblood! but you will not hear me! (Iago offers Roderigo a drink.)
I want to make him defensive about insulting my honor.
If ever I did dream of such a matter, abhor me.

Roderigo *I want to verify the possible lie he told me. I want to stay sober until he tells me the truth.*
Thou told'st me thou didst hold him in they hate. (Roderigo pushes the bottle away.)

Iago *I want to win his confidence.*
Despise me if I do not.
I want to quench my thirst from all this arguing with him. (Iago takes a sip.)
I want to get him to drink, too. I want to lure him into drinking. (Iago takes another small sip, smacks his lips, and offers the bottle to Roderigo again, forcing the bottle into his hands so that it will drop unless Roderigo really grasps it.)

decisions Did you take the time to think through every beat, or did you skip over lines that might have been effectively broken into tiny units to give the scene more variety and enrichment? Did any segments seem nebulous? Was your inner dialogue as interesting as the written scene? Was it consistent with the characters both of you were playing?

THE SILENT-ACTION EXERCISE

procedure If you feel that you lack a firm sense of your physical movement throughout your scene, or if your movement seems illogical, repeat the scene *without using words.* As you and your partner move from place to place, relate to each other, but communicate by relying on your bodies and gestures to convey your objectives. However, don't move to another position until you feel that your partner has given you sufficient motivation. Stand there and wait until you are sure of what he is attempting to convey. Speed up the movement of the scene; don't stand in one position so long that you allow time for a lengthy tirade or soliloquy—just take enough time to clarify what you need from your partner.

discussion Did you demand specificity from each other? Did your movements suit your objectives? Did you meander along when you should have been angry? Was part of your body (for instance, your arm) moving within your emotion, while the rest of you seemed totally at ease? An actor's entire body must give the impression of involvement within his action and objective.

FACE SHAPING

Face shaping is particularly effective for romantic scenes in which the performers seem a little shy of each other. You may be having a hard time finding affection for each other, or you may be allowing yourselves to indicate your affection with worn-out gestures.

procedure Take positions at opposite ends of the work space with at least twelve feet between you. Keeping this distance, reach toward each other, focusing on the general outline of each other's face. Trace specific facial features. Caress them. When you feel that the physical task of caressing has helped your concentration, begin the scene. Remain standing twelve feet apart and keep reaching toward each other's face, caressing with both words and gestures. Eventually you may stop caressing with your hands and allow just your words and your lips to do the caressing for you.

Begin to approach each other very slowly, one step at a time per line, until you are directly in front of each other. Go on concentrating and caressing each other's face with the words, but do not touch each other, even if the script indicates doing so. Begin the scene again, using any of your old blocking that you need, but continue the face-shaping game as you say your lines.

decisions Did the physical act of caressing lead you into new line readings and rhythms? Did the scene seem to be "going somewhere"? Caressing solely with words can be as sensual for the audience as giving in to real physical contact.

ALTERING TYPES OF PLAYS

If you are working on a scene from a play that is essentially tragic, like Arthur Miller's *Death of a Salesman,* you may be making purely tragic choices in your actions and line readings. If the scene is making you miserable, your undertones are being totally immersed in your overtones.

procedure Imagine that you and your partner are doing the dialogue between songs in a Rodgers and Hammerstein musical. Direct the first two words of each sentence at each other, and then share the rest of the lines with the audience, enjoying the possible comic values in the play. You may even be able to improvise a tune to the lines as you sing-say them to each other! You may feel foolish at first, but you may also find a human balance in the script that will intrigue the audience.

If you are performing an obviously funny scene in a play that is basically a comedy, like the opening scene in Abe Burrows' *Cactus Flower*, you may be milking the entire script for laughs from the audience because you are concerned only with the comic values. Remember that the play begins with Toni's attempted suicide, and that Igor is an *unsuccessful* playwright. Of course, it would be deadly to wallow in their problems, but you must give the impression that Toni and Igor do take them seriously. Pretend that Henrik Ibsen wrote *Cactus Flower*, and repeat the scene, just as if the play were going to be a tragedy. Forget the audience and concentrate on each other's dilemma. If you seem to be playing the scene too fast, try to think of yourselves as being underwater. Speak very slowly, and "swim" toward each other to make physical contact.

decisions Are you able to make the transition from a comic to a tragic attitude with ease? Do you find yourself falling into one comfortable, generalized emotion when working on a scene, instead of bringing out the various values that may be in the script? An actor does not consciously have to choose ways to play the tragedy in a tragedy or the comedy in a comedy. Trust the playwright, and play your objectives with your partner.

MAINTAINING FIRST-TIME ILLUSION (THE INHALATION GAME)

If you and your partner feel that you are no longer making discoveries with each other as you rehearse your scene, you may want to try a technique that creates the illusion of the first time.

procedure As you go through the scene, vocalize a sharp inhalation, as if you were surprised, before speaking any of your lines. Try to incorporate the inhalation logically as an honest reaction to your partner's lines. Vary the rhythm and length of the inhalation to suit your objectives.

decisions This exercise may seem silly at first, but if you try to make the inhalations sound like real parts of your speeches, you will find that you can motivate many of the inhalations logically. Did you realize that a lot of the lines you had taken for granted in the scene were really fresh discoveries that your character was experiencing? Try to incorporate the better-motivated inhalations into the scene.

CREATING A NERVOUS IMPRESSION (THE HICCUP GAME)

Perhaps you are working on a scene in which you know your character is upset; for example, you may be playing Laura Wingfield in Tennessee Williams' *The Glass Menagerie* or Serafina in Williams' *The Rose Tattoo*. Laura's scene with Jim and Serafina's scenes with Alvaro begin with a sense of near-trauma;

however, after rehearsing the roles for a long period of time, your excitement may be waning and the scene may be going flat.

procedure Superimpose a hiccup within the rhythm of your character's lines, or try to incorporate a stutter into your role. Be logical and economical. Use the hiccups or the stutter only when you feel threatened by your partner within the circumstances of the scene. Play the hiccup as if it were real.

decisions Did you take the exercise seriously, allowing yourself to become embarrassed by hiccups? If you approach these externals with *economy*, they may help you reform the elemental feelings of your character. The next time you work on the scene, begin with the stutter or the hiccups, allow yourself to feel embarrassed, and then consciously try to stifle the hiccup. Remember that your character does not *want* to stutter or hiccup in front of someone else. His energy would be directed at controlling his nervousness, not at accentuating it.

You can create more of these exercises for yourself if you use (or learn to use) the power of observation. For example, have you noticed that when some people are intent on learning something, their mouths fall open? If you need to give the audience the impression that your character is going through a learning process, focus on your partner and listen to him. Rehash his logic in your mind by silently repeating his last line to yourself and let your jaw fall open. Merely doing the external can give you as your character an internal justification for your action. As long as you relate to the other actor onstage, the audience will probably accept your actions as credible, but the moment you try to act alone you risk destroying the audience's belief in your character.

chapter 8

EXPERIMENTING FOR CREATIVE CHARACTERIZATION

Professional directors usually select actors for their productions who closely resemble the roles they will play. However, few theatres have the financial resources to allow directors to typecast unrestrainedly in every play, especially in a repertory situation. In most cases, an established theatre has on call older people from the community who can play character roles with age requirements. However, you may be expected to play a variety of character roles within your general age bracket (your natural age plus or minus five years).

Creating a character who is very different from yourself requires skill, patience, and imagination. Nearly all the acting that you do might be called character work, because you are giving an audience an interpretation of a role that you are consciously performing. To play any role you should find the most economical way to give the audience the impression that you want and need what your character wants and needs as much as he does and for the same reasons. You must construct a logical series of human choices for your character. You actually create his ego.

Be honest with yourself. Can you play roles like yourself with simplicity? You should be able to play yourself before you attempt to play someone else. Paradoxically, the more removed the character is from you as a person, the easier it is to put yourself and your own experiences into the role. For example, if you are a handsome juvenile playing a good-looking young man like Ferdinand in Shakespeare's *The Tempest*, you may be embarrassed to substitute your very real feelings for your own girlfriend as an emotion-memory basis to relate to the actress playing Miranda. But if you step into the role of Angelo in Shakespeare's *Measure for Measure* or of De Flores in Thomas Middleton's *The Changeling,* you may find it easier to use your vulnerable love for your girlfriend as a basis because the role is further removed from you as a person.

The initial set of exercises should help you find a logical, playable way into your character. The latter exercises are designed to help you explore a new rhythm, a new emotional pattern, and a new external attitude based on the internal life of your character. Film actors as well as stage actors may employ these creative methods, though film actors must be more subtle in order to please the discerning eye of the camera. The more distance you have from your audience, the freer you are to experiment with external characterization.

Remember that there is a difference between cold, objective analysis and creative, objective analysis. It isn't necessary to write lengthy psychological studies of the characters you are to play; in fact, overwriting will bleed the life and joy out of playing a role. Your personal tendency may be more adapted to writing about a role than playing it; therefore, outline form is better than paragraph form for an acting study of a role. Make your choices logical, specific, and decisive.

In selecting conscious choices for your role, you may find that you know things about your character that your character does not know about himself. Reread the play to determine the author's intent. Try to structure your character's needs to bring out the theme of the play.

Even if the theme of the play, as in Luigi Pirandello's *Right You Are, If You Think You Are,* develops the idea that no one can ever know anyone else completely, you as the actor must make definite choices about your role. Pirandello's theme deals with a social injustice; you must deal with artistic, playable facts.

ANALYZING A CHARACTER FOR SCENE WORK

Use the following chart to analyze your next role for class critique:

Character Analysis for Scene Work[1]

A. *Objectives* (Stated—in positive terms of "I want"—whenever possible in referring to direct or indirect objects, and always in relating to the other actor or actors on the stage.)

1. Super-objective. Your central purpose from which all your actions in the play spring.
2. French-scene objective. The central purpose or motivation that characterizes all your actions from each entrance to each exit you make in the play.
3. Unit, Beat (sometimes called Action) objective. Every tiny

purpose that instigates or alters any single piece of business you have in any French scene. The more physically (body or prop) oriented these are, the more successful they are in putting you into action.

All of these are worded in the same way; they are interrelated and are aimed solely at putting you into action. You cannot be passive onstage, even if your action is to ignore another actor. Ignore him dramatically!

B. *Script analysis*

1. What the author says about your character in stage directions by other non-dialog remarks.
2. Lines you say about yourself as a character. Any lies?
3. Lines other characters say about you. Any lies?
4. Your attitudes toward every other character in the play with whom you come into contact.
5. Changes in your attitude toward other characters in the play and changes in their attitudes toward you that influence the way *you* play a scene. Major discoveries you make during the play.

C. *Specific sensory and background choices*

1. Extent of education and favorite or hated subjects studied.
2. Favorite foods, restaurants.
3. Favorite music.
4. Most frequently used expressions.
5. Grooming habits.
6. Ways of exercising or relaxing.

D. *Creative abstractions*

1. Characterization method: life study; animal study; direct-object study; secondary characteristic.
2. Individual psychological gestures; major sense or emotion memories to flesh out your reality.

---

discussion

Examine the segment on sensory choices (item C) closely. Character choices selected here will not be helpful if they are not gut-level for you as the actor. If these choices are not apparent in the lines of the script, make them up yourself. If you are playing Oedipus, second-guessing about neighborhood night spots in ancient Thebes or such foods as yiaprakia and moussaka is worthless.[2] Instead, try to relate ancient Thebes to the city in which you live, and to consider the functions Oedipus would have to perform were he the mayor of your city.

Used properly, the chart should give you a creative framework to tackle any role. Be sure that your work with the chart relates solely to the character you are going to play. Deciding attitudes for characters other than your own tends to spur you into directing yourself because you will be responding to what you feel the other characters *should* be giving you onstage. Train yourself to react to the first-time discoveries that your character ought to be making about the other persons in the play.

The following example is an outline for Happy Loman in Arthur Miller's *Death of a Salesman,* dealing basically with Happy's first French scene in Act I.

A. Objectives

1. Super: I want to find a way to get everyone to acknowledge me as successful at something.
2. Scene: I want to convince Biff to stay here in town and take over responsibility for Willy.
3. Units: I want Biff to agree that Pop is falling apart.

   I want to establish common ground with Biff by recalling old times.

   I want to prove to Biff that he has changed for the worse.

   I want to convince Biff that he is the reason that Pop is falling apart so that Biff feels guilty.

   I want to force Biff to define his own failure.

   I want to get Biff to compliment me on how I got what I wanted.

   I want to prove to Biff that the real challenge and the real money are here in the business world.

   I want my brother to admit that I'm extremely successful with women.

   I want to encourage Biff to see Bill Oliver.

   I want to get Biff angry enough to do something about Pop.

B. Script analysis

1. Author: "Happy is tall, powerfully made. Sexuality is like a visible color on him, or a scent that many women have discovered. He, like his brother, is lost, but in a different way, for he has never allowed himself to turn his face toward defeat and is thus more confused and hard skinned, although seemingly more content."

   "(with a deep and masculine laugh)"

   "(combing his hair)"
2. Self: "Oh, I still am [bashful], Biff. . . . I just control it, that's all." [I use it.]

   "I'm lonely." [Somewhat true.]

"I have to take orders from those common, petty sons-of-bitches till I can't stand it any more."

"I want to walk into the store the way he walks in. . . . Maybe I just have an overdeveloped sense of competition or something."

"I take it and—I love it!" [Bribes and women.]

"I don't know what to do about him [Pop]."

3. Others: "I bet you forgot how bashful you used to be. . . . You're a success, aren't you?" [I think so.]

   "You'd never come home." [To a wife? Probably true.]

4. Attitude: I was always jealous of him and still am, but by the end of the scene I feel superior to him.

5. Discoveries: Biff is very uptight about Pop.

   Biff considers himself a failure, a kid.

   Biff doesn't enjoy women as much as he once did.

   I know I can get him to take care of Pop.

C. Sensory and background choices

1. Education: I got through high school. I liked physical education and history best. I dig heroes. Eventually I spent more time in baseball to avoid comparison with my brother who was in football. I also took the business curriculum in high school because Biff had chosen the academic curriculum.

2. Foods: I like a good steak, medium-rare, in a place where I can make my own salad and heap on the blue cheese. I also like Italian and Greek restaurants on a date, and I joke about how to pronounce the names of foods.

3. Music: Stuff with a flair, like Herb Alpert, is best. I always think lyrics are distracting.

4. Expressions: Y'know.

   Like I said (I have to repeat myself to the stupid people I work with).

   Hey, hey, hey, come on now!

   I don't swear much, because it's a bad habit.

5. Grooming: I comb my hair before I go to bed every night, and I comb it again before I go the bathroom in the morning. I like to have one curl come down over my forehead. I use Right Guard and High Karate. I firmly believe in using dental floss after meals.

6. Exercise: I don't like to dance too much on a date. I have a regular handball partner twice a week. I keep a set of springs in my apartment in a closet and I pull them sometimes while I watch the late

movie. I always pull them before I shower when I get ready to go out on a date with a chick.

D. Creative abstractions

1. I watched a tomcat for a while, and I analyzed a set of weights. I liked the way the cat cleaned himself, and the weights made me feel tight and sure of myself.

   Happy has a strong handshake.

   As a secondary characteristic I used the change that comes over me when I tell old army stories.

2. Happy stands around at work with his arms folded and his hands under his biceps to make them bulge more. I remember the way I felt playing second-string offensive tackle watching the first string play football.[3]

FINDING AN INNER RHYTHM WITH MUSIC

In this instance the word "rhythm" refers to the basic energy pattern manifested by your character as he thinks, moves, acts, and pursues his objectives. Your rhythm, tempo, and pace all reflect the same thing—the way you physicalize your character's plan of attack to get what he needs from the other characters in the scene.

needs Clear the work space of any furniture. Find a phonograph and several pieces of music with different types of sound and beat, such as Bedrich Smetana's "The Moldau," Sergei Prokofiev's Sonata No. 7 for Piano, Bela Bartok's "The Miraculous Mandarin," Jean Sibelius's "Finlandia," Richard Strauss's "Also Sprach Zarathustra," and Peter Ilyitch Tchaikovsky's "March Slav."

procedure Play one of the records. Try to move with the music in a rhythmic and spatial plane that seems suggested by the music. Have your partner join you. Relax into working with each other and allow physical contact as the music leads you into a relationship and into a movement pattern. Allow each record to play for at least five minutes before selecting a new one.

decisions What would your objective regarding your partner be if you surrendered to the mood of the music? Did you feel light, or were you heavy with responsibility? Were you moving mercurially, or were you moving smoothly? Did you move with direction or were you somewhat aimless?

After listening to and moving with "The Moldau," you may feel that your movement was light, that you were buoyed up or carried up and down along a flexible plane. Was the steady growth of the music evident in your movements? Did you feel a floating sensation that induced you to take a long time in finishing your gestures with your partner? Or, on the contrary, did you feel an undercurrent of fast, up-and-down movements that gave you the impression that you were flicking along an indecisive path?

What was the impact of a more frenetic and nervous type of music, such as Prokofiev's Sonata No. 7 for Piano? You may have had various subjective responses to the music, depending upon your hedonic reaction, though you probably felt that your movements were like tiny jabs—light and quick and purposeful. However, you may have been unnerved by the music and you may have tried to work against it, letting it tense you into a stiff or heavy movement pattern that caused you to run up and down with great purpose and decisiveness, as if you were wringing the life out of your partner.

Work with each piece of music to determine which selections make you feel like slashing at or pressing each other, gliding or soaring along with each other, punching at or wringing each other. If you allow yourself to be swept along with the music, you will find yourself creating what Michael Chekhov calls "psychological gestures."[4] Such gestures stem from the inner rhythm and life of a character's emotions.

You can manipulate yourself into an internal pattern by telling yourself, "My character always feels the way that piece of music makes me feel." In fact, you may be able to freshen your character merely by humming the piece of music in the dressing room or the green room. You may even be able to use it onstage on the rare occasion that the director feels that it "works." Laura Wingfield has a favorite piece of music she keeps playing in Tennessee Williams' *The Glass Menagerie,* just as Joe Bonaparte has a tune he whistles to soften Lorna's façade in Clifford Odets' *Golden Boy.*

CHARTING A CHARACTER'S ESSENCE

procedure Impersonate a famous television or movie personality. Only a few vocalized sentences are necessary. Ask your partner to guess who the star is.

decisions A few well-chosen gestures that typify a star are more effective than a barrage of clichés. Jack Benny's stance and his slow burn—with that measured turning of his face toward the audience—may be all that an actor needs to do to perform an effective impersonation. Impersonations may require a certain knack on the part of the performer; however, the final result of this exercise is not the creation of a perfect imitation, but rather the discovery of what specific traits contribute to the formulation of an identifiable human type. Even if your partner did not guess whom you were imitating, you may still have latched on to a certain essence that you can perform onstage. Originality is more creative than mere mimicry.

Begin analyzing various stars by asking yourself how each star handles the major physical variables of time, space, weight, and flow of action. Does he move very fast, whether he is decisive or jerky, so that he may be described as "quick"? Does he move with consistency over a length of time, whether his movement be deliberative or continually nervous, so that he may be called "sustained"? Does he pursue his objective within a single plane of movement, whether it be high, medium, or low, making his use of space seem "direct"?

Does the direction in which he plays his objective appear to vacillate so that his use of space is "flexible"? Is there a serious tension or a ponderousness in his movements that makes his weight seem heavy or "strong"? Are his movements bouncy, airborne, bird-like, perhaps nervous or even flighty, so that his movements seem "light"? Lightness does not entail weakness. Weight in this sense suggests a way in which a character pursues his objective. Shakespeare's Ariel and Oberon may be generally typed as "light," whereas his Iago is heavy with intention.

Is the star uptight, stubborn, or "bound," or does he seem capable of change so that his movement seems "free"? What music reminds you of his personality? For example, if you are working on the role of the Bandit in Fay Kanin's *Rashomon*, do you find the "slashing" quality in Bartok's "The Miraculous Mandarin" (similar to the movement you might associate with James Cagney or Frank Gorshin) suggestive of the Bandit's movement?

Compare the divisions on the following chart with the stars' names, the musical compositions, and the animals suggested in each category.[5] The eight basic variations or possibilities of types within this system are not as limited as they appear at first. There are no hard and fast rules for categorizing. The chart presents a springboard to creativity rather than a scientific method of bleeding the life out of a characterization.

A character may deviate slightly from type to type, depending upon his function in the play, though he will generally remain within the variables true to his category in playing his objectives. A star or an animal is most frequently found within his type when he needs something desperately or is vulnerable. Watch him when he performs socially with other characters, and when he is hurt or distracted. Flow of Energy is impossible to chart because the choice between bound or free energy is so personal that it varies completely even within a category. Perhaps this is why Carol Burnett and Anthony Quinn may both be classified as "punchers." Bound energy suggests that a character or a star may see himself locked into an expected mode of behavior, whereas Free energy suggests that a character or star does not accept restrictions on his creativity even though he still shapes space around him in one basic way.

variations

Listen to Modest Moussorgsky's "Pictures at an Exhibition," Camille Saint-Saëns' "March of the Animals," and Peter Ilyitch Tchaikovsky's "Peter and the Wolf." Where might certain movement patterns of these multifaceted compositions belong on the chart? Watch dancers shape the space around themselves as they move to varying kinds of music. Respond to the music as *you* feel it, not as you think you should feel it to satisfy anyone else.

Compare Igor Stravinsky's "The Rite of Spring" with one of the many excellent choric sections in *The Eumenides*, the third play in Aeschylus' trilogy, *The Oresteia*. Chant a choric section of *The Eumenides* until you have mastered it. Move freely to the sounds of the words themselves.

Examine the collective objectives of the chorus of Eumenides. They are a community of Furies (Harpies) whose job is to inflict pain, both mentally and physically, on human beings who have violated Natural Laws. The Eumen-

Character Quality Chart

	Variables			
	TIME	SPACE	WEIGHT	FLOW OF ENERGY
Elements *(Polarities)*	Quick Sustained	Flexible Direct	Strong Light	Bound Free

Strong WEIGHT	Light WEIGHT
PUNCHER (direct and quick) German shepherds, lions (big cats that pad rather than slink along) Anthony Quinn and Carol Burnett Rossini's "William Tell Overture"	DABBER (direct and quick) Starlings, small lizards, squirrels, wasps Sandy Dennis and Jack Lemmon Prokofiev's Sonata No. 7 for Piano
PRESSER (direct and sustained) Tigers, orangutans, goats (when they butt), large constrictor snakes Rod Steiger and Geraldine Page Tchaikovsky's "March Slav"	GLIDER (direct and sustained) Eagles, hawks, otters, peacocks, spiders Burt Lancaster and Diana Rigg Richard Strauss's "Also Sprach Zarathustra"
SLASHER (flexible and quick) Barracuda, panthers, game cocks, poisonous snakes James Cagney and Julie Newmar Bartok's "The Miraculous Mandarin"	FLICKER (flexible and quick) Ducks, sparrows, pan fish, small monkeys and fruit flies Jerry Lewis and Lucille Ball Dukas' "The Sorcerer's Apprentice"
WRINGER (flexible and sustained) Chimpanzees, hyenas, raccoons, nervous birds of prey Kirk Douglas and Judy Garland Stravinsky's "The Fire Bird"	FLOATER (flexible and sustained) Hummingbirds, honey bees, swans and jellyfish Dick Cavett and Mary Martin Smetana's "The Moldau"

Source: Based on Rudolf Laban, *The Mastery of Movement,* 3d ed. rev. and enl. by Lisa Ullmann (Boston: Plays, Inc., 1971). For an in-depth description of these subjective classifications, see pp. 128–131.

ides are all part of a non-human group. They should have sort of an ugly or frightening appearance. They have a job in common—they are reactionaries bent on restoring the old order. Their first entrance proves them to be capable of tracking, and they are especially fond of blood. In order to carry out their objective, the Eumenides would most probably have to be "light" to travel fast, "direct" to track well, and "quick" to attack their quarry. A glance at the chart suggests that they may be effectively performed as "dabbers," perhaps animal types like small lizards or wasps. Since the Eumenides operate as a community, wasps—community insects—might provide the best image.

To solidify the image, observe wasps, especially while they are carrying on some function. For instance, watch the way the deep-blue mud-dauber wasps build their homes. Study their weight, their movement pattern, their buzzing sounds. Impersonate these wasps with your own body as well as you can. When wasps settle, they tend to lean forward and clean their back legs by rubbing them together. Such a position may be a good one to use as the first Eumenides enter, settle over Orestes' blood, and try to decide which way he has gone.

Aristophanes used wasps as animal images in *The Acharnians* (*The Wasps*), and Jean-Paul Sartre chose to represent the Eumenides as flies in *The Flies,* which is Sartre's version of Aeschylus' *The Oresteia.* There are a number of variables to consider in choosing wasps, and you may feel that the Eumenides are better depicted as "gliders" or "slashers" than as "dabbers." You may feel more comfortable with a piece of music like Sergei Prokofiev's "The Scythian Suite," or perhaps even a piece of modern popular music. However, you must remember that your image should still perform the function that the Eumenides must carry out in the play.

CREATING A HUMAN CHARACTER WITH ANIMALS[6]

procedure Visit a zoo or park. Of course, it is more desirable to watch an animal in his natural habitat, because captivity changes an animal's behavior. Try to find an animal that reminds you of a character that you are working on for presentation in class. The animal image ought to parallel your choice of objectives and to reflect what other characters say about you. For example, several characters in Henrik Ibsen's *John Gabriel Borkman* refer to Borkman as an old gray wolf with yellow fangs. If you were playing Borkman, it would obviously be ridiculous for you to choose a pussy cat or a chicken for your animal image.

Try to observe the animal you have chosen carrying on a part of its daily function, especially if it is playing or feeding, because it is truest to its nature at these moments. Your observation *must* be firsthand; an animal seen on television simply won't do. Animals are just as individual as human beings. The camera will not pick up the individuality and little quirks of character that may help you flesh out your role. The television director is using the animal for his own purposes, not yours.

Personal pets are poor choices for study, too, because you have formed preconceptions about your pet. If you cannot approach your animal with an open mind, you cannot really learn from it. Instead, you will end up copying whatever your own pet does that fits your conception of the animal; you will not be reconstructing how the animal really acts in its natural state.

decisions Watch how the animal undulates its backbone and how it carries its pelvis. Do its feet move in symmetry or in opposition? Is it graceful? Is it economical? Is it very nervous? Does it have a sense of being caged? Does it seem to perform for people watching? What does its intelligence level seem to be? What is its weight and its action pattern when performing its objectives in daily life? Is its movement sustained or quick? Does it have any specific qualities or habits that distinguish it from other animals of the species? How can you imitate the animal economically for your partner? What parts of its body correspond to yours? Can you see this animal with the strengths and fears your character has? Can you justify every move you see it make? Mimic the animal for your partner.

Reduce your animal study to a single essence for stage-worthy presentation. Animal studies require individuality in movement and action. Was your animal identifiable? Where does your animal fit on the Character Quality Chart?

Now you must explore ways to translate your animal into a human being. Does your animal have any specific habits that resemble those of a human? Very old people often rub their lips together in order to moisten them before they begin to speak, just as crickets and praying mantises move their mandibles to eat. It is extremely important to decide exactly why the insects, as well as the older characters that you play, do what they do. A young actor playing an old character with his lips in constant, unmotivated motion can destroy the aura of believability for the audience. But if the old character is nervous or getting ready to speak, such a habit may be properly motivated. What are the play and French-scene objectives of the character in question? Do they fit with this animal image?

variation Straighten up and use your animal's posture as fully as you can in an upright position without straining yourself. What voice would the animal have as a human being? Over-perform the animal's traits as you move around the work space. Relate to your partner's animal character as your own animal character. If your animal characteristics vanish during your improvisation, return to your animal study again. Simply do the animal until you "lock in."

Place several chairs in a line representing an aisle at a movie theatre. Decide what the movie is. Bring along an imaginary bag of popcorn. Sit down and face the wall in front of you as if you were at a movie. After a few moments your partner joins you and tries as secretly as possible to steal your popcorn as you watch the movie. Try to translate your animals into human beings with human motivations for actions that began as animal habits.

discussion Though your work may be very external in an improvisation or in early rehearsals, the animal should not be extremely obvious in the final performance of a scene or play. This technique is a creative means, not an end. The audience can get caught up in the clever way an actor is playing an animal onstage and forget the rest of the play. Never let your technique show!

You must humanize the entire process. For example, a performer using a seal as the Professor in Eugene Ionesco's *The Lesson* may make use of the "uh, uh" vocalization of seals, as well as the way seals roll on their sides and clap their flippers. Ionesco's Professor occasionally hunts for words; and his initial compliments to the young student motivate his clapping. Of course, an actor working on the role of the Professor may find a snake or a lizard just as inspirational as the seal. Use an image that excites you!

You must restrict your study to one animal. An amalgamation will not do. No animal can be half giraffe and half tortoise. Nor could you imitate such an animal, for there would be no central rhythm or basic movement pattern to your character. Sometimes you will have difficulty making the translation from animal to human being. If you become bored with the idea of working with animals, try the next characterization method. No single system will work for every actor.

IMPERSONATING YOUR PARTNER AS A LIFE STUDY

procedure Appoint a time for you and your partner to meet at the work area. Start impersonating each other from the moment you arrive. Do the impersonation economically, regardless of your respective sex. Don't undermine the exercise by, for instance, assuming a falsetto voice. Mimic basic habits. Choose a game to play, using real props—perhaps play catch with a football or play a game of chess. Whatever you choose should be fairly simple, because you already have your impersonation to concentrate on. Your game should demand some physicalization to put your impersonation into action.

decisions Did you see yourself in your partner's work? In which category on the Character Quality Chart are you? Which one is your partner in? Did you have to use a different category on the chart to perform the impersonation of your partner? Could you incorporate his vocal mannerisms and tone of voice? What animal is your partner most like? If you could change one element in his impersonation of you, what would it be? Is his impersonation stage-worthy? Is his impersonation a caricature, or is it capable of being shaped into a full characterization? Did your partner step beyond sheer mimicry?[7]

USING A LIFE STUDY

procedure Though animal studies must be confined to the examination of one animal, they may be profitably combined with life-study work on the same character. If your animal and your life study are similar, you may derive your spark of inspiration from the same rhythm and character essence.

Find a person who resembles a character you are working on, and bring in an "impersonation" of the life study for your partner to observe. Just as with the animal, it is best to watch a human being while he is concentrating on performing a specific task; otherwise his consciousness will force him to adapt his behavior because he knows you are staring at him. Life studies do not necessarily take long periods of time; quite often, in just a few minutes you can capture another human being's walk, smile, handshake, posture, routine, and so on. Pick a task with a beginning, middle, and end that your life study either did under observation or might have done if you had watched him long enough.

decisions

Where would you chart the life study you observed? Does your partner agree? Are your gestures well motivated? Have you gone beyond mere mimicry? Is the character you observed similar to any animal? Try combining both methods, animal and life studies.

Focus on one age level—for example, middle age, because maturity is so difficult to perform economically. As a person grows older, parts of his face and body begin to settle. Elements of his spirit and energy usually settle as well. Rehearse one of the excellent scenes with middle-age characters in Edward Albee's *Who's Afraid of Virginia Woolf?,* August Strindberg's *Easter,* Henrik Ibsen's *John Gabriel Borkman,* or any of the major plays by Anton Chekhov.

Variations

Leading with what you want

After you and your partner have chosen a scene to rehearse, solidify a past history for your study. Choose a life history that would mold your character into the kind of person he seems to be. Justify his choice of objectives, his needs, and the way he places claim on other people.

Use your stage space constructively and sensitively. The space that your character shapes may be directly related to his occupation or to the way he plays his objectives to fulfill the needs he sets up for himself. For example, a butcher who is used to slicing up meat may figuratively carve up his partner in a scene, slicing with his words and his hands from sheer force of habit. In other words, as the butcher moves across a room he may lead with his hands like meat cleavers as he pursues his objective. On the other hand, a professor whose entire life revolves around his thinking process may walk with his head extended forward, just as if his body were an appendage to the center of his focus of attention. An absent-minded professor may have the top part of his body moving in one direction to meet a present need while the bottom half is moving in the opposite direction to fulfill a past or even a future need. For example, if he is going to teach a difficult class, the top part of his body may be moving toward his classroom while the bottom part discovers that he has to go to the bathroom; his contrary objectives set his body into opposite movements.

procedure

Ask your study group to sit on one side of the work space. You will take turns walking from one side of the space to the other in front of the rest of the group. (If only you and your partner are working, just keep taking turns.) Each person who performs a walk must lead with a specific part of his body. Begin at the top and work down: the first volunteer should lead with the head jutting forward; the second, his neck (like a turkey); the third, the chest (the hero-heroine); the fourth, the middle body (the bully); the fifth, the belly (the glutton); the sixth, the pelvis (the sexist); the seventh, the knees (the coward).

Decide on an occupation for each walker and repeat the exercise. See what combinations you can create by using two parts of the body to lead your walk; for example, the lecherous professor leads with both his head and his pelvis. Find a reason to improvise attending a Parent-Teacher Association meeting. Your motivation may be that you do not believe that your child is getting a fair chance to succeed in the district school. Your partner may play the child's teacher. Use the temperament and physical traits typical of the role you are studying. Incorporate your character's occupation in the improvisation and lead with the part of your body that corresponds with the way your role places claim on other people.

CREATING A CHARACTER FROM A SECONDARY CHARACTERISTIC OF YOURSELF

procedure This method can be employed at any time. It may be used alone or in conjunction with either or both of the last two methods. A "secondary characteristic" is personal inner feeling that you may heighten and surrender to, altering your posture and demeanor as if you felt that specific emotion most of the time throughout your character's life.

For example, in his early films with Jerry Lewis, Dean Martin usually seemed alert and energetic. Suppose that Martin became a little tipsy at a party once; in fact, he began to slur his words a bit and hum or sing over the break in his voice as he allowed himself to feel more and more free. A director who was also at the party said to him, "Dean, you're really great when you're a little high. You're fun and you make people around you relax. Why don't you pretend you're always a little high when you act or sing. It would sell!" This example is fictitious (I think) but it serves the purpose. It is possible to discover a hidden personality within your own self.

Relax and try to pinpoint an emotion that you have felt fairly strongly in the last few days. Try to recapture the emotion at its strongest peak. Explore the keenest moment of the recall sensorily. Flash the images through your mind, and draw the breath up through yourself from deep in your body, synchronizing your breath rhythm with the way you remember you were breathing at the time you experienced the emotion. Try to make the sensory responses part of the emotion as a whole; in other words, if you are recreating frustration while driving, try to use the hard, cold, metallic feel and smell of the car, as well as the spasmodic pressure of your leg as the car stalls at a red light.

If the moment was happy, texture the sensory responses with a happy feeling, a sense of buoyancy. Allow yourself to move around in the skin of the character who seems to be taking over your personality. Let the emotion engulf you. Think of your own home and kitchen. If you felt this way all the time, what would your home look like? Pantomime getting up in the morning and making breakfast for yourself as this new personality. Relate to your partner. Think of the new space you are shaping and check yourself on the Character

Quality Chart. What would be your usual objectives in life? Create a past for your character.

decisions An actor must learn how to be his own creative stimulus, especially in refreshing a character during a long run. A secondary characteristic has no external subject to examine, so it can be the most free and most original form of characterization.

How consistent were you as you built a fictitious past and began relating to your partner? Were you able to find snatches of moments that you felt were especially real? Try to enlarge those moments of "locking in" so that they encompass more than just a few seconds.

variation If you are meeting with a study group, set up some chairs to indicate rows of shelves at a food store. Each member of the group creates a secondary-characteristic study and explores the shelves for items that would be typical purchases of his new character. After each person selects what he needs; he goes to the check-out counter; however, no one is there to check the items. Your group motivation is to find out what the hold-up is from the other people in the line. You can do just the latter part of the exercise, perhaps substituting a welfare line. Once again, the motivation would be to find out why the line isn't moving, or if you're in the right line.

CREATING A CHARACTER BY USING AN OBJECT STUDY

Phase 1

The desk set

procedure Each of six volunteers from the study group is going to represent a particular inanimate object on a desk on which a letter is about to be written: an inkwell, a fountain pen, a round ink eraser with a whisk, an art gum eraser, a blotter, and a piece of paper. Bring these articles to the work area and let the volunteers take their time in handling and examining them closely. Each volunteer should project himself into his object imaginatively. A seventh volunteer will stand at the edge of the work space and act as the letter writer.

When you are playing an object, you must consider the shape, weight, function, and manipulation of your object, and how you can best represent it with your body. You may even find a vocal sound that typifies your action, such as sucking in air between pursed lips as you fill yourself from the inkwell, should you be playing the pen. If you are unhappy with the way you first chose to represent your object, alter your actions in any way you like.

The performer playing the letter writer should try to find a way to incorporate each of the objects (that is, each of the volunteers) into the writing of the letter as often as possible. His procedure might go something like this: "I arrange my desk with the piece of paper in the center, the pen at the right of the paper, the inkwell at the top left corner of the paper, and—ranging from left to right at the top of the paper—the ink eraser with the whisk, the art gum eraser, and the blotter. Now, I use the art gum to clean a smudge off the top corner of the paper. [The volunteer playing the art gum eraser moves to the volunteer playing the paper and tries a soft, pliable method of erasing the smudge, in contrast to the way the rather grainy and tough ink eraser would work. The art gum might tickle the paper, but the ink eraser would scratch and hurt.] I unscrew the top of the inkwell and bring over the fountain pen. I slide the lever on the side of the pen up and down to fill the rubber bladder inside the pen with ink from the well. I clean the tip of the pen with the blotter and reseal the inkwell. Now I begin to write, 'Dear Mom,' comma, then I go down to the next line, indent, and write, 'I hope you and Dad and Ellie, the two cats, and the three dogs are all fine,' period. Oh, I slopped too much ink on the period. I soak it up with the blotter and then use the ink eraser to remove the whole period. Damn! The way I wrote the word 'dogs' was messy, too. So I use the ink eraser again. Now I brush the bits of eraser and paper away with the whisk on the ink eraser, bring back the art gum to clean up little smudges, and then use the whisk once more. I take the pen and clean the tip on the blotter again, and then rewrite the word 'dogs' and add the period. Now I continue writing. . . ."

decisions You can use nearly anything as the inspiration for a role. If you handle a special prop, or if you can carry your prop as part of your stage business, you will have a way of refreshing yourself in the role and rejuvenating your character merely be re-examining the prop from time to time, possibly even during a performance! Did the volunteer playing the fountain pen find a way to represent the lever for the filling process and the way the pen writes with the point downward on the piece of paper? Did the movement of the pen seem to develop an attitude toward interaction with the inkwell and the paper? Were the erasers distinguishable? Was the blotter effective in soaking up the slopped ink? What sounds were particularly effective? Can these sounds suggest ways to speak that would differentiate one character from another? (For example, the soft swishing of a whisk would sound a great deal different from the scratchy, possibly bumpy sound of the pen.) Did any volunteer find a purely subjective and abstract movement that captured the essence of a writing tool effectively?

The volunteer playing the paper should either stand in the center of the space or find a comfortable sitting position rather than lie on the floor, because the recumbent position would not allow the performer much freedom of expression, nor would it provide a stimulus that might be easy to translate into a human action.

Phase 2

The dentist's office

procedure Create a dentist's waiting room by placing six chairs around the center of the work space. The volunteers who played inanimate objects in Phase 1 sit down and start using the character traits they have developed as objects.

The players try to remain true to their newly found characters, and experiment with a vocal rhythm and quality based on the object study. Each volunteer has the same objective—to convince everyone else in the group to let him go into the dentist's office first. Each must choose a motivation for this objective, as well as any type of painful dental work that might seem natural to the character he has derived from the object study.

decisions

As one of the players, did you merely take on some external qualities of the inanimate object, or did you motivate your actions? Did you fall into performing for an audience? Did you pursue your objective with simplicity and believability? Were there moments when your new character traits helped you lock into relating to a fellow performer?

You may find that object studies help you particularly with the vulnerability of your character. Remember the two lead balls that Humphrey Bogart nervously rolled about in his hand as Captain Queeg in *The Caine Mutiny?* The split in Queeg's personality may be represented by these *two* balls. You can base a character voice on the sound suggested by the click of the balls as they strike each other. The lead balls are small and can be hidden. Rolling them back and forth in your hand heats them. They are like tiny cannonballs, which are probably misshapen rather than perfectly round, but an oval shape will force them to roll in a circular fashion. All these ideas suggest a man who presents a formidable exterior, yet is really bent and imperfect; a man with a harsh metallic-sharp voice. He may be a "small" man who hides despite his assertion that he is a leader, a man who talks in circles because he is incapable of really thinking things through and coming straight to a decision. Physically, he may even tend to roll constantly, though at times imperceptibly. The space he creates as a character might be "heavy," "sustained," and "flexible," like a "wringer."

The object study may be coupled with the animal study or the life study as long as the traits do not conflict. Only one object and only one animal or person should be used. Take the time to glean all you can from a single study source. You can see object-animal similarities in a character who is a combination of a rusted anchor and an irascible old camel, like a tough old sea captain in the Eugene O'Neill one-act play *Ile.* Felix in Neil Simon's *The Odd Couple* could be a chicken and a silk tie. Nevertheless, any study—be it an object, animal, or life study—is at its best when used *alone* in conjunction with the character's objectives. No study should dominate an actor so much that he becomes mechanical and his technique becomes obvious.

SUGGESTIONS FOR CHARACTERIZATION SCENE STUDY

Noël Coward, *Fallen Angels:* Jane and Julia

Jean Genet, *The Balcony:* Irma and the Police Chief

Henrik Ibsen, *John Gabriel Borkman:* John and Ella

Arthur Kopit, *Oh, Dad, Poor Dad . . . :* Madame Rosepettle and the Commodore

Arthur Miller, *The Crucible:* John and Elizabeth

Clifford Odets, *Waiting for Lefty:* Sid and Florrie or Joe and Edna
Eugene O'Neill, *A Long Day's Journey into Night:* Mary and James
Harold Pinter, *Night* (one-act play): Husband and Wife
George Bernard Shaw, *Major Barbara:* Undershaft and Cusins
Neil Simon, *The Odd Couple:* Felix and Oscar
Neil Simon, *Plaza Suite:* Jesse and Muriel
John Steinbeck, *Of Mice and Men:* Lennie and George
Oscar Wilde, *The Importance of Being Earnest:* Cecily and Gwendolen
Thornton Wilder, *Our Town:* Mrs. Gibbs and Mrs. Webb
Tennessee Williams, *The Rose Tattoo:* Serafina and Mangiacavallo

chapter 9
PLAYING UNDER SPECIAL CIRCUMSTANCES

Have you ever been accused of playing an "attitude" onstage instead of sharing the scene with your fellow actors? You can easily fall into this trap when you are assigned a role that requires you to give the audience the impression that you are drunk, addicted to drugs, or mentally unbalanced. The temptation to isolate yourself onstage in such a role can be deceptively delicious because it requires less energy on your part and it allows you to indulge your ego by wallowing in an abstract emotion.

The drama in these scenes usually derives from the human conflict instigated by your character's inability to communicate with your partner's character because in your roles one of you is "drunk," "drug-addicted," or "mad." Conflict cannot spring out of playing such a quality alone. Once the audience sees you enter "drunk" or "mad," it knows what to expect from you, and your effect will wear off quickly unless you try to relate to another person onstage. Objectives require transitive (action) verbs in relation to your fellow performers. You *are* what you *do* onstage. Try to incorporate the madness or drunkenness into the way you place a claim on your fellow actors when you play Ophelia in Shakespeare's *Hamlet* or Jamie in the last act of Eugene O'Neill's *A Long Day's Journey into Night.*

Remember that your character is not trying to be "out of control"; in fact, he is probably fighting to control both himself and, possibly, another actor onstage. You cannot play "I want to be drunk . . . addicted to drugs . . .

mad." Just as with crying and laughing, you will have more success if you direct your energy against the quality. For example, try to give your scene partner the impression that you are *not* drunk or mad. During the second act of *A Long Day's Journey into Night,* Mary Tyrone will attempt to keep her family from seeing her dilated pupils, perhaps by doing some crochet work. Ophelia, in her "mad scene" in *Hamlet* may try desperately though *indirectly* to warn Laertes to distrust Claudius—she may give the rosemary to Laertes, begging him to "remember"; and she may give the rue (shame) to Claudius, exhorting him to wear his rue "with a difference." Claudius can silence her at any moment. Of course, such actions are a matter of personal interpretation. The minute you surrender control of your character onstage, you risk losing audience identification with your role. Try to find real, human, physical actions to accomplish while relating to your fellow performers.

The following exercises are proposed as explorations of the external manifestations of drunkenness, madness, and drug addiction. The exercises are designed to be experiential; they are not aimed at projected results. There is no wrong or right to these games, only a realization of how to be more efficient at playing under special circumstances. Although the exercises call for several participants, they can be adapted for two partners. Use your entire work area and your rehearsal furniture to create as flexible a space as possible. Choose real tasks to do with the other participants as you improvise freely. Relate to your fellow performers as directly as you can.

CONFLICT UNDER INEBRIATION

needs Arrange several tables and chairs and a small platform in the center of the work area.

procedure You and four or more volunteers will try to create the atmosphere of a drunken party at an informal neighborhood bar. Begin the exercise by concentrating on a sense memory of the last time you were "under the influence." Each of you attempts to recapture the contours of the kind of glass that is customarily used to serve your favorite type of drink (for example, try to shape a beer bottle or a glass for an old fashioned with your hands). Choose one of the following objectives:

a. I want to impress everyone here by singing so that I can get a job as a vocal stylist.
b. I want to beg everyone here to be quiet to keep my head from throbbing.
c. I want to pile all the furniture up against the rear wall so that I can dance.
d. I want to set all the chairs on top of the tables and sweep up so that I can go home.
e. I want to compel everyone to keep everything exactly as it is so that

I can remember how it was here last week when my boyfriend left for the army.

f. I want to hustle as much money from everyone here as I can.
g. I want to find the contact lens that I've dropped.
h. I want to find someone to give me real affection.
i. I want to coax everyone, without offending anyone, to leave as quickly as possible so that I can lock up.
j. I want everyone to agree that alcohol is the root of all evil.
k. I want to find someone who has a television set who will let me watch the late show at his home. I'm afraid of the dark, and I'm an insomniac.
l. I want to find someone to help me jump cables and get my car started to get my girlfriend home.

Pretend you are drinking. Relax and let the alcohol do its work. Handle your props as if you were high. Sturdy objects, walls, and the floor are securities to you. They will help you steady yourself. Avoid circular movements or you may vomit. Focus your gaze on a partner who is also performing the exercise. Put your glass down beside you. Place your hands over your face vertically so that your fingers cover your hairline. Slowly let fingers caresss your hair, forehead, and face as you draw them gently down to your chin and throat. Relax each muscle that your fingers caress. Let your face and head droop. Surrender forehead tension, eye tension, tension around the cheeks and lips. Let your jaw fall open. Drop your hands by your sides and let your back fall into a curve. You will have to squint a little to see, and your tongue is so relaxed and thick that you will have to concentrate on your partner when you speak. Your tongue feels like a ball of lead in your mouth. It is difficult to lift it or to point it inside your mouth. Using these "symptoms," try to say "Round the rock the rugged rascal ran" and "She sells seashells down by the seashore." Focus on a partner and play your action.

decisions Did you react to the burning sensation of the alcohol? Did you take your objective seriously? Did you overdo the results of drunkenness? Did you get progressively drunk as the scene played, or did you try to plunge into inebriation so fast that it trapped you into playing an attitude? Ask any observers if they believed you. Remember that you cannot play a result (drunkenness); you can only play out the *means* to that end.

variation The exercise for inebriation can also be used for drug addiction, despite the fact that drugs and alcohol affect the system differently. Focus on a single object or idea as you play your objective. Compare the variation in physical activity among the characters in both acts of Jack Gelber's *The Connection.* List the effects that heroin produces in the second act.

CONFLICT UNDER MENTAL PRESSURE

needs Place eight or nine chairs in either a circle or a semicircle to accommodate as many volunteers as there are to perform the exercise. Any group members who have a history of mental problems should make a private choice of participating in or abstaining from the exercise. All observers should comment upon the believability or the theatricality of the participants. Occasionally in both this exercise and the exercise for inebriation, "true to life" believability and theatrical effectiveness do not necessarily go hand in hand. There are quite a few dramatic liberties in *David and Lisa,* dramatized by James Reach from the book by Theodore Isaac Rubin, and in *One Flew over the Cuckoo's Nest,* dramatized by Dale Wasserman from the book by Ken Kesey. Drama is conflict, not scientific fact.

procedure After the initial eight or nine volunteers have chosen seats, one more volunteer will play the "group analyst." His job is to maintain a reciprocity among the "disturbed" participants, encouraging the participants to relate to one another in real terms. The "analyst" should try to burst all the illogical bubbles he encounters. The participants each choose one of the following motivational objectives as a basis for their improvisation.

a. I want to touch everything and everyone around me to be sure that I still exist and have not begun to vanish.
b. I want to force myself and others to see humor in everyone around me and in everything that is said.
c. I want to find a word to rhyme with every word I hear.
d. I want to impress everyone with how clever and normal I am by diagnosing all their problems.
e. I want to hold onto people and objects to prevent myself from falling; I feel there is no security under me.
f. I want to avoid germ infection and/or clammy, sweaty people's bodies by abstaining from physical contact with people.
g. The faces of people who look at me decay or distort. I want to find out why that happens, and why these people are lying to me.
h. I want to sit absolutely still and avoid responsibility for anything that goes on around me. (Make this a *conscious* choice.)
i. I want to prove to everyone that prayer is the only answer for all our problems.
j. I want to invent a number system (or any self-created system of security), using words that people say to me so that I can tell whether or not to trust them.

   The number system should have personal significance for the member of the group who elects to try it. He may simply count off the number of letters in selected words that his fellow participants use and freely associate those words with arbitrary words of his own choice, such as the following:

   I is a one. One is alone and frightened.

   By is a two. Two together are dishonest; they need a third eye.

   God is a three, but God is not always to be trusted, for *God* can also be a *dog* or *bad,* which is also a three.

Hate, Love, Pain, Good, and *Evil* are all fours and are very complicated. Asserting one also asserts the opposite.

Devil and *Saint* are both fives—therefore ultimately liars.

Mother and *Father* are sixes, which are twice as creative or procreative as threes. They can also hurt twice as much.

Baptism is a seven, which is man's number. The world was created in seven days. Seven is a safe number, because it is basic and true, even if it hurts.

Confined is an eight, the worst number. The eighth floor in most hospitals is the mental ward. Eight is an *eight ball,* always to be feared.

Beginning is a nine. Danger! It takes three times the courage to use a nine.

decisions Did any members of the group appear to be indicating "madness"? Who seemed to be attacking his objectives honestly and with economy? Who were the most involved with their objectives? Did their involvement include or exclude their fellow participants? If there were any exciting moments, what were the ingredients that led to their success? Could the observers identify with the performers? Did the participants try to control themselves and relate to one another normally, or did their energy appear to be diffused? Who was bewildered or embarrassed? Did the person with the number system find it easier as he progressed? Did the "analyst" really get people to work together?

discussion Madness is rarely the inability to choose between many possible alternatives; madness is closer to seeing something through only one set of uncompromising eyes. When you are analyzing the objectives of any character who has mental problems, try not to comment on your character from the outside as the actor who is to portray this person. Trust your character's illogical logicality and simply play your needs as straightforwardly as possible. Stay alert to what is going on around you. Resist the impulse to "create great drama," and avoid the temptation to play your role as a "nut," or you will certainly offend and alienate your audience. Always look for the beauty and the strength in your role. Rather than pandering to your audience's prejudices, try to find a way to lift both yourself and your audience by imbuing your role with human inspiration.

Because of the uniqueness of the demands, playing under special circumstances is a more difficult task than most acting assignments that you will receive. You must find a way to play your character's "symptoms," the "conditions" under which he operates, as well as his needs and wants. The danger is that the symptoms may remove you from playing the real conflict with the other actors onstage. Symptoms should never get in the way of the conflict of the scene; instead, your symptoms should help accentuate the obstacles that you must surmount in order to achieve your objective with the other actors. Of course your symptoms will modify the way in which you choose to fulfill your needs.

In addition to seeing the world in only one way, people under mental pressure generally evidence a number of physical problems—extreme constipation, either a pronounced nonchalance or an inordinate fastidiousness about their personal appearance, and either an "effervescent up" or a deep depression induced by drug therapy. It is extremely important to choose a logical side effect to accompany your "world view." If your assigned task involves people around you decaying, you must decide whether to relax your eyelids from the effects of a hallucinogen drug (in which case scrutiny will require real effort) or to widen your eyes with the excitement of discovery. A person who is attempting to find a sense of order in his changing world by imposing a number system would probably pay little attention to his personal appearance.

Remember that your symptoms should augment conflict with the other actors onstage. Approach your symptoms with economy. Let them grow as the scene progresses after you and your partners have laid the groundwork for your exercise.

variation Decide upon the super-objectives of the major characters in Mart Crowley's *The Boys in the Band.* How do Crowley's characters react to the circumstances that surround them? Each character has a uniqueness, a roundedness. Playing your objective with sincerity and economy, especially if it is socially provocative, will help demonstrate your author's intent.

Remember that your job is to give the audience the impression that you want what your character wants in the manner your character wants it. Choose real tasks that you can perform simply. If you do more than you have to in order to satisfy your character's needs, you are violating your role. You are never playing a "drunk," an "addict," or a "homosexual"; you are playing a human being.

You think of yourself as a complete person, not as a type. Of course, there are some hard and fast facts about you as a person. By the same token, there are certain facts about your character in the script, and you must know them in order to play the role well. However, if you generalize your character into neat little bundles and categories, you will strip the humanity from the role. Try to approach your role with a view to human dignity, just as you would like to have people approach you in your life.

chapter 10
FINDING AN APPROACH TO DIFFERENT TYPES OF COMEDY

Comedy is a complicated genre for any actor to approach. Comedy operates on more levels than tragedy generally does. By its very nature, comedy must be more audience-oriented than tragedy. To be successful a tragedy may not need to elicit tears from the audience, but a comedy requires laughter. You must discover how to share the joke with the "house" as well as with your partners onstage. In addition, comedy is more reliant upon first-time illusion than tragedy for its success. You must give the impression that your repartee and your zany activities are being formulated in front of the audience.

All of these qualifications contribute to certain often elusive elements essential to acting in comedy: you must listen to the audience as well as to your fellow actors; you must react to stimuli as if you were "living" the role; and you must maintain a fund of energy to keep the action moving at a bouncing pace. Above all, you must give the audience the impression that you are enjoying what you are doing. Emmett Kelly, the famous "sad clown" of the Ringling Brothers' Circus, displays a doleful exterior, but the actor underneath the make-up is obviously having fun.

Both Jackie Gleason and Red Skelton construct characters who seem always to be caught in a quagmire, yet they succeed in making their audiences laugh. Neither Gleason nor Skelton intimates that he is "pretending" as he performs. They both appear to take their dilemmas seriously. Of course, these two create "stock" characters the audience may identify with, but they also perform in situations in which compromise is always possible. Neither Skelton nor Gleason ever really finds himself trapped in a comic dilemma that offers no escape from mental or physical pain. Comedy can be serious without being tragic. Smile whenever you logically can, and you will encourage the audience to smile, too.

If you see yourself exclusively as a dramatic ("serious") actor, you are not only underestimating comedy, but you may also be limiting yourself to impressing your audience with emotional feats. In addition, you are probably limiting your choice of roles. Most audiences prefer comedy to tragedy for their social outings (which makes comedy a good financial risk for a theatre).

The following exercises will help you explore the varied forms in which comedy operates. Most of the exercises are designed to be performed with one or more partners, preferably in front of some observers so that you may learn to use audience feedback.

DEVELOPING COMIC INCONGRUITY

definition This form of comedy derives from a set-up series of events in which the audience is led to expect a certain logical outcome. Suddenly the audience is surprised by developments that seem to be in opposition to the original set-up. The audience may also be predisposed to anticipate conventional developments from a usual life situation, when the opposite occurs, creating the incongruity.

After the ball was over

needs Assemble a table and two chairs and perhaps a bench to represent a sofa in the middle of the cleared work area.

procedure Select a male and a female to play a young couple returning from a high school or college (military) ball. The couple have been married as teachers or students for over a year. The performers may compose their own circumstances as they create the scene. Her objective is to criticize all the sexist comments and actions he was guilty of during the evening, including any crude or rough behavior. His objective is to defend himself on any grounds he can find.

As the exercise progresses and the woman gets more and more angry, she begins to "meow" with frustration. During the conversation her meows grow into throaty roars, her brows furrow, her back begins to arch and she is slowly transformed into the Catwoman (of the typical horror-show variety). The man sees this metamorphosis taking place and, though he is alarmed, he continues to defend himself because she is so intent on criticizing him.

She stalks him, bent on attack. He begins to run away from her, trying to find somewhere to hide in the work space. The chase is on. He may ask people in the audience to defend him. As soon as she catches him and is about to strike, he begins to snarl and furrow his brows. Slowly he evolves into Lon Chaney's Wolfman. The Catwoman and the Wolfman circle each other, watching for an opening to attack, roaring all the while, just as a wolf and a tiger might. Very slowly the animosity subsides. The two may go off together hand in hand; the mollified monsters may turn into a puppy and a kitten, or the husband and wife may return to themselves and pick up their earlier conversation, depending upon what the volunteers decide to do.

decisions Discuss these questions about the performers in this and each of the following exercises in this chapter:

a. Were their objectives and actions clear and consistent?
b. Could you identify with them?
c. Was their progression gradual and logical? Did they parody the exercise? Did they do anything that was unexpected, though believable, for the world they created in the exercise?
d. Did they take their actions seriously?
e. Were they capable of compromise?
f. Did you see the performer under the character?
g. Did they try to complete every action they started?
h. Did they react simply when they were frustrated?
i. Did they continue speaking, even while the observers were laughing?
j. Was their rhythm interesting, or did the pacing lag?
k. Did it seem obvious that they were thinking?
l. Did they seem to enjoy what they were doing?
m. Did they try to include the audience in the action?

An audience tends to reproduce what it sees an actor do. If an actor feels sorry for himself in a comedy, or if he really seems to be hurt, an audience will stop laughing because it cannot help but empathize with pain onstage.

suggestions Read Murray Shisgal's *Luv* and Neil Simon's *The Odd Couple.* Underline passages in which you can lead the audience to expect a logical outcome and then surprise them with incongruities. Dick Van Dyke and Lucille Ball usually perform in scenes rife with incongruities. Can you name other stars who use similar techniques?

PERFORMING ABSURDITY

definition This form of comedy does not really require a set-up; it features an unexpected piece of characterization or a surprise situation.

needs Set up one small table or a platform turned over on its side to be used as a butcher block.

procedure One volunteer will play a detective, another a butcher. The butcher may begin by setting up his shop and cutting or trimming the fat off some meat. The detective enters, checks over the shop, and inspects several cuts of meat while the butcher watches him out of the corner of his eye. The detective begins to question the butcher about the source of the meat to find out if he knows much about the animals slaughtered for his store's supply. The detective asks the butcher to identify photographs of a particularly mean bull, and then shows him photographs of seven murdered men, pointing out that each of them has grease stains around his collar and throat. The victims had operated either the ranch or the slaughterhouse where the bull was taken. The detective's objective is to explore the link between the bull and the murdered men to see if the butcher is implicated. The detective has followed a trail of grease stains from the last murder to this butcher shop. At first the detective is suspicious and on his guard; the skeptical butcher tries only to maintain his innocence.

Suddenly the butcher remembers that specific murderous bull and that he did grind down parts of it for beef sausage. Recently meat has been disappearing from his counter. He had thought this was the work of thieves, but a new idea occurs to him. Perhaps the salami has developed a mind of its own and gone out to revenge itself on the raisers and the killers of the bull. The detective admits that a salami was seen leaving the scene of the crime. An imaginary salami leaps up from the counter and wraps itself around the detective's throat. The butcher may decide to help the detective, or he may be exposed as a brilliant but demented scientist who is out to conquer the world. Of course, the butcher is a vegetarian.

decisions In what ways must the performers incorporate elements of incongruity with absurdity? Did both performers accept their situation with believability? In order to be effective, you must approach your material as seriously in absurdity as you would in any other form of comedy; otherwise the audience will not identify with the action onstage. If the audience realizes that you *know* you are doing a parody, your technique is too obvious.

suggestions Compare Samuel Beckett's use of absurdity in *Waiting for Godot* with Thornton Wilder's in *The Skin of Our Teeth* and Leonard Melfi's in *Times Square*. Ernie Kovacs, Jonathan Winters, and Woody Allen acquired reputations for their repertoire of techniques that capitalize on absurdity.

SETTING UP LOSS OF DIGNITY

definition The actor playing a character in this type of comedy must establish that his character respects himself as someone special in society. During the action, either he or the other characters in the play will break down his self-image.

Swooning for a swan dive

procedure Three volunteers—a man, a woman, and a third volunteer of either sex—set up a table and two chairs in the center of the cleared work space. First, the female sits alone at the table pretending to be in a fancy restaurant. The male joins her, introducing himself. They both have the same objective: I want to get him (her) interested in me by creating a romantic image of myself. The two may get competitive, using the following topics:

a. Foreign countries I have visited.

b. Important dignitaries I have known (even intimately).
c. The great talent I have in the arts.
d. The vast number of women (men) I have sexually satisfied.
e. The gifts members of the opposite sex have purchased for me.
f. Financial holdings I have in important companies.
g. Honors, trophies, and citations I have won.
h. The number of college degrees I have (including honary degrees).

After the first two volunteers have established the tenor of their conversation, the third volunteer enters. The third volunteer may be either the man's wife or the woman's husband; or he may be the restaurant owner. His function is to destroy the self-image of one or both of the other two by playing one of the following objectives:

a. Since he hasn't paid his bill, I want to get him back into the kitchen to finish the next load of dishes or I'll call the police.
b. I want to get her back to the "house" across the street because some of our best customers are asking for her.
c. I want to get him (her) to come home and make dinner and quiet down our six kids.
d. I want to hustle him by seeing how much cash he'll pay for her (I pimp for her).
e. I want to get him into the bathroom to fix the restaurant toilet that's running over (he's my plumber).
f. I want to force her to tell me why she missed her last parole meeting.
g. I want to get him (her) to leave my establishment because he (she was arrested here once before for "molesting a child" (or for picking pockets).
h. I want to warn him (her) that his VDRL test came out positive.

decisions Loss of dignity is more effective if the comedown really seems justified. The actor playing Malvolio in Shakespeare's *Twelfth Night* must create a pompous façade from the beginning so that his eventual comedown is both comical and well-deserved; otherwise the audience may wind up pitying him, and the humorous situation will miscarry.

suggestions Compare Molière's *The Ridiculous Young Ladies* with George Bernard Shaw's *Misalliance* and *Man and Superman.* Concentrate on the loss of dignity that Tarleton, Summerhays, Tanner, and Mascarille suffer. Loss of dignity can operate on a mental as well as a physical plane. Jack Benny used this motif as part of his basic repertoire of comic business.

EXPLORING COMIC ENDURANCE

The triple affair

procedure You will need a hand mirror and several adjacent chairs for this exercise, which requires three partners. The first partner sits in the first chair and uses the hand mirror, playing Narcissus (Narcissa) with this objective: I want to admire myself and use all the means I can to get everyone else to compliment me. The second partner sits in the second chair with the following objective: I want to get Narcissus (Narcissa) to admire me and tell me that he (she) loves me. The third partner sits in the third chair and plays this objective: I want to get the second volunteer to admire me and tell me that he (she) adores me. Figure out as many ways as you can to play your objectives; your aim is to find the comedy by persisting in an impossible situation.

decisions Did you avoid self-pity? As long as a compromise is possible, audience identification will work for you; but if you allow yourself to wallow introspectively, you will lose the humor in the scene.

suggestions Compare Nina in Anton Chekhov's *The Seagull* with the aristocratic Ranevskis in Chekhov's *The Cherry Orchard.* Compare Jason in William Faulkner's *The Sound and the Fury* with the lovers in Shakespeare's *A Midsummer Night's Dream.* These people seem to strive pitifully onward, slipping on one banana peel after another, only to rise again; however, each of them could compromise if he wanted to. A character's inelastic view of himself creates the humor in these situations. Charles Chaplin, Stan Laurel, and Oliver Hardy were all masters of comic endurance.

All four comic motifs—incongruity, absurdity, loss of dignity, and endurance—can appear in the same play, overlapping each other successfully. Reread George Bernard Shaw's *Misalliance.* The actors playing Summerhays, Tarleton, Johnny, and Bentley must help to set up the speech in which Lena Szczepanovska exposes their incongruities and provides them all with a loss of dignity by putting them collectively into a compromising situation. The acrobatic entrance that Lena and Joey Percival perform, smashing into Tarleton's greenhouse with their airplane, is certainly absurd. Though the other characters onstage seem to react to Lena and Joey seriously, no one is really bothered about the greenhouse.

Later in the play a character named Gunner appears. He eavesdrops from inside Tarleton's weight-reducing cabinet. Gunner carries both a gun and a locket containing a picture of his mother, who, he says, was wronged by Tarleton. Though Gunner's situation is dramatically the most serious, its level of humor is the broadest and the most absurd of that of all the characters in the play, which is why Shaw saves Gunner for the last part of the play, introducing him only after the major philosophical segments have been performed.

Choose a scene from the following list to perform with your partner:

Aristophanes, *The Birds:* Peisthetaerus and Euelpides.

Anton Chekhov, *The Boor:* Smirnov and Natalia

Mart Crowley, *The Boys in the Band* (I,i): Michael and Donald

Ben Jonson, *Volpone* (I,i): Mosca and Corbaccio

Niccolò Machiavelli, *La Mandragola* (III): Timoteo, Lucrezia, and Sostrata

Molière, *The Misanthrope* (III,i): Clitandre and Acaste

William Shakespeare, *As You Like It* (IV,i): Rosalind, Orlando, and Celia

George Bernard Shaw, *Heartbreak House* (I): Ellie and Mrs. Hushabye

Richard Brinsley Sheridan, *The School for Scandal* (II,i): Sir Peter and Lady Teazle

Neil Simon, *Barefoot in the Park*: Corrie and Paul

Thornton Wilder, *The Matchmaker* (II,i): Minnie, Mrs. Molloy, Cornelius, and Barnaby

PLAYING GAMES WITH COMIC TECHNIQUES

Try the following exercises with your partner the moment you arrive for rehearsal. Experiment freely and try to find the right exercise for your specific scene!

Cluing in your audience

procedure Begin doing your scene. After every line that any character says to you or to anyone else onstage, turn to an imaginary or a real audience and tell it exactly what your reaction to your partner's line is. Immediately after defining your reaction in an ad-lib style, turn back into the action and continue the scene. Stay in character, even when you address the audience. After going through your scene once in this manner, repeat the scene, still turning to the audience. However, this time you must define your reaction nonverbally, using only mimetic gestures. Never let yourself go "dead" onstage.

decisions Defining your reactions is less taxing than telling the audience your objective. Avoid being analytical. Give in to your immediate response. Did you find yourself "mugging" (indicating what you feel rather than communicating with economy)?

Defining your comic attitude

extension 1. Instead of telling the audience your reaction to the last line that was spoken, try to tell it what motivation may have prompted the last person to speak. Stay in character and avoid being coldly objective as an actor. Simply state your character's reaction to the last line that was spoken.

extension 2. Try telling the audience what you feel that it as the *audience* may be thinking about the last line your partner spoke.

extension 3. If you feel that you are still mugging, overacting, over-reacting, or degenerating into open exhibitionism, modify your task by trying to make silent contact with the audience. Communicate your task quickly and efficiently. No other actor onstage should ever catch you at it. In other words, you play the game the same as everyone else, but you are not allowed to get caught sharing your reaction with the audience.

illustration Take a look at Tartuffe's scene with Elmire early in the third act of

Molière's *Tartuffe.*[1] The cluing-in game as it is originally set up might be played like this:

Tartuffe: May the bounty of heaven ever bestow on you health of body and of mind, and extend you blessings commensurate with the prayers of the most humble of its devotees!
[Elmire to the audience: I'm so lucky to have such an eloquent and holy man here in my home.]

Elmire: I'm very grateful for these pious wishes. Let us sit down. We shall be more comfortable.
[Tartuffe to the audience: She's falling for me again, and when we sit I can get closer to her bosom.]

The same opening to the scene played as in Extension 1, defining the possible motivation for your partner's line:

Tartuffe: May the bounty of heaven ever bestow on you health of body and of mind, and extend you blessings commensurate with the prayers of the most humble of its devotees!
[Elmire to the audience: Goodness is oozing out of him because he's so interested in my health.]

Elmire: I'm very grateful for these pious wishes. Let us sit down. We shall be more comfortable.
[Tartuffe to the audience: She feels completely at ease with me, and she's infatuated with my purity.]

The same opening to the scene, played as in Extension 2, with the actors telling the audience what they feel the audience must be thinking:

Tartuffe: May the bounty of heaven ever bestow on you health of body and of mind, and extend you blessings commensurate with the prayers of the most humble of its devotees.
[Elmire to the audience: I know you're thinking that Tartuffe is so sincere that my husband and I are absolutely right to trust him.]

Elmire: I'm very grateful for these pious wishes. Let us sit down. We shall be more comfortable.
[Tartuffe to the audience: I bet you're wondering what I'm up to.]

decisions

When an audience really lets go and laughs, the worst thing you can do is freeze. The last exercise and its extensions can be a means of filling in reaction time during the audience's laughter. Reactions in the hands of tasteful comedians may be performed as fleeting glances that do not call attention to the reactions themselves, but seem to add to the rhythm and humor of the written words. This form of extended reaction can develop an individual style of ad-libbing, a style that seems to spring from the moment, creating a first-time illusion that gives the audience the impression it is being clued in to something that was not necessarily planned. Both Groucho Marx and Dean Martin use this method of departing from the script.

Of course, such a method destroys the "fourth-wall" naturalness of certain plays. The ad-libbing technique should not intrude on the words and the rhythm of a scene as they were set up by the playwright. This exercise is suggested as a *means*, not an end. In its essence, this game technique is similar to the Restoration convention of asides. Study the ad-lib method that John Gay built into *The Beggar's Opera*. Try the nonverbal communication method with any of George Bernard Shaw's comedies, where the fourth-wall is not as requisite to the performance of the play as it would be in his *Saint Joan*. An ad-lib to the audience is generally considered a pretty low form of comedy; however, sharing a subtle moment with the audience can bring down the house.

BUILDING STEP BY STEP

The sportsmen

procedure Five or six men either sit around an imaginary campfire or takc chairs and sit in a circle in the center of the work space. The men all do a brief recall of the last time they were "tipsy." Spend some time relaxing into the feel of the bottle, the glass, or mug in your hand. Your group objective, one by one going from right to left, is to brag about what you caught on your last hunting (fishing) trip. Individually, each one of you must better the last performer's story of his catch. Try to take the exercise as seriously as possible.

decisions Did your stories get increasingly implausible? Did any of you describe such an impossible catch that the next actor was forced to lie quite obviously? How long was believability in the situation sustained, even though the stories became progressively more phony?

If a physical level of humor is introduced too early in a comedy, it sets the pace for cheap, obvious bits. A flamboyant first act in George Bernard Shaw's *Pygmalion* makes it very difficult for the actors to sustain the philosophy of the fourth act. Did any performer in the exercise seem to let the pace bog down? Did he dwell on fishing technicalities, or could all the observers continue to identify with his action and story line? Did the spirit of competition alter any of the men's characters so that the observers ceased to like him? Remember that an audience seldom laughs at or with a character when they don't care what happens to him.

RIDING THE CREST OF A LAUGH

procedure Underline the last few words of the phrase that leads up to the punch line. Try to find a prop, an object, or an action that would be logical at that time, and note it in the margin on the page of the script next to the underlined laugh. Choose some type of physical action to involve yourself with during the laugh. For example, if your character is expecting the arrival of another character when the audience might sustain a long laugh, try looking out the window for him, and then look at your watch.

If your theatre has a sound-effects recording with canned laughter on it, try an experiment with your prepared comedy scene. Act your scene and simply let the record play at the same time so that the laughs will fall where they may, regardless of the logicality or motivation for the laughter. Every time a laugh occurs, try to find a way to cover the length of the laughter by getting involved with an object or an action; or try heightening the intensity of your emotion by maintaining eye contact as long as the laugh persists. As soon as the laugh crests and *begins* to peter out, the actor with the next line should begin speaking at a vocal level slightly louder than the laugh.

decisions Did you flounder around at all, or could you find logical business to occupy your time? Did anyone begin his line during the crest of a laugh, when you could not hear him? Canned laughter on television has proven to be successful in enhancing the home viewers' enjoyment. Study this acting technique in your favorite television comedy series.

TESTING YOUR COMIC PERCEPTION

If you and your partner did not get an honest laugh where you expected it, the following check list may help you ascertain where the problem lies.

a. Is the straight man helping the comic by setting up the laugh for him? Is the straight man too obvious, or does he try to get laughs himself, crowding the punch line with unnecessary actions? The seriousness of your comic situation rests with the straight man, which is why he should usually perform with a straight or poker face.

Bud Abbott and Oliver Hardy were successful straight men. They seldom intruded on their partners' laughs, and they posed direct physical opposites to play; for example, if your partner appears to be "pressing" you, try "floating" or "flicking" back at him.

b. Is either of you "walking" on the other's lines or laughs by anticipating his motivations? Is either of you moving during a moment when your fellow actor should have the focus? An audience may be attracted enough to any actor who is moving to forget about the actor who should have the spotlight and the focus. Be sure that you can deliver all punch lines downstage toward the audience with clarity.
c. Is your most obvious, sure-fire physical gimmick saved for the last minute, or do you allow your scene to climax in laughter too soon?
d. Which laughs are "honest" laughs that *any* audience might give you? Are there any laughs that spring from "in" humor because only a group as intimate as your class would get the joke?
e. Do either of you attempt to talk while a laugh is still at its peak? The people in your audience may feel cheated out of a second possible laugh because you do not wait for them to quiet down. Eventually

they will stop laughing in order to hear you unless you wait for them. Conversely, waiting too long for a laugh can drag out the pacing, or possibly insult members of your audience by boring them.

f. Can either of you get a second laugh in your particular scene by making contact with the audience as you share a reaction? Jack Benny's "slow burn," in which he shares his reaction with the house, is as close as most modern comedians come to the Restoration technique of asides.

If you choose to use the cluing-in game, do either of you make direct contact with the house, or do you "splash" an area (taking in several seats but avoiding eye-to-eye contact)? Some members of the audience may be distracted by direct contact; others may feel cheated because they cannot hear everything you say if you splash only a few select seats.

g. Did you sustain your energy to keep the comic spirit of the play alive? If a comedy looks like work, no audience will appreciate it.

EXAMINING THE COMIC SPIRIT

definition In order for a scene to be effective in a comedy, the actors must be free enough to enjoy what they are doing; there must be an element of good will between them; and they must be capable of compromise.

procedure Repeat the exercises for "contrary objectives" (see pp. 47–49). Infuse each situation with a comic spirit. The underlying circumstances you develop for each other must contain the element of compromise. You should take each situation seriously, and you can even get angry at each other; however, this time add incongruities and absurdities. Try the exercise in which a boy and girl, who have steadily dated for two years, are sitting together in church during Mass. He wants to coax her into agreeing to his elopement plans, and she wants to convince him that she would have a more meaningful life if she became a nun. The dialogue might go like this:

He: Honey, I've got everything ready, just as you suggested.

She: Hush, John, this is one of the most sacred parts of the Mass.

He: I'll only be quiet if you hold my hand, sweet.

She: I can't, John. Mother is sitting right next to me, and she's never really approved of your seeing me because you're an avowed atheist. My family has always been very devout.

He: You've always said rebellion is delicious to you, dearest.

She: It is, John, so don't touch me.

He: That's not what you said last Friday night at the drive-in movie. You were awfully affectionate that night, my rabbit.

She: I was freezing, John, it was 34 degrees outside. Still, it was my only chance to see *The Song of Bernadette* on a twin bill with *The Ten Commandments.* I wanted to share them with you.

He: You certainly didn't spend much time watching the movies.

She: That's true, but I had to find the contact lens I lost in the lavatory.

He: Come on, honey, you were a hot little number that night!

She: Be careful! Father and Mother are looking at us. Smile at them.

He: I want them to ask us to leave!

She: You behave or I'll never speak to you again. I mean that!

He: Sweetheart, you told me that you were pregnant.

She: Yes, pregnant with the knowledge of what I must do.

He: Right, marry me and have our child.

She: No, become the bride of God and atone for the sins you almost led me into, but thank heaven nothing ever really happened.

He: Our eloping was your idea, honey. I've got the car packed with everything we need. I've got the license and I've even prepaid that little motel you liked so much last summer.

She: Oh yes, that wonderful little motel that we stopped at on our family trip last summer. You had such a good time with my brother.

He: Well, sweet, everything's paid for, so I feel we're committed.

She: Yes, you need to get away and calm down. Why not take Charlene? You've dated her all week long, and she's the cheapest girl in town. I can't rely on you the way I can on God.

He: Darling, I just wanted to be sure of my love for you by dating someone else. Now I know I can't live without you! And you know how violent I am. Don't make me take my own life!

She: Pray for guidance with me now, John. Prayer is so calming. I have to say my Penance. The Father told me to say two hundred Our Fathers and three hundred Hail Marys. I love to pray.

extensions

Try the following list of contrary objectives:

a. Man: I need your help; I've just been bitten by a snake.
Woman: I need you to protect me from the pack of wild dogs that are chasing me.
Locale: The north woods of a state park.
Adjustment: She faints at the sight of blood.

b. Son: I need to convince Mom that I should be a Navy nurse.
Mother: I want to get him to agree to take over Dad's barber shop.
Locale: The barber shop; she's cutting his hair.
Adjustment: Mother develops hiccups and a nervous twitch whenever the military is mentioned.

c. Daughter: I want Dad to help me find a way to keep my illegitimate baby.
Father: I need her to help me organize a meaningful speech on birth control.
Locale: The reading room of a college library.
Adjustment: He's the local coordinator for Planned Parenthood. She's four months pregnant and a chronic gum chewer.

MILKING A LAUGH OR A PAUSE

Phase 1

Study the following two plots; then perform them for some observers. Try to stretch out each piece of comic business as long as you can.

Put a chair and a table in the center of your cleared work space. Pantomime all props. You will play a librarian; your partner will play a devoted student. The situation is as follows: the library is on fire; the librarian dashes in; the student shushes her (him) without taking his eyes off the book on the desk. The librarian tries nonverbally to tell the student that the library is on fire, but the student, oblivious of the librarian, keeps on reading the book as long as possible. The librarian makes at least six vain nonverbal attempts to get his attention before speaking. The student finally listens to the librarian's whispers and gets all his things together while still trying to read the book as long as he can. The exercise is over when the student, with the librarian trying to hustle him out of the room, says, "Shouldn't we put the book back up on the shelf?"

Alternate situation: The same chair and table are needed, but this time the scene is a fancy restaurant. Once again, pantomime all props. The waiter comes in with an imaginary tray and a beautiful lobster dinner for a well-to-do lady (gentleman). He serves it exquisitely, and the lady compliments him lavishly. The waiter stands by the table and looks over the rest of his imaginary customers as the lady gets ready to eat. However, as she picks up her knife and fork, the lobster moves slightly. She cleans her glasses, grasps her knife, tries to stab the lobster, but it moves again. The actress may indicate that the lobster is alive by shifting her head as she watches the imaginary lobster crawl across the table.

Finally, the waiter notices that the lobster is moving, and he also cleans his glasses. The lady waits, hoping he'll say or do something. But he is too embarrassed to say or do anything. She is speechless, too, but since she is famished she tries to stab the lobster again. This time it defends itself and snatches her imaginary knife away from her. The lady must keep on trying to hint to the waiter, and the waiter must continue to busy himself with his own logical business (menus, orders, adding totals, cleaning glasses, etc.) until it is no longer possible to avoid the lady's plight. The exercise ends as both the waiter and the lady are forced to duel the lobster in a life-and-death struggle.

decisions

Were you able to accept your objectives and your circumstances with a sense of reality? Did your exercise develop slowly enough or did you involve yourselves in physicality too quickly?

Analyze the structured scene you are working with now. See how long you can stretch a moment by filling a silence with growing embarrassment.

Phase 2

This exercise may be done separately, or it may be used in a scene in which you and your partner must laugh together onstage. Clear the work space and set up a table and two chairs. Either sit side by side or share a corner of the table. One of you brings a huge imaginary pizza, and the other a large antipasto. Begin to eat slowly, enjoying your imaginary dinners. Eventually, each of you gets envious of the other's meal until, after at least two minutes of silent hinting to your partner, you switch plates. However, in your haste, you switch plates too fast, and your food winds up on both your lap and your partner's. At first you are embarrassed; then one of you initiates a laugh, snorting through the nose. Both of you begin to laugh, slowly accelerating the laugh as long as possible. At first, laugh with your lips closed, then open them an eighth of an inch, then a quarter of an inch, then a half an inch, and so on, until you are laughing hysterically and slapping your legs. Slowly come back to reality. Slapping your thigh reminds you of the mess on your lap. Begin to pick the food off your lap. Slowly, one of you begins to snort again until you are both laughing uproariously once more. See how many times you can continue to create an infectious laugh that will titillate your observers.

Try the exercise for milking an infectious laugh with one of the structured comedy scenes from Aristophanes' *The Birds,* Niccolò Machiavelli's *La Mandragola,* Shakespeare's *As You Like It,* Thornton Wilder's *The Matchmaker,* or any of Noël Coward's plays.

MILKING A REACTION

This exercise is an adaptation of an old vaudeville or burlesque technique that can be used in some types of presentational stand-up comedies as a way of filling pauses over audience laughs and possibly adding a second or third laugh. The technique can be practiced separately and then added to a scene that has been prepared for in-class criticism.

procedure If a character says something embarrassing to you or asks you to do something embarrassing, first look down at the floor or at your feet; then look up at the person who spoke to you; next, look at the audience, and then back at the person again. Finally look back at the floor or at your feet, raise your head, and speak your next line. The performer who demands justification for such an obvious presentational technique might ask himself the following sequence of questions:

Did I hear what I think I just heard?

Did you say what I think you just said?

Did you (the audience) hear him say what I think he just said?

Do you (the character) understand the consequences for me?

Do I really understand what I'm getting myself into?

In some cases, an actor can repeat the entire movement sequence and get another laugh.

variation Try repeating the earlier exercise for clarity in facial expression, "Masks of Emotion" (see pp. 32–33). Face your partner and try to capture the emotions most frequently found in comedy scenes—for example, bewilderment, embarrassment, devilishness, innocence, comic lechery, and awakening to a new solution or a new idea. Try adding these specific masks of emotion as you milk a reaction. Everyone's facial morphology is different, and a knowledge of the reactions your face can create that will tickle an audience can be very important in performing a presentational comedy. Catalogue your effective expressions and add them to your comic bag.

In some situations you can successfully dare an audience to laugh by looking directly out into the house and making the right eye contact. What masks of emotion might you wear to do this effectively? Can you imagine this technique being used in Hal Holbrook's *Mark Twain Tonight; Beyond the Fringe* by Alan Bennett, Peter Cook, Jonathan Miller, and Dudley Moore; Aristophanes' *Lysistrata;* or John Gay's *The Beggar's Opera?* Try to enjoy your audience. If you can project a warmth and a spirit of fun to the audience, it will respond to you in kind.

chapter 11
STYLE ACTING 1—THE ANCIENT GREEKS

INTRODUCTORY NOTE ON STYLE IN GENERAL

The term "style acting" can be awfully nebulous to deal with in performance. It usually conjures up images of extravagant gestures and costumes, replete with artificial manners and artificial speech. Unfortunately, many attempts at classical theatre wind up looking so contrived that the human element with which an audience might identify lies buried under a heap of external tricks. Art generally strives to copy human nature in every period of man's development, and despite the fact that we humans are susceptible to fashion and various forms of exhibitionism, people are people. With style acting as well as with in-depth characterization, external manifestations should stem from a logical inner need to communicate with another character onstage. Every gesture must have real motivation.

If your only response to a prepared scene from classical theatre is "That was clever," the actors are showing off their technique, not genuinely performing the scene. Ballet lessons were quite popular among the aristocracy during the Restoration period; and royal and noble personages often took part in amateur, pageant-like performances marked by the stiff conventions of the ballet of that time. The upper classes nearly monopolized the theatre of that period for themselves, which is why Restoration plays tend to have a cliquish, artificial, and expensive quality all their own. Nevertheless, even the most contrived of characters—Sir Fopling Flutter from George Etheredge's *The Man of Mode,* for example—poses because he wants to communicate some human need either to his fellow performers onstage or to the audience. His poses will be effective only if they are locked into his objectives. Regardless of the extent of your training, no one moves in fourth position or speaks in iambic pentameter naturally as part of his everyday life; but his *choice* to do so onstage can be quite dramatic, impressive, or, on occasion, ludicrous.

A director will usually define the mannerisms and artificialities he wishes you to use in the production, but a bit of research in the library will help you flesh out his demands. Find out how intricate the dances and the clothing of your character's era were. Tortured material, distorted costuming, and complicated dance steps tell you something of your character's mode of life. Glance at the contemporary paintings and the architecture, and listen to the music of the period's eminent composers. Remember that you must rationalize all your study from the standpoint of the play as it was written. Reject what you cannot play intelligently within your character.

The collective objectives of all the characters in a play are the greatest contribution to the acting style of the production. Regardless of how unreal the demands of the play seem to you at first, you must still create an identifiable if anachronistic world for your audience by giving the impression that you want and need what your character wants and needs.

The following style-acting exercises and those in the next three chapters are designed both to help you familiarize yourself with the manners and social artificialities of a period to help you attack some specific acting problems inherent in the period's dramaturgy. Relax into yourself as you begin each exercise. Find out what's underneath your scene first, then add on your externals simply and economically.

EXAMINING THE ROLE OF THE GREEK CHORUS

The prayer exercise

procedure Gather your study group around the cleared center of the work area, and darken the whole area as much as possible. The members of the group should stand slightly apart from one another. This exercise is very personal; however, there will be no individual demonstrations. Take the exercise seriously. Respond to the following steps. Be careful not to rush along too quickly or to dwell so long on one step that your group gets bored.

Recall the last time you felt really sorry for yourself; for example, when you were a child you may have tried to envision your parents crying at your funeral, and remembering, above all, how mean they'd been to you. Find the moment when this emotion reached its peak. Explore this moment sensorily, associating each sense recall with your feeling of self-pity. Protract your breathing rhythm and drop the breath deep into your abdomen. Imagine that your breath is going through you into the floor or chair under you. Sigh gently on the inhalation and use the exhalation to cool and moisten your throat. Maintain a yawn in your throat and make the vocalization staccato, as in the earlier exercise for crying (see p. 54). Raise the pitch and flash the images of the sensory recall through your mind.

Remember the last time you were extremely hungry—absolutely famished (any type of appetite will do). Repeat the same steps that you used with self-pity. Instead of vocalizing over the inhalation, find an outward sigh that epitomizes your hunger. Sigh up the sensory recall and peak your pitch slowly.

Ask yourself, "What is it that I want more than anything else in the world?" Be honest. After you have decided what you want most in your life, be it success in your career or some physical enjoyment or wealth, see yourself achieving your aims. See the changes that there would be in your current life. See yourself at the pinnacle of success in attaining your desire. Quicken your breath rhythm and find a new sound that epitomizes success. Let it out with relaxation and enjoyment on your exhalation. Peak it! Stop for a moment and realize how truly far you are from the achievement of your goal. Vocalize this pain. Yawn up a free sigh if you can.

What is your favorite song (especially hymn)? Create your own incantations alone here in the dark, humming your song—no matter what it is—over and over, as if it were a Jesus Prayer or a Hare Krishna. Wash your feelings of sorrow and unhappiness away in the song. Let it rise and engulf you. Give in to the song and sway to it. Find movements or gestures that help you give in to the song. Peak the movements or the gestures.

Listen to the sounds around you. Relax and analyze the gestures that you made. Locate these gestures on the Character Quality Chart. Decide how they represent grief or misery and how such gestures might be made theatrical.

decisions Try to find a group life that seems natural to the emotions that a Greek chorus might express. The sounds that the chorus makes should not be a cacophony of sound but a single cry from a group mouth. A chorus performing the opening ode from Sophocles' *Oedipus Rex* might use the same gestures as the ones your group discovered.

variation The participants choose one song or rhythm that all of them associate with the emotion caused by hunger. They then draw closer together so that each can touch the partner next to him. As you hold on to your partner, try to find the same level of participation that you found earlier while alone. Allow five minutes or so to pass. Make contact with your partner and heighten the impression of the emotion of "hoping for relief." Both of you are joined in a group effort. Do you feel tensions creeping into your limbs? Try to maintain the outward impression of the emotion while doing a relaxation exercise, such as panting like a dog. Really working with your fellow chorus members should free you rather than tighten you. *You* never need to be tense, even if the character you're playing is involved in a life-and-death struggle.

Improvising a ritual

needs Bring a loaf of bread and some wine or grape juice in a large flask. You will also need two candles and a symbolic weapon, like a rope or a rubber knife.

Your group task will be to create a shared believability in your self-constructed ritual.

procedure The attitude for the exercise is serious fun. The group does another recall-improvisation of despair. This time, each participant tries to outdo the others to get the group to pity him the most. As the group relaxes and falls into the exercise, each member in turn tells his "pain."

Dim the lights as low as possible and light the candles. The participants divide into two groups, and one person from each group takes a candle to a corner in the work space. A second person from each group takes either the wine or the bread (whichever the group has) to the same corner of the room. Every participant must keep one hand on either the wine bottles (flask) or the bread (depending upon which article his group has), and the other hand on the person holding the candle for his group.

The person holding the candle for one of the groups lifts the candle high and creates his own incantation, such as "Lord of the sky give us water," and the fellow member holding the wine or bread raises it three times; then the person holding the candle for the other group intones, "Lord of the earth give us food," and the fellow member holding the wine or bread raises it three times. The aura here is pure improvisation, and it may linger until one of the persons holding a candle runs out of incantations.

Each of the two with the candles begins to lead his group around the work space with the member holding the bread or wine close behind him and the rest of the group following in procession. Both groups walk slowly around the work space in procession three times, holding the candles and the bread and wine high as if offering it to the gods.

Combine groups and create a circle. Choose the member of the group who got the most pity in the first part of the exercise. He becomes the "victim," and lies down in the center of the work space. The members with the bread and wine come toward him and deposit their fare on either side of him. Next, the persons holding the candles enter the circle and place their candles at the head and foot of the victim.

These two members then pick up the symbolic weapon and hold it up in the air. They walk around the circle together three times. The group around the victim starts a chant like "Now, now, now" as a whisper that gets louder and louder. Finally the two bearing the symbolic weapon pretend either to strangle the victim with a rope or to plunge the rubber knife into his heart, cut it out, and raise it overhead. Everyone in the circle moves in and kneels around the victim. The two members who symbolically destroyed the victim open the wine and break the bread. Everyone in the circle kneels and takes a piece of bread and drinks some wine. A choice piece of bread is left on the victim's chest and some wine may be poured into a (paper) cup for him.

The members of the group maintain the circle around the victim after they are through eating, and chant, "Come to life!" As the victim rises, he eats his bread and drinks his wine and stands up fully. Now the lights are turned on. The people in the circle fall prostrate. Each one crawls toward the center and touches a person on the floor next to him. Slowly everyone in the circle begins to chant, "Long live the King."

decisions It is easier to fall into doing such an exercise when everyone else in the group is doing it. Do you feel a sense of group life? Of course, this exercise is "campy" and it may fail spectacularly, but at least the group will be happily appeased by the bread and the wine. This exercise may help you get into the spirit of the mock ritual in Aristophanes' *The Peace,* as well as the serious prayers in Sophocles' *Oedipus Rex* and Aeschylus' *Oresteia.*

discussion One of the most prominent scholars on the Greek theatre, H. D. F. Kitto, urges today's directors to abandon many stodgy misconceptions about the Greek theatre and Greek acting styles. Kitto suggests that Greek performances were probably innovative and occasionally free in form. In Euripides' *The Bacchae* and Aeschylus' *Seven against Thebes,* expressionistic and chaotic movements are necessary to accommodate the needs of the script.[1] Costumes certainly had to have been designed to allow flexibility of movement in *The Bacchae,* in which it would be impractical to expect cothurni and heavy chitons, as well as awkward masks, to be worn. Nor would one expect the chorus in *The Bacchae* to move in carefully choreographed symmetrical patterns.[2] On the other hand, an orderly procession seems to be in keeping with the initial choric odes in Sophocles' *Oedipus Rex.*

suggestions Read the first choric prayers in *Oedipus Rex* together as a group. Choose a Chorus Leader and two High Priests. Place a set of chairs upstage left to represent a palace door, and a set of chairs upstage right to represent an altar. Try to improvise the opening sequence of choric odes. Use the John Gassner version of *Oedipus the King* in the series *A Treasury of the Theatre.*[3]

The following observations and suggestions concerning blocking the chorus may provide material for group discussion:

a. What is the collective objective of the chorus in this play? How do the lines phrase this need?
b. Every choric ode is broken into segments called strophes and antistrophes. Is the emotional flow of the ode bound or free? In other words, is the emotional content variable between the strophe and the antistrophe? Does the opinion of the chorus fluctuate, or is it straightforward with little variation? If the chorus is fickle, try to find a different movement pattern for each stanza.
c. Try a group improvisation to find a set of gestures typical to the emotion being expressed in each strophe. Plot your choric movement pattern on the Character Quality Chart. Don't be afraid to experiment broadly with physical opposites. The very names strophe and *antis*trophe indicate that there should be opposition and great variation in choric movement. Take one stanza moving stage left, the following stanza moving stage right.

d. Choric movement in ancient drama is occasionally described as "dactylic" (analogous to the verse form in which a long stress is followed by two short stresses). Dionysus even trains Pentheus to do such a dance step in Euripides' *The Bacchae.*
e. Generally, a fifteen-member chorus is blocked into five rows of three or three rows of five for the entrance to the stage (the down-center dancing circle for the chorus).
f. Once onstage, the chorus rarely leaves the stage; in fact, the chorus usually is the major character in the play. An actor doing a scene from Greek theatre must remember that the chorus (within its function) is often onstage watching him, even if it is not *directly* involved with him. You should plan your objectives to include the chorus within your action.
g. Violence invariably happens offstage, and the action of the play is generally continuous over a short period of time. The aim of good choric blocking is to dramatize the suspense and tension generated by recounting an event that has occurred or is occurring offstage.

USING A MASK

needs

Try to locate at least two masks. These can be of any type and construction as long as they allow easy breathing, a decent amount of peripheral vision, and enough exposure of the mouth to permit easy vocalization. Certain types of Halloween masks may do, or you can fashion your own masks out of paper bags. A medium-sized grocery bag will do. Take a pair of scissors and cut the top off the bag about nine inches up from the bottom. Cut one side down to six inches from the bottom. This side will provide a front to the mask and plenty of exposure for the mouth. Slip the bag over your head with the six-inch side of the bag in front and locate where two holes might best be cut for vision. Cut out the eye holes, making them at least one-and-a-half inches in diameter. Reinforce the edges of the bag and of the eye holes with some masking tape.

Paper bag mask

Create a set of charades and write them out on tiny pieces of paper. Familiar book titles like Richard Llewellyn's *How Green Was My Valley* are too easy to guess. Get some fortune cookies if you want fresh sentences to use in this exercise.

procedure

The study group relaxes in a semicircle on one side of the room. One by one, each member comes into the center of the work space, puts on some sort of mask, and acts out his charade. Time each performer as the rest of the group tries to guess the words that are being acted out. Establish a code for playing charades, such as physical symbols for "songs," "book titles," "operas," "plays," and "famous sayings." Create gesture symbols for the number of syllables and the number of words in each charade, as well as symbols for the short words

Code for charades

book song opera film

melodrama play whole idea sounds like

number of words number of syllables small word longer (stretch it)

(such as "a," "the," "on"), and a general symbol to indicate that you are miming the whole idea of a phrase.

decisions

Is your face moving behind your mask? How heavily do you rely on your face to get your ideas across? You must find a way of transferring your expressions from your face to your whole body so that every gesture you make clearly communicates your character's needs. Extraneous movements are easier to detect with a mask on. What are your extraneous nervous habits? An audience may wind up watching your nervous habits rather than what you are trying to convey. When you wear a mask, all your gestures must be economical and immediately understood.

Did you try to "show" an action or a need instead of "being" or "doing" it? If you should get a book title like James Westman's *Why Fish Bite and*

Why They Don't, avoid the mistake of trying to indicate the word "fish" by casting bait like an angler. Your observers will certainly jump to the word "fishing," or "casting," or "fisherman," in which case you will have to indicate that you want your audience to focus on what you are fishing *for.* Just simulate the action of a fish itself. Your task will be simpler and more direct.

EXPLORING CLICHÉ GESTURES

procedure You and your partner stand on opposite sides of the work space. Put on your masks. Take turns performing a cliché gesture that is immediately recognizable, such as "Halt!" (with the arm outstretched and the hand vertical in a forbidding position). Perform the gestures as long as you can come up with new ones. Neither of you is allowed to repeat any gesture.

decisions Which cliché gestures are the easiest to identify? Gestures explaining directions, such as left or right, north or south, can help to solidify an aura of physical reality in a play that does not feature a naturalistic setting.

As you begin to rehearse your scenes from Greek drama, consider these suggestions concerning physical gestures:

a. Express your emotions through your voice and body rather than through your face.
b. Economize on gestures that do not define physical locality or spatial areas. Gestures that come *directly* out of the emotion of your objectives in the scene are also permissible.
c. If you are in doubt about the need for a gesture, cut it.
d. Plot your objectives carefully. See which gestures seem natural to your objective in relation to the sound of the sense of your words. Heighten the *natural* music of your voice and the *natural* movement of your gestures. Discard movement that boils down to an "external show" of what your character is feeling. Perform only what your character *needs* to do.
e. You never have to work hard to try to appear to be bigger than life. Excessive gesturing will make you look smaller to an audience. Name several actors who seem bigger than life. Such performers are generally quite economical, smooth, and direct in their movements. "Gliders" and "pressers" often appear to be bigger than life because their rhythms and their gestures are specific and sustained, like those of W. C. Fields and Mae West.

EXAMINING UNIVERSAL CHARACTERS (THE DORIAN GRAY EXERCISE)

procedure Ask your partner to watch you. Put on your mask and walk slowly across the work space, trying to give the impression that you are growing progressively older with every step you take. Try to run the gamut from youth to extreme age.

Tilt your pelvis backward so that your butt sticks out as you assume a posture typical of youth. Bring your pelvis under you and tilt it up toward your chest to approach middle age and old age. Avoid strain in doing old age. Elderly people seldom permit their bodies to undergo constant strain. Keep your shoulders aligned with your knees. Avoid leaning too far backward or too far forward.

Physical progression to illustrate age

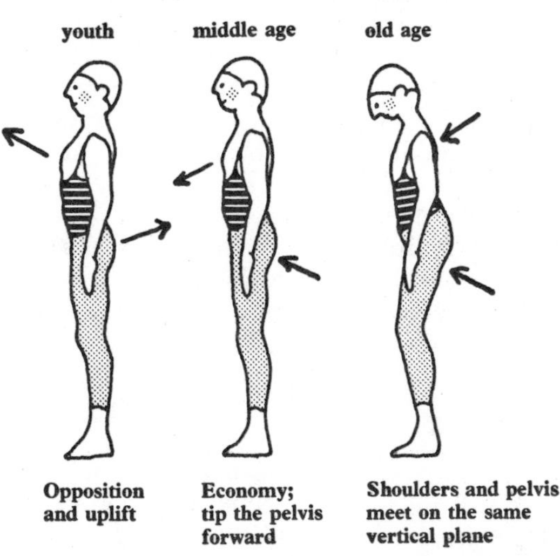

variation Give yourself a real purpose to get to the other side of the room. For instance, imagine you're dying of starvation and there is food over there. Pretend you are nearly under water as you *begin* to walk, but by the time you reach the other side you are gradually getting to dry land, though you are also dying in the process. Trying to keep your head above water at the beginning of this variation should help you lengthen your spine, creating a youthful posture that will disappear as you reach the other side of the work space.

decisions Use the Dorian Gray exercise for character studies in Sophocles' *Oedipus Rex*. Decide upon the elements of old age called for in the physical descriptions of Tiresias and the Herdsman. The performance of old age requires a loss of flexibility in your joints. You can appear to be stiff in such areas as the neck, elbows, and knees without tensing your body if you refuse to lock your joints in straight lines.

Older people seldom give in to diagonal movements. They tend to reset themselves as they approach new tasks, squaring off with each new job. For example, if you were ironing several articles of clothing, instead of squaring off to the ironing board and leaning over to one side to sprinkle water on the clothing, square off first to the hamper to pick up an item, then to the table to sprinkle it, and finally, to the ironing board to iron it.

Try to find enough details of characterization to give some variety to your role, even if you are playing one of many elders in *Oedipus Rex.* An actress playing the role of Jocasta must find an individual movement pattern that gives the impression of maturity as well as sensuality. Begin by analyzing Jocasta's superobjective and her progression during the course of the play. Jocasta's physical rhythm and her way of handling herself should change drastically after she learns who Oedipus is. You can approach such an emotional transition externally by shifting from a "glider" or a "presser" to a "dabber" or a "wringer" as you perform your scene.

It is often a good idea for a person who is basically a "glider" in life to work on a role that should be done by a nervous "flicker" or a "wringer," just as it can be a telling experience for an insecure performer to work on a role that forces him to give the impression of being in command.

Oedipus Rex is excellent to study because it contains some weaker characters, like the Herdsman, as well as characters who maintain their power, like the Stranger from Corinth, Creon, Tiresias, and several members of the Chorus. In addition, Oedipus and Jocasta make fine studies, for they lose their stature gradually during the course of the play.

PHYSICALIZING TRANSITIONS WITH A PARTNER: THE CLOSING CELL

procedure You and a partner put on your masks and face each other in the center of your work space. Take your time in performing the following steps. Pantomime each segment clearly and precisely, *sharing* each experience.

Together, perhaps one partner high and one low, create the four walls and the ceiling of a cell. It's a dark cell in which you can barely see. On one side of the cell establish a small door (it is more like a small sliding panel). The door is tightly locked. Find a place in the cell to relax. Together, establish a sense of the cold and a need for mutual body heat. Rest and fall asleep.

One of you awakens suddenly and discovers some food has been pushed into the cell through the panel. Establish what kind of food it is and share it. Try to rest again.

One of you becomes aware that the walls are slowly moving in. Share this discovery and shock. Both of you try to keep the walls from closing in and killing you. Share each other's body strength. Establish that the ceiling and walls are coming in uniformly and that it is impossible to stop them. As the walls and ceiling force you down onto your knees, try to share the space left to you as well as you can. Collapse together into a small ball.

decisions Mental and facial transitions in a mask are useless. The body must learn to do the job that the face and voice once did. Did either of you get ahead of the other in creating the room so that your walls, and particularly your ceiling, were at different levels?

Were either of you disquieted about sharing each other's body warmth? Did the person who discovered that the walls were moving in demonstrate his shock with his body, or did he make the discovery internally so that it was not clearly shared?

If there were moments when the action of one partner was obscure, he should be asked what he was doing and for what purpose. If he has a good answer, it may be possible that he made his transitions mentally, trusting the other partner to grasp what he was doing. Once you have a mask on, you cannot expect an audience to guess blindly at what you are doing. Physicalize all transitions. You must learn to use only enough effort to accomplish your needs. Did both of you really use each other's body and strength to press against the walls? Did you use your backs and legs or did you merely use your arms?

Arm gestures cannot be controlled if you are in full extension. Try lifting a chair with your arms fully extended. Now do it again, but this time move in closer to the chair and bend your elbows. Use your pelvis, legs, and back to straighten up and lift the chair so that the motion is easier and more controllable. Try pushing against your car and see if you don't keep your arms and hands in close to your chest and pelvis as you lean in, letting the trunk of your body do the work. In any acting exercise you do, the use of the trunk of your body suggests an organic involvement. Effective use of the center part of your body can replace many arm and hand gestures. Your audience will believe your actions more readily if your entire body is organically involved with your objectives, but your involvement should *begin* from your center, not from your limbs.

USING THE TRUNK OF THE BODY

procedure You can do this exercise alone or try it standing and facing your partner at a distance of about ten feet.

Drop your arms to your sides and close your eyes. Imagine that the sun's warm rays are tanning your entire body. Relax! Cut all arm and hand gestures.

Begin a graceful contraction with the lower part of your body, using the image of a large beach ball (about twenty-four inches in diameter) rolling slowly up your body from the back of your ankles, past your calves and knees, up to the backs of your thighs. Tilt your pelvis gently forward and feel the ball roll around to your belly. Now begin a contraction with the upper part of your body as the ball rolls upward from your stomach area to your chest, to your neck, and then over your face. Let your body conform to the shape of the ball wherever it rolls. Do the exercise five times without straining. Imagine that you are undulating like a wave on a gentle sea.

Extension 1

Shaping an image with the center of your body

procedure Face your partner with your eyes open and alternate doing the next steps as you criticize each other's movements. Repeat the above exercise but instead of using a beach ball as an image, pretend first that a boa constrictor is slithering up your body, then that a fuzzy bunny is crawling up your body. Watch each other from the side and from the back. Try to be just as expressive with your back as you are with the trunk of your body in profile and full front.

Extension 2
Remote-control puppeteers

procedure In this exercise alternate positions with three partners. Stand in the center of the work space. One partner stands directly on your right and will control the right side of your body; another stands on your left and controls the left side of your body; the third stands directly in front of you and controls your head and neck movement. Concentrate first on your right-hand partner; move as he directs you, responding to his nonverbal gestures with the part of your body that he seems to indicate. If he appears to be lifting your right arm or leg, allow your right arm or leg to correspond to his gesture. Your partners should help you shape the space around you with direct pressing or lifting gestures just as if you were a puppet and they were pulling the strings.

After you have the feel of your right-hand partner's rhythm, add your left-hand partner's rhythm to it. Watch both partners out of the corners of your eyes. Try to move as both partners simultaneously direct. Be patient and concentrate. After you have tuned into these two partners, take on the additional task of watching the partner in front of you and responding to him with your head and neck movements. Continue the exercise five or ten minutes and then switch positions with one of your partners.

decisions Can you adjust to and use the impetuses given to you by three people at one time? If you have any trouble, go back to focusing on one partner at a time until you tune in; then slowly add responses to your other partners' stimuli. Always take your time. You may find that your partners' movements evolve into a dance-like grace, with you sharing aspects of three types of movement. This relationship is fine as long as you have all gone through the puppet-puppeteer process first. Mutually tuning in is the desired result.

Because the torso, the neck, and the legs comprise the bulk of the body that the audience sees, an actor should remember that he does not act merely with his face and hands, but with his entire body. Restricting yourself to using only the often neglected areas of your body—torso, neck, and legs—will help you in two ways: you will find that your emotions must be expressed organically in performance so that your whole body feels "love," "fear," etc., and you will learn more efficient control over your gestures so that your performance will elicit immediate identification and empathy from the audience.

EXPERIMENTING WITH GESTURE

procedure Put on your mask and ask your partner to watch you. Using only mimetic gestures, describe a segment from a horror movie you have seen recently (the more action-oriented the movie was the better). All hand gestures are out—use only the trunk of your body (especially your pelvis), your neck, and your legs. Your partner should tell you when you are being obscure. Repeat anv nebulous moves, using different torso gestures.

Variation 1
Physicalizing objectives

procedure Gather your study group into a circle. Everyone puts on a mask. A volunteer moves into the center of the circle and decides upon an objective that can be accomplished only with the aid of one or more persons. Choose an objective that involves some immediate danger, such as: "Because the river is flooding very quickly, I need two people to help me carry sandbags down to the levee" or "A tornado is coming toward us, and I need help to carry Grandma down to the cellar." Without words, the volunteer in the center must define his need and enlist assistants. Now he and his helpers try to carry out the task in pantomime, their movements suggesting weights and maneuvers.

Variation 2
The fish and the angler

procedure Both you and your partner put on your masks and come into the center of the work space. One of you will play a fish, the other a fisherman. Pantomime the following steps: Decide first where the edge of an imaginary pond would be. The fish swims around looking for food. The fisherman approaches the pond and baits his hook and line. The fisherman casts his line hopefully and waits. The fish notices the ripples in the water. The fisherman reels in and the fish watches the bait.

The fisherman casts again, this time less happily and hopefully. The fish sees the bait and examines it, swimming around it. The fisherman slowly starts reeling in the line, not realizing that the fish is in close pursuit of the bait, but then he quits. He sits down dejectedly, leaving the bait in the middle of the pond. The fish eyes the bait and cautiously watches it settle. The fisherman falls asleep. As he allows his pole to go limp, he jerks the bait and the fish bites the hook. The angler is startled. He jumps up and begins a tug of war with the fish, letting it have its run and reeling in the line as the fish tires.

The rest is up to you and your partner. Either the fisherman will net the fish and bring him home or the fish will get away, perhaps crossing the fishing line and cutting it at the last second if the fisherman gives the line enough slack. Be specific.

decisions Did either of you violate the limits of the pond? Did the angler use a spinning reel or a fly casting rod? Was the fish consistent in its movements and in its attraction to the bait? During the tug of war, did the fish and the angler work together to keep the length of the fishing line constant, or did each of you "do your own thing"? Did you involve your entire body? Were your partner's needs and efforts clearly evident in his gestures? Remember that you can play only objectives, not abstract emotions. Every effect produced onstage requires a human cause that can be communicated to an audience. Every form of play requires logic. A child at play may get very angry at anyone who attempts to destroy the logicality of the world he has created. Your audience is just as demanding.

Variation 3

The departing ship[4]

procedure Ask your partner to watch you perform this mimetic exercise. Alternate using and not using a mask.

You have come to a wharf to say good-by to a friend or loved one who is leaving on a *huge* ocean liner. Be specific in regard to who this voyager is. There is a large crowd gathered at the dock in front of the ship. Survey the ship and the crowd. Inch your way through the crowd, filling in the spaces you create for yourself between imaginary people. Come to the front of the dock and sight across the line of voyagers high above you. Look for your friend. Wave slowly as you look for him. Suddenly you find him. His presence is like the sun to you after a month of rain. Alter the speed of your waving.

Try wildly to attract his attention. Continue waving as the truth dawns on you that the person you are waving at is not who you thought it was. Keep on waving, but change your rhythm with each transition. Lean in and scrutinize the person you were waving at, and then lean back to get visual distance from him. Decide that he's not the right person. Continue waving, though you are embarrassed and less hopeful of finding your friend. Notice that everyone around you is still waving. Try to save face by waving at anybody up there, though you are still looking for your friend.

Suddenly the ship moves out. A moment of panic seizes you as you realize that you may never make contact with your friend. Keep waving as the liner slowly pulls away and eventually disappears far off on the horizon.

Try to use your entire body to demonstrate each transition you make.

decisions Discuss the following questions with your partner.

a. Did your entire body indicate who the friend was? Was it a lover, your mother, or a close pal?
b. Did you lay out the basic task well before plunging into the exercise, or was your partner baffled?
c. Did you create people in the crowd with different sizes, shapes, personalities, and with real human qualities? Did your gestures indicate that you were pressing through a crowd or did it seem as though you were pushing your way through a field of wheat? Remember to keep your arms close to or against your body, just as you would in a real crowd; don't allow your arms to spread out, even when you wave. A female performer should remember to protect her breasts as she inches through the crowd.

d. Did you remember to keep the deck of the ship consistent? Did you appear to be searching for your friend? *Real* searching is smooth, not flexible or staccato.
e. Did your partner believe that you thought you saw your friend?
f. Was the embarrassing moment when you discovered that you were waving at the wrong person apparent?
g. Did the angle of your body alter when you realized that you had made a mistake?
h. What happened to your pelvic line as you tried to save face? Did your partner notice organic changes in your pelvic line when you saw the ship pull out and when you finally gave up hope of saying good-by?

suggestions Experiment with a real crowd. Go to a crowded intersection and try to inch your way to the front of the crowd as it waits for a red light to change.

If you are female, alter the exercise this way: play a girl who is six months pregnant saying good-by to her sailor boyfriend. Be careful to make real space for yourself as you move through the crowd.

BUILDING TO A VOCAL CLIMAX

procedure Memorize and prepare from fourteen to twenty consecutive lines from the section of Greek drama that you are to perform for your group at a later time. Your objective is to intensify your speech and raise your volume slightly with each successive line until you reach the optimum amount of sound within your basic range. Work your way up the decibel scale slowly from a whisper to a shout. Try to peak your volume as you reach the natural climax of your speech. Your partner should tell you when you are taking too great a leap in volume. See if you can build each step of the speech methodically and technically first, then try to add emotion the second time you do the speech.

You may also do this exercise alone. The most fruitful way of approaching it by yourself is to do the speech while standing about three to four feet from a corner of a room. Do it "live"; no tape recorder will pick up your progression accurately, and the time it takes to rewind will destroy your continuity.

When working with a partner, share the exercise progression: let him say the first line from his speech; next, you take the first line from your speech; then he says his second line, and so on. Share the build. You should each take your volume level from the other and top it slightly when you take your turn again. Try to avoid any harsh straining. Breathe and support your tone.

Repeat the exercise, but this time add the element of rhythmic speed to volume as you interchange your lines. Accelerate from the slowest possible speed you can manage to the fastest speed at which you can utter distinctly while maintaining the emotion necessary to the performance of your respective speeches. Cooperate with each other; avoid any feeling of competition.

decisions Any performer who practices such an exercise on his own must avoid the tendency to listen to himself for long periods of time, because he will disclaim the need for a partner. He will become a loner. This exercise is designed as a means, not a sure-fire way, to polish a final performance.

If you were working with a partner, ask him the following questions:

a. Were you too quiet for him to hear you?
b. Were you straining for that last blast of volume?
c. Did you really get louder (or faster) that time, or did you go too far that time in volume (speed)?
d. Are you motivating what you're saying? If your energy of communication dissipates, say the lines to your partner as mere conversation, then repeat the exercise, heightening your volume and speed.
e. Were you too loud for him to top without "pushing"?

Every so often a speech hits a plateau or a level at which the succeeding lines may modify what has already been said. Perhaps this segment of your speech can be called "parenthetical" (it may be part of a subordinate clause, or it may be in opposition to the main part of the speech that you have already spoken). For example, consider the second speech in Sophocles' *Oedipus Rex,* that of the Priest (brackets added):

> Oedipus, ruler of my land,
> you see our generations at the altar—
> [the nestlings here too weak to fly far,
> the priesthood bent with age,
> and the chosen young.]
> The rest sit with branches in the marketplace . . .

The three bracketed lines are subordinate to "generations at the altar." These three lines do not need a rising level of intensity; therefore, they do not need a rising level of volume or speed. However, "The rest sit with branches" introduces a new group of people and a new thought; therefore, this introduction should pick up the same volume and speed that you used for "generations at the altar," and you should accelerate the speed and raise the volume just a bit. Every actual transition you make needs a real rise in intensity, speed, and volume to introduce it.

Decide where the modifying segments of your speeches belong. Put parentheses or brackets around these modifiers to remind yourself of them. Try your speeches once again. Ask your partner to listen and tell you when you are over-emphasizing or under-emphasizing a particular spot.

ANALYZING THE ACTION OF YOUR ROLE

procedure You may use this method to examine every beat objective you play, or to break down the organic, French-scene objective into its progressive components. First, try to use the method with a simple "Three-Task" exercise.[5]

Phase 1

Three-task exercise

procedure Make up a list of uncomplicated actions, such as: close a window, lie on the floor, slam down a book, yell something, stand on a chair, turn on a light. After assembling a list of about twenty actions, either you or your partner should take a position in the center of the work area. The observer then chooses any three actions for the performer to carry out as a beginning task, a central task, and an ending task, regardless of the process involved. Don't try to be "theatrical." *Let* yourself find a logical way to do the three tasks in order without doing a lot of superfluous actions. Use your most direct motivation.

This exercise is designed to help you achieve two aims: always to find the most straightforward motivation to do your tasks, and to finish one task before beginning another. You can link all three segments of your exercise into one motivated sequence of actions; nevertheless, you will still be doing three distinct actions. For example, if you are given the tasks of first standing on a chair, then lying down on the floor, and finally slamming down a book, you may find yourself gravitating toward a prop (the book) right at the start. Try to read the book. Decide it is too dark and turn on the light. No light. Stand on a chair to see if the bulb is burned out or just loose. Tighten the bulb. The light works! Lie down on the floor under the bulb. Realize that there is still not enough light and that you are straining your eyes. Get angry and slam down the book. Always try to use real stimuli from real sources in your work area.

decisions Were you conscious of your partner watching you as you performed? Were your actions logical, coherent, and simple? Busy little movements will make you look smaller than life. The Greek theatre often deals with gigantic human needs in the simplest, straightforward terms. No gestures at all are better than too many little movements. If you give in to the one big gesture you feel you *need* to make, you will find that you can easily eliminate many meaningless little motions.

variation Perform any one minute task from your daily routine, such as brushing your teeth. The task should have a beginning, middle, and end. In other words, it should be clear from the changes in your attitude, rhythm, and speed that you are starting to do something, that you are getting into the purpose of your task, and that you have completed your task.

Phase 2

Breaking down a Gestalt action

procedure Every objective (task) goes through five definite steps, whether it be your superobjective, your French-scene objective, or a unit or beat objective. The five stages in order are: Focus, Determination, Preparation, Attack, and Release.[6] In the case of units or beats, your final Release usually carries you into your next Focus. The system is psychologically sound and economical. A person is attracted by a stimulus (Focus); he decides to do something about it (Determination); he gets together whatever he needs, including the guts to deal with the problem (Preparation); he does what he discovered he needs to do (Attack); and he relaxes to see the effect of his actions (Release).

Apply this system to the same sequence as Alan H. Monroe's motivational sequence for the Persuasive speech.[7] Focus complements the Attention Step, in which the speaker attracts his audience with his material; Determination complements the Need Step, in which the speaker explains why the people to whom he is talking must take action; Preparation complements the Criteria Step, in which the speaker defines possible alternatives to the problem; Attack complements the Solution Step, in which the speaker demonstrates to the audience that the particular answer he has will meet with the requirements of all the criteria and solve the problem with the least amount of repercussions; and Release complements the Urge to Activity, in which the speaker incites the audience as well as he can and watches his audience to check the effectiveness of his exhortations.

This system can be a valuable tool for dissecting a difficult scene or a problematic action. For example, it may be apparent that either you or your partner has jumped from Focus into Attack without having taken the time to make any real decisions at all. This can be a common problem in emotionally charged Greek scenes. Performers often jump into Attack too early and leave themselves nowhere to go in the rest of the scene. An actor should never show his top too soon. Play against your emotion as long as possible, though your audience sees that your emotion is growing and that it is about to explode.

Any actor playing Oedipus should use this concept. Oedipus attacks fully only when he blinds himself. If he allows himself to attack Tiresias at a high level, he will never be able to sustain the later scenes in the play. The actor playing Oedipus should think of his Tiresias scene as part of his Determination for his overall super-objective, rather than as his Attack. Of course, Tiresias' final prophecies in this scene *are* part of Tiresias' Attack, because this is the only time in the play that Tiresias appears. Oedipus has a much longer way to go. An actor who shows his anger too soon will exhaust or bore an audience before the climax occurs.

If you try to use this system scientifically, you may wind up destroying the spontaneity of first-time illusion in a piece of work. However, if you use the system with discretion, the Focus step can help you find where your discoveries are throughout the script. Sometimes you may see an actor jump from the Release of one action directly into the Determination of a succeeding action without taking the time to receive the stimulus for his new action. The stage jargon for this fault is "anticipation." Such a problem generally occurs when performers are over-rehearsed in their roles, when they are in a long run, or when they are nervous and anxious to finish a scene quickly.

decisions

With your partner, explore both your scene and a few Three-task exercises, using the following check list:

a. What was the beginning, middle, and end of the piece of work you just did?

b. Were the stimuli for your actions clear and direct?
c. Did you take your time, even if only a second, to *decide* to do an action?
d. Were there many possible solutions to your dilemma that needed consideration?
e. Was your Attack late in the piece of work, or did you show your top too soon?
f. Did you really check your effect? Did your effect lead you logically to your following action?
g. Was your entire sequence simple? Was there evidence of audience-consciousness?
h. Were your actions complete?

CRITICIZING THE GREEK SCENES IN CLASS

The following suggestions for discussion topics are based on the material in this chapter.

a. What was good about the scene?
b. Where did the actors carry their tension?
c. Did the mask enable the performers to give in to their emotions?
d. Did the mask get in the way of the scene? Were any movements too busy or cluttered rather than economical and descriptive?
e. Was the situation believable within the context of the play and style? Were the movements those that would be natural for a character in the world of this play?
f. What type of character did the performers select from the character Quality Chart? Was their choice of animal and quality categories consistent with the objectives they had to play?
g. Did the performers reveal any hedonic movements that might be distracting to an audience?
h. Did every gesture have a function of reference or stem directly from the emotion of the scene? Did the actors cloud the gestures with the implied use of personal pronouns by pointing to themselves ("I," "me,") or to others ("you")? Is there any need for such gestures? Occasionally, they can aid an actor to show contrast—for example, "That's mine [gesture], not yours!"
i. Were the number of gestures so excessive that the really important ideas were lost in a barrage of movements?
j. Did the actors listen to each other?
k. Was there first-time illusion?
l. Did the actors share the scene, supplying the right motivations for each other?
m. Were transitions accompanied by changes in rhythm and gesture?

Did one gesture seem to carry over into the next beat, even though the actor had made a new vocal transition? Did either of the actors seem to fall into a position that suggested he was "holding large rocks"?

n. Were each of the steps logical and motivated in the Gestalt system?
o. Did either actor peak too soon? Was the piece of work vocally sustained?
p. Was your criticism constructive?[8]

chapter 12
STYLE ACTING 2—THE JACOBEANS AND THE ELIZABETHANS

PREPARING A VERSIFICATION STUDY SHEET

procedure

Choose a dramatic scene to work on with your partner. A scene from Shakepeare's *Othello* or *Macbeth* would be a fine choice for several reasons. Both plays have sharply defined circumstances and explicit objectives to lock into easily. Both make definite technical demands on actors in regard to creating characterizations, sustaining the vocal and physical requirements, and peaking the dramatic moments. Both contain excellent scenes for two or three people; *Othello* has especially good trio scenes that you can use if you are working with two partners. And finally, both plays feature strong emotional builds that are constructed into the rhythms of the poetry. Versification, speech rhythm, and the kind of colorful wording that requires a familiarity with the sound of the sense of each word are carefully developed to bring out the emotional progression in each scene.

Outline the ways in which your words seem to reflect your objectives and the inner life of your character. For example, in Shakespeare's *Macbeth* (II, ii) the staccato rhythm, the short replies, the explosive "K" sounds, and the number of cut-off thoughts in this scene just after Macbeth murders Duncan reflect the confusion and anxiety in both Macbeth and Lady Macbeth. Macbeth's objective is to get his wife to help him understand the distractions he experienced during and after the murder; her objective is to calm him down in order to cover their tracks as completely as possible. His rhythm seems to accelerate and hers seems to slow down during the scene as they relate to each other. "K" is a glottal sound made at the back of the throat—it may indicate a dryness in your mouth, a nervousness typified by either Macbeth or Lady Macbeth.

The second half of your outline deals directly with versification. Select twelve to fourteen lines from your speeches in the scene. Write them, word for word, on a piece of lined paper using every other line, or type them double-spaced on a sheet of paper. Carefully reproduce on this analysis sheet each line of poetry *exactly* as it appears in the script you have chosen. Use the following guides and suggestions to divide each line of poetry into feet, accent beats, and stress words that will help you perform the speech with clarity and economy.

There are few rules in versification that *must* be followed. Nevertheless, in order for verse to be verse, it must be formal; therefore you should have some knowledge of the disciplines found in verse drama. Shakespeare generally maintains and shapes character, emotion, and suspense by balancing his poetic lines so well that by simply finding the most efficient and inclusive manner of phrasing his words, you will be able to produce the natural sound and effect needed. Versification is a means of breaking down and analyzing a line so that when you put it all back together, the character you are playing becomes at once more human, natural, and individual. Always ask yourself why your character uses each particular word the way he does, but don't be too scientific or you may bleed the joy and life out of your role.

Work for what sounds natural and human, as opposed to what sounds mechanical and planned. Read the speech over twice. As you go over the speech the second time, simply add a mark over each syllable to indicate whether that syllable should take a stress or remain weak. If you are doing the study in longhand, pencil in over the stressed (long) syllable the straight mark the dictionary code gives for the letter "a" in the word "pāy." Over the unstressed (short) syllable use the curved mark given for the "a" in "păt." If you are typing you may substitute an apostrophe for the curved mark, like this: "pa̓t." Working in pencil is always best. Even experts not only make mistakes in versification, but also may later decide to change an idea or to try a different type of motivation for a line, thus altering their earlier choice of long and short sounds. Stress what sounds natural to you first, then see if you have at least four strong (stressed) syllables in each line of ten syllables. If a word has more than one syllable, always stress the syllable that carries the natural accent; for example, hit "sȳl lă bl̆e," not "sy̆l lā bl̆e."

The best way to decide what a playwright wants in a troublesome line of verse is to count the number of syllables in the line. If the words add up to an even ten syllables in a line, the verse is called "pentameter." The "meter"—the measured rhythm of verse—is made up of units called "feet" (each foot consists of stressed and unstressed syllables). "Pente" is the Greek stem word for five. Therefore, the word "pentameter" means that there are five feet in the line.

Technically, no verse form contains just one syllable per foot; there should be at least two syllables. The most common foot, the iambic, has two syllables—an unstressed syllable followed by a stressed one.

Sometimes a playwright may feel that another form of verse is best for his dramatic intention, so he may decide to use six feet in a line rather than five. Instead of pentameter he may choose hexameter (from the Greek stem word for six, "hex," and the usual word for feet, "meter").

If a playwright begins a piece of work in iambic pentameter, he will most often continue with that form throughout the piece. He will rarely depart from his overall verse form unless he wishes to make a special point, as Shakespeare does with Vincentio, the Duke of Dark Corners, in a peculiar speech from *Measure for Measure* (III, iv). Shakespeare has the Duke shift from iambic pentameter to iambic tetrameter ("tetre" meaning four). Any audience would hear the shift easily as Vincentio begins, "He who the sword of heaven would bear/Should be as holy as severe," and so forth. Many critics argue that this speech is not one of Shakespeare's; however, the Duke seems to be a holier-than-thou politican who never bothers to practice what he preaches, therefore it may be to Shakespeare's purpose to call attention to the Duke's rather sanctimonious soliloquy, or to the Duke's godlike power.

Thumb your way through any complete works of Shakespeare for other significant deviations from his standard iambic-pentameter form. You will find many lines in any of Shakespeare's plays that do not balance out to ten syllables. If the line has more or less than ten syllables, it does not necessarily mean that the playwright has shifted form. Rather it indicates that the playwright has decided to place a special emphasis on this segment by using a different form of verse.

If a particular line has more than ten syllables, it is called "hyperlectic." If it has less than ten syllables, it is called "catalectic." A catalectic line sometimes has a mark of punctuation which signifies that a word has been deliberately left out of the line. For example, in *Othello* (III, iv, 55), Othello begins a rather long speech with a catalectic line, "That handkerchief–." Obviously there are four syllables in this line, but the next line, "Did an Egyptian to my mother give," has all ten syllables. In such a case, Shakespeare has given you great dramatic freedom with this line because it is up to you to find a way to pause long enough to fill six more beats of rhythm. You don't need to use all six beats where the dash indicates. Instead of pausing *after* the word "handkerchief" and destroying the dramatic continuity of the line, pause *before* you begin the line. Desdemona has just admitted that she cannot find the handkerchief. It would be logical for Othello to pause for a moment before he decides what to say next. Shakespeare orchestrates the rhythm in a scene this way by letting the actor fill in the pauses meaningfully. Try to motivate taking a tiny pause before and after the word "handkerchief."

Occasionally, you will find a speech ending with a line of verse that has only a few words. This line is not necessarily a catalectic line! If the next line in your script begins halfway or part of the way across the page, it indicates that Shakespeare may intend that the actor with this next line should pick up his cue quickly in order to maintain the poetic flow. Your final line is catalectic only if your partner's next line begins at the extreme left and has a full ten syllables of its own. Look carefully at both of the lines in question and decide where a long pause would be effective.

Othello (IV, ii, 32–35) provides a fine example of both a catalectic line and a set of lines in which you and your partner should pick up your cues quickly.

Desdemona: I understand a fury in your words,
But not the words.
Othello: Why, what art thou?
Desdemona: Your wife, my lord; your true
And loyal wife.
Othello: Come swear it, damn thyself,/

Desdemona ends her first speech with a four-syllable line. Othello picks up his rhythm with another four-syllable line, but Desdemona completes his line with the six syllables of her own next line, "Your wife, my lord; your true. . . ." etc. She defends herself quickly and openly, picking up Othello's cue instantly. Othello should also jump on her cue, "And loyal wife," with his "Come swear it, damn thyself," which completes the balance of ten syllables for line thirty-five.

This text, as it appears in the folio, attributes only four actual lines of verse to the section under analysis. We have established ten syllables for line thirty-two and for lines thirty-four and thirty-five, but how about line thirty-three? You may assume that Shakespeare suggests that the actor playing Othello should take a pause equivalent to six syllables (three feet) on the period after Desdemona's "But not the words" before he begins "Why, what art thou?" It would be easy to motivate such a pause, and the pause is necessary to keep the poetic flow balanced in the next lines. The actor playing Othello can also give his line more variety by breaking his three-foot pause into two shorter pauses. For example, he may wait a beat after Desdemona's line "But not the words"; then he may say "Why," and take a two-beat pause before he finishes his question, "what art thou?" Use what you can motivate best. In determining such a spot, check whether the preceding line and the following line each have ten full syllables; then see whether the text gives the line a number of its own, and if so, look for a logical way to motivate the pause.

Try to retain the iambic pattern of an unstressed (short) syllable followed by a stressed (long) syllable wherever possible. Iambic verse is the most typical verse form in the English language. There are basically eight major forms of verse feet: the iambic (short-long), which is considered to be "more aggressive" and more masculine than the other verse forms;[1] the trochee (long-short), which complements the rhythm of the French language best and which is considered (not necessarily by sexists) to be "graceful and placid" and the more feminine of the verse forms; the dactylus (long-short-short), which is often labeled "grave and serious"; the anapestus (short-short-long), which suggests a "march rhythm"; the paeon (long-short-long), which Rudolf Laban calls the rhythm for "excitement and foolishness"; the Ionian combinations of the long-long-short-short, typical of "violent agitation," and the short-short-long-long, typical of "profound depression." In addition, the Ionian can be broken into its components: the spondee, which has two stressed syllables (long-long) and makes for strong emphasis or emotion; and the pyrrhic, which has two unstressed syllables and simply aids the flow between ideas. The paeon and the four-syllable Ionian combinations are strangers to the English language, but you will find a great many pyrrhic and spondaic feet in Shakespeare's verse. Do not try to use any short-long-short combinations within your foot divisions. Such combinations simply do not exist. Restrict yourself to using iambic, trochaic, anapestic, dactylic, spondaic, and pyrrhic feet.

Every line of verse can be broken into the number of feet that fit comfortably between its first and last words, depending upon the phrases, pauses, and punctuation marks. Every syllable in every word represents part of a foot. Versification categories may be used as a means of helping you to feel out the best emotion to use in performing a line of poetry. These suggestions are merely possibilities, not hard and fast rules.[2]

In order to divide a line into the right number of feet, begin by counting in two syllables from the front of the line and then two syllables from the end of the line. The most difficult section of the line invariably falls in the middle, so it usually helps to establish the first and fifth feet first. Look at the first of the twelve to fourteen lines you have chosen for analysis and try to find the first and the fifth feet. After the first foot and before the fifth foot put in a slash (/). Now count in from the front another two syllables and insert a slash for the second foot. If there are an even ten syllables, there is a good chance that you can just add a slash every two syllables and you will have divided your verse line into five feet. If there are more than ten or less than ten syllables, you've got more work to do. Remember that it takes at least two syllables to make a foot.

A catalectic line with a word that ends in "-ed" should retain the ending as a soft sound (unstressed syllable) in the rhythm of the line. In *Othello* (I, i, 162), Brabantio states, "And what's to come of my despised time," in which the "-ed" of the "despised" is needed to fill out the rhythm. On the contrary, in *Othello* (III, iv, 141), Desdemona has the hyperlectic line "Either from Venice, or some unhatched practice," in which the "-ed" is not really necessary to the rhythm. Brabantio is an older man, and the use of "-ed" in his line might lend him a kind of dignity; whereas Desdemona does not need the pedantic "-ed" as part of her character. In her line, the word "unhatched" becomes a two-syllable word.

The major pause in every line of verse is called the "caesura." The caesura usually falls slightly to the left or right of the middle of the line or in the middle of the third foot. Caesuras work best when they fall on a mark of punctuation that ends a sentence or separates two clauses. But they may also appear around a prepositional phrase if a pause at such a spot would help you clarify the meaning of the line, or if it would help you catch your breath, providing the pause can be motivated. There is not necessarily a caesura in every line; but sometimes there may be two! Indicate a caesura with parallels, that is, two slashes (//). This will remind you where to pause when you go over your lines.

It is not incorrect form to have a mark of punctuation in the middle of a foot. Punctuation functions best when it appears on the slashes (single or double) you have applied in pencil, though this is certainly not a rigid rule.

The choice of long and short sounds should conform to the natural accents of the words; for example, "hūmăn/ bēiňg/" would sound ridiculous as "hŭmān/ bĕiñg/." There will be times when Shakespearean pronunciation will deviate from modern American speech. You should accent your words the way your audience will understand them best.

Shakespeare sometimes alters pronunciation for dramatic effect; for example, in *Othello* (V, ii, 25), Othello asks Desdemona on her deathbed, "Hăve yŏu prāy'd tŏ-nīght, Dĕsdēmŏn?" Shakespeare deliberately omits the final "a" to bring out Othello's feeling about her as the "demon" in Desdemona. In the same line, Desdemona replies, "Āy, mўy lōrd." Othello's words "tŏ-nīght" and Desdemona's "Āy" flank the word "Desdemon" with two strong sounds which seem to indicate that the pronunciation ought to be "Dĕsdēmŏn." Naturally, the actress doing the role of Desdemona must react to the pun on her name. He has never called her that before.

The second foot should almost always remain an iambic (short-long) to carry the rhythm from the first foot and to keep the caesura centered around the third foot. You should also try to keep the fifth foot iambic in order to preserve the definite quality of the verse and the strong, "masculine" ending, especially if the line has no punctuation at the end and seems to "run on" to the next line. Occasionally, this is impossible to do with the fifth foot because the very last word must end in an unstressed syllable or else it will sound unnatural. For example, in *Othello* (III, iii, 173), Iago ends the line "Bŭt rīchĕs fĭnelēss ĭs ăs pōor ăs wīntĕr" with a soft "feminine" ending. The word "winter" just won't go iambic here without destroying some of the sense of the line and calling attention to itself. You would certainly confuse an audience by saying "wĭntēr."

A line with a fifth-foot "feminine" ending that seems to "run on" to the next line because there is no punctuation to stop it will sound better with an upward inflection or with a rising or a level intonation on the last syllable—almost like a "masculine" ending. The word "cases" is always accented "cāsĕs," though in *Othello* (III, iv, 143, 144), when Desdemona says, ". . . ănd ĭn sūch cāsĕs/ Mēn's nātūres wrāngle wĭth ĭnfēriŏr thīngs," she may lift the "-es" in "cases" at the end of the line so that she carries the tone into the next line. There are a great many places where you can do this effectively to help the poetry and support the sense of the line. When you find such a spot, try putting in an asterisk just after the last word on the line. As you study the script, the asterisks will remind you to either lift or level the final tone and "run on" to the next line, keeping the sound of the piece alive.

The simpler and more straightforward a character's objectives are, the more his verse will tend toward simple iambic pentameter. Desdemona is simpler than Emilia; Macduff is simpler than Macbeth. As Macbeth becomes more and more of a plotter, his verse becomes more and more complex. He shifts from a direct physical means to a cerebral means and eventually back to a physical means of expressing himself. Iago's verse is far more difficult to dissect than that of Othello, for Iago is a devious character capable of complicated plotting. Iambics are the easiest for your audience to hear and understand. But sometimes deviations from the iambic are needed to clarify meaning, to help the sound of the sense of an emotional phrase, or to provide some variety after a long string of iambics.

The most common deviation from iambic is the initial trochee. The initial trochee often occurs when it is necessary to introduce a new thought or a new series of ideas, but it generally comes after a run-on line that has an upward inflection or intonation on the fifth foot. In this instance it is often the verb of the sentence, especially when the verb is in the progressive tense (ending in "-ing"). The only test for using an initial trochee is to ask yourself if it sounds more natural to lead off the line with a long-short foot.

Your character's objectives are implicit in his scansion, in his rhythm, and in his specific choice of words. Coloring or painting each word verbally is absolutely necessary. When a strange word comes along, find out its precise meaning from the glossary of the text you are using; or go the library, get out the variorum copy of the play, and see what may be suggested as the meaning of the word. You cannot act if you do not know exactly what you are saying.

Shakespeare usually writes in blank verse; that is, he writes without a rhyme scheme. There are exceptions: Gower, the ancient Chorus in *Pericles*, uses rhyme as a formal convention in every one of his choric introductions; therefore, the audience expects it. However, there are times when Shakespeare uses rhyme to call attention to a particular moment or character. If your words shift into rhyme, you must explore the purpose for this shift.

In comedies, rhyme becomes a vehicle for winding up the moral of the play. But when rhyme appears in a tragedy, it is definitely the playwright's way of calling attention to a character. In *Hamlet*, Polonius, Laertes, and Ophelia share the family trait of summarizing whatever they say with a couplet used as a moral or as a parable. All three of these characters are a bit shallow. Moralizing is part of their family characteristic of not looking beneath the surface. Polonius, Laertes, and Ophelia, though sensitive, have little common sense; they generalize in neat bundles. This shortsightedness may be partially responsible for the suffering that all three undergo.

After deciding where the various notations belong—the foot slashes, the long and short marks, the asterisks to indicate run-on lines and upward or level intonations—you are ready to insert the stress marks (underlines) on your sheet.

If you have jotted down objectives or transitions in the margin, this is the way to make them work as you perform the text.[3]

Stresses should be made in pencil with a ruler. Draw them under the word to be emphasized. You should be judicious with these marks: too many underlines are impossible to perform because nothing is subordinate; too few underlines, on the other hand, give you no framework upon which to build. Use a single underline if the word or phrase is important to the clarity of an objective or helps elucidate an obscure idea. Try to avoid overdoing your adjectives. Nouns tell the audience what you are talking about. Try giving the respective words in an important noun-and-adjective combination equal vocal stress.

Use a double underline if the word or phrase carries the story line of the plot. A phrase designated by a double underline should help provide immediate clarity, but if people in the audience miss such a phrase they may be bewildered by what happens next. A double underline can also be used to indicate strong emotional involvement, as well as plot information. You can apply a triple underline to denote extremely full emotion—but use it sparingly. Remember that the rhythm and climax of your speech should grow as long as possible before you allow yourself to crest your speech vocally and emotionally. A triple underline early in a speech is a dead giveaway that you are showing your top too soon.

Not only should words or phrases in a series grow in intensity, but they ought to be performed differently every time. Purposefully choose a trochee if you used an iambic with the phrase before. Always strive for a fresher music, a stronger sound to the verse, as long as that sound is natural to the needs of your character. Occasionally, you may want to express all the words in a series the same way for a dramatic purpose, as in Macbeth's famous "Tomorrow, and tomorrow, and tomorrow" in *Macbeth* (V, v, 19). You might want these words to sound like bells tolling a funeral dirge; or you might want them to demonstrate Macbeth's total boredom with life now that all he wanted has been lost and his wife has died. You may just as easily sigh out the last "tomorrow" as an exclamation of despair, in which case there would still be a build. A negative build in volume can be just as theatrical as a positive one. It is perfectly acceptable to decrease the volume and pitch for words or ideas in a series, as long as you do not drop the intensity. The *intensity* must always grow.

These suggestions are designed to give you freedom, not to restrict you. Try to master these disciplines before you bend them to suit the individual purposes of your character within your scene.

The following analysis tackles a Macbeth speech using the preceding rules and suggestions. Macbeth's objective in this speech could be "I want to decide whether I have the guts and the right to kill Duncan." The steady iambics from lines three to seven and from lines fifteen to twenty-six develop two strong rhythmic growths as Macbeth ponders his desire and convinces himself that he can't really rationalize or get away with murdering Duncan. Macbeth's "if's" and "but's" reflect his indecision. He actually constructs a list of dangers to consider.

This is one of Macbeth's key speeches. Making versification decisions about this speech will help you plot Macbeth's character growth during the first half of the play. Used creatively, versification will help you over the problem spots in poetic drama. Use it when you need it, and always find real character motivation for your choices.

Step 1
Establishing your objectives and your progression of action

MACBETH
(I, vii, 1–28)

	Beat Objectives
FOCUS If it were done when 'tis done, then 'twere well It were done quickly. If th' assassination Could trammel up the consequence, and catch, DETERMINATION With his surcease, success; that but this blow	I want to decide whether the shock of Duncan's murder will so stun the country that my wife and I will be able to take the throne with no questions asked.
Might be the be-all and the end-all—here But here, upon this bank and shoal of time, PREPARATION We'd jump the life to come. But in these cases	I want to convince myself that my wife and I would venture hell to enjoy the throne *now* in our earthly life.
We still have judgment here; that we but teach Bloody instructions, which, being taught, return To plague th' inventor; this even-handed justice Commends th' ingredients of our poison'd chalice	I want to consider whether by killing Duncan I will initiate a chain reaction that will eventually catch up with me and my wife.
To our own lips. He's here in double trust: First, as I am his kinsman and his subject— Strong both against the deed; then, as his host, Who should against his murderer shut the door,	I want to list all the honors I enjoy under Duncan's leadership at this time.
Not bear the knife myself. Besides, this Duncan Hath borne his faculties so meek, hath been So clear in his great office, that his virtues	I want to weigh Duncan's reputation with the other thanes.
Will plead like angels, trumpet-tongu'd, against	I want to decide whether

The deep damnation of his taking-off;
And ATTACK pity, like a naked newborn babe,
Striding the blast, or heaven's cherubim, horsed
Upon the sightless couriers of the air,
Shall blow the horrid deed in every eye,
That tears shall drown the wind. RELEASE I have no spur
To prick the sides of my intent, but only
Vaulting ambition, which o'erleaps itself
And falls on th' other side. How now! What news?

the thanes will let me get away with the murder or whether their feeling for Duncan is so strong that they will persist in investigating his death.

I want to prove to myself that I have no reason to kill Duncan except my shameful desire to have more power.

Step 2
Saying the lines naturally for meaning and inserting accent marks

If it were done when 'tis done, then 'twere well
It were done quickly. If th' assassination*
Could trammel up the consequence, and catch
With his surcease, success; that but this blow
Might be the be-all and the end-all—here
But here, upon this bank and shoal of time,
We'd jump the life to come. But in these cases*
We still have judgment here; that we but teach
Bloody instructions, which, being taught, return
To plague th' inventor; this even-handed justice*
Commends th' ingredients of our poison'd chalice*
To our own lips. He's here in double trust:
First, as I am his kinsman and his subject—*
Strong both against the deed; then, as his host,
Who should against his murderer shut the door,
Not bear the knife myself. Besides, this Duncan*

Hitting the "if's" in the first two lines sets up Macbeth's wishful thinking. Try to alter the accent marks over each of the three "done's" in a series so that each sounds a bit different.

Add an asterisk wherever there is no punctuation to indicate a run-on line. Decide whether a level or an upward inflection on the fifth foot maintains the poetic flow and clarifies the meaning better.

Lines 10 and 11 are thirteen-syllable hyperlectic lines that seem to deviate from pentameter to hexameter. The number of strong accents indicates that Macbeth's mind is racing to make an emotional decision.

Making "strong both" an initial spondee brings Macbeth's argument home.

Line 16 is tricky.

Hath borne his faculties so meek, hath been
So clear in his great office, that his virtues*
Will plead like angels, trumpet-tongu'd, against
The deep damnation of his taking-off;
And pity, like a naked newborn babe,
Striding the blast, or heaven's cherubim, horsed
Upon the sightless couriers of the air,
Shall blow the horrid deed in every eye,
That tears shall drown the wind. I have no spur
To prick the sides of my intent, but only*
Vaulting ambition, which o'erleaps itself
And falls on th' other side. How now! What news?

Keep the natural accent in "Duncan" and forget "this"; there is only one Duncan to think about in the play.
Macbeth drives straightforward, peaking his major build to decide what to do. His lines here are loaded with simple, direct iambics.

Macbeth shifts rhythm and sums up his answer here. Line 26 is another tricky one. In order to balance, the line you will probably have to make the third foot an anapestus. Hit both syllables in "intent."

Step 3
Adding the foot slashes and decide where to put the caesuras

If it/were done/when 'tis/done//then/'twere well
It were done/quickly./ //If th' as/sassi/nation
Could tram/mel up/the con/sequence,/ //and catch
With his/surcease,/success;/ //that but/this blow
Might be/the be-/all and/the end-/all—//here
But here,/ //upon/this bank/and shoal/of time,//
We'd jump/the life/to come./ //But in these/cases
We still/have judg/ment here;/ //that we/but teach
Bloody in/structions,/ //which be/ing taught/return
To plague/th' inven/tor;//this/even-/handed/justice
Commends/th' ingre/dients/of our/poison'd/chalice
To our/own lips./ //He's here/in dou/ble trust:

Hitting "it" seems too effeminate for Macbeth. "If th' as" might be a trochee as well as a dactylus. The apostrophe in "th' " is substituted for a vowel that might make "the" a full syllable. Wedging syllables together to maintain the poetic flow is called enjambering. Enjambering may also be used in lines 10, 11, and 28.

Punching "this" establishes Macbeth's belief in an eye for an eye, in contrast to any other type of justice.

First, as/I am/his kins/man//and his/subject—
Strong both/against/the deed;/ //then, as/his host,//
Who should/against/his mur/derer//shut/the door,//
Not bear the/knife my/self.// Be/sides, this/Duncan
Hath borne/his fa/culties/so meek,/ //hath been
So clear/in his great/office,/ //that his/virtues
Will plead/like an/gels//trum/pet-tongu'd/against
The deep/damna/tion of/his ta/king-off;//
And pi/ty,//like/a na/ked new/born babe,//
Striding/the blast,/ //or hea/ven's che/rubim,// horsed
Upon/the sight/less cou/riers/of the air,//
Shall blow/the hor/rid deed/in e/very eye,//
That tears/shall drown/the wind./ //I have/no spur
To prick/the sides/of my in/tent,//but/only
Vaulting/ambi/tion,//which/o'erleaps/itself
And falls/on th' o/ther side./ //How now!/What news?

Hitting "am" in the second foot acknowledges that Duncan is superior in power. It is emphatic! "Am" tells more about Macbeth than "I" does because Macbeth is alone onstage. There is seldom a need to hit "I" or "me" unless you have to show a contrast; however, hitting "his" in the fourth foot of line 18 proves that Macbeth feels that the thanes respect Duncan's qualities as a leader more than his own.

Giving two strong accents to "intent" in the middle of line 26 preserves the natural accent in "only" and also reflects Macbeth's inner motivation by forcing the audience to focus on his intent.

Step 4
Putting parentheses around subordinate modifiers

If it/were done/when 'tis/done//then/'twere well
It were done quickly. If th' assassination
Could trammel up the consequence, and catch
With his surcease, success; that but/this blow
Might be/the be/all and/the end/all—(here
But here, upon this bank and shoal of time,)
We'd jump/the life/to come./ //But in these/cases

Examine alternate ways of performing each line. The first line can be done in a myriad of ways that are all consistent with the rules of versification. See how the subtleties of meaning may alter. A final iambic or spondee is acceptable in line 4. The first foot in line 5 may also be a spondee.

Hitting "we'd" includes Lady Macbeth in the crime.

We still have judgment here;/that we/but teach
Bloody instructions, which (being taught) return
To plague th' inven/tor;//this/even-handed justice
Commends th' ingredients of our poison'd chalice
To our/own lips./He's here in double trust:
First, as I am/his kins/man and his subject—
Strong both against the deed;/then, as/his host,
Who should against his murderer shut the door,
Not bear the knife myself. Besides, this Duncan
Hath borne his faculties/so meek,/hath been
So clear/in his great office, that his virtues
Will plead/like angels trumpet-tongu'd against
The deep damnation of/his ta/king-off;
And pi/ty,//(like/a naked newborn babe,
Striding the blast, or heaven's cherubim, horsed
Upon the sightless couriers of the air,)
Shall blow/the horrid deed in every eye,
That tears shall drown the wind./ //I have/no spur
To prick the sides/of my in/tent, but only
Vaulting ambi/tion,//which/o'erleaps itself
And falls on th' other side. How now! What news?

The fourth foot in line 7 may be dactylic or anapestic, depending upon your choice of emphasis. The third foot in line 10 may be either iambic or pyrrhic.

If you feel that hitting "our" is strong enough, weaken "own" in line 12. Hitting "his" in line 13 strengthens Macbeth's feeling of allegiance to Duncan.

In lines 17 and 18 you may alter the accent on either "so," or keep them both strong and thus give these lines a very modern sound. Using the alternative spondees in lines 19 and 20 as well as the iambic (instead of pyrrhic) in line 21 heightens Macbeth's decision not to kill Duncan. This idea is also fortified by the possible spondee in line 24. "Shall" is emphatic. The fourth and fifth feet of line 25 may also be definite spondees. Using a dactylus instead of an anapestus in the third foot of line 26 maintains the natural accent in "intent," although it draws attention to the word for no real purpose.

Step 5
Underlining the words to stress for clarity, plot, and emotion

If it were done when 'tis done then 'twere well
It were done quickly. If th' assassination
Could trammel up the consequence, and catch

You should never underline an unaccented word. Check your decisions here with those in Step 2. Give the words you underline more volume or a longer duration of sound.

With his surcease, success; that but this blow
Might be the be-all and the end-all—(here
But here, upon this bank and shoal of time,)
We'd jump the life to come. // But in these cases
We still have judgment here; that we but teach
Bloody instructions, which (being taught) return
To plague th' inventor; this even-handed justice
Commends th' ingredients of our poison'd chalice
To our own lips. // He's here in double trust:
First, as I am his kinsman and his subject—
Strong both against the deed; then, as his host,
Who should against his murderer shut the door,
Not bear the knife myself. Besides, this Duncan
Hath borne his faculties so meek, hath been
So clear in his great office, that his virtues
Will plead like angels trumpet-tongu'd against
The deep damnation of his taking-off;
And pity, (like a naked newborn babe,
Striding the blast, or heaven's cherubim, horsed
Upon the sightless couriers of the air,)
Shall blow the horrid deed in every eye,
That tears shall drown the wind. // I have no spur
To prick the sides of my intent, but only
Vaulting ambition, which o'erleaps itself
And falls on th' other side. How now! What news?

Accelerate words in a series. "End-all" should be stronger than "be-all."

Macbeth climaxes his first build and begins his new reversal in line 7. This mental transition requires a vocal transition to clarify such an important shift for the audience.

Line 12 also ushers in a whole new line of thought. Macbeth begins to compile a list of reasons why he should not kill Duncan.

The second of two underlined words usually needs more emphasis to promote the on-going feeling in the speech. In line 16, "myself" clarifies who would bear the "knife" and therefore carries plot connotations. As a modifier, "deep" does not require the strength of emotion that the "damnation" does. Test your choice of stress words. If you can say the sentence without the word you underlined and still grasp the plot and meaning, you probably don't need to punch that word.
Macbeth climaxes the build of the speech in lines 20 to 25. He sums up his final decision in lines 25 to 28. Once again, this mental transition requires a vocal transition for clarity.

The preceding analysis is only one efficient way of doing this soliloquy. Another actor and director may wish to bring out other emphases and ideas; different motivations and justifications may change several of the choices here.

Nevertheless, Macbeth's progression from his testing whether he might be successful in killing Duncan to his final negative conclusion should be a constant in almost any production. Macbeth's reversal takes him from one polarity to another so that Lady Macbeth will be able to come onstage and coax him into reversing his entire decision again! However, Lady Macbeth doesn't try to convince him that he has the *right* to kill Duncan. Instead she reinforces his desire and his machismo, bringing his decision full circle.

Notice that nowhere in this lengthy soliloquy does Macbeth say that he doesn't *want* to kill Duncan or that he has given up the idea of being king. He decides only that he can't get away with the murder. As soon as his wife puts pressure on him, he changes his mind in the space of four of his speeches. Macbeth needs his wife to help him fulfill his French-scene objective; she helps him find the "guts" to kill Duncan and convinces him that he *can* get away with it.

In order to find some variety in playing the remainder of this scene between Macbeth and Lady Macbeth (I, vii), try approaching it as a love scene. Lady Macbeth probably wouldn't make very much immediate headway with her husband by screaming at him, but she certainly must know how to use her femininity. As Macbeth agrees to kill Duncan, he urges his wife to "bring forth men-children only." Whenever you can justify it, choose an opposite to play. For instance, plotting Duncan's death as you and your partner cuddle gives you an extremely diversified variety of tasks and emotions to perform.

CREATING A BUILD WITH PIANO NOTES

needs Find a practice room with a piano in it. You do not have to know how to play the piano. You will need to hit only a simple succession of keys. Remember that vocal tension and strain are antithetical to the purposes of this exercise.

procedure Begin by doing a vocal warm-up. Pay special attention to your final drop-overs as your pitch travels up and down your natural scale. You never need to go into falsetto—trust your own natural head tones. Avoid going so high or so low that only dogs can hear you.

Yawn down your scale to your lowest natural low. Find this note on the piano. You might ask a piano player from your study group to hit the notes for you. In this case, you should work in profile to your pianist so that he may help you avoid tension. If he sees you begin to strain, he should place his hand gently on the back of your neck where your spine joins your skull. Be especially aware of relaxing as you hit high notes.

After you figure out which note is your low, move up the scale, hitting the next three piano keys (black or white) to the right. The third note you hit should be close to your optimum pitch (the lowest relaxed pitch that you can support easily with good volume). Begin to say the first line of your speech on the same pitch as the note you found to be your optimum pitch. Whenever you move into a new thought line in your speech, you should move slowly up the scale, one note at a time, merely by hitting the next piano key to your right.

Yawn up your lines. Slowly accelerate your rhythm as you raise your pitch. Have enough patience to go up the scale slowly. If you are in doubt about where your new thought groups begin, try raising your pitch with every caesura you meet in every line. Speak your lines on the pitch. Do not try to sing the speech. Nor should you attempt to sing the note struck on the piano. Simply try to let the piano lead you into a greater intensity for performance.

Decide where the Focus, Determination, Preparation, Attack, and Release lie within your speech. After you have plotted your Attack, decide exactly where the climax of your speech is. This point should correspond to the highest natural note that you can hit. If there are any subordinate, modifying thoughts, they may be performed without a rise in pitch. Set off these ideas with parentheses. If a pianist is helping you, put a copy of your speech in front of him so that he knows when to raise the pitch and when to keep it level.

You may have to drop your pitch if there is a lengthy natural build within the new subordinate thought itself. In this case, begin a new build within the parentheses at a point low enough to allow yourself to raise your pitch slowly to the same note at which you left off before you began performing this modifying thought. This technique will help you maintain the continuum of your speech, raising your pitch gradually from your Focus to your Attack.

After reaching your Attack, try going slowly into your Release as you retrace your way *down* the scale, possibly going full cycle back to the note on which you began. This cycle is especially effective if the character you are playing winds up with the same mental framework that he began with when he started the speech.

Take another look at the Macbeth speech used in the last exercise. If you were to have a lowest comfortable pitch about two A's down from middle C, you or your pianist might raise your pitch to C below middle "C" as your optimum pitch, the note on which you would begin the Macbeth speech. Remember that the bulk of your pitch changes will be on the caesuras in the lines. This happens because the caesura, being the major thought pause of the line, is also the logical place to breathe. A new breath facilitates a pitch change, as well as a new level of heightened intensity. Of course, you will have to find your own lowest relaxed optimum pitch in order to tailor this exercise to your individual ability.

Using piano notes with dramatic verse

Beginning at C below middle C, and taking a tiny breath at each caesura or at each //, go through the following speech, increasing your intensity as you work your way up your scale. Do not push! Go as far

MACBETH
(I, vii, 1-28)

(C) If it were done when 'tis done,// (C#) then 'twere well
It were done quickly.// (D) If th' assassination
Could trammel up the consequence,// (D#) and catch,
With his surcease, success;// (E) that but this blow

D
Might be the be-all and the end-all—// (here
D#
But here,// upon this bank and shoal of time,)//
E D
We'd jump the life to come.// But in these cases
D#
We still have judgment here;// that we but teach
E D# E
Bloody instructions,// which, (being taught), return
F
To plague th' inventor;// this even-handed justice
Commends th' ingredients of our poison'd chalice
F# G
To our own lips.// He's here in double trust:
G#
First, as I am his kinsman// and his subject—
A
Strong both against the deed;// then, as his host,//
A# B
Who should against his murderer// shut the door,//
C C#
Not bear the knife myself.// Besides, this Duncan
D
Hath borne his faculties so meek,//hath been
D#
So clear in his great office,// that his virtues
E
Will plead like angels,// trumpet-tongu'd, against
The deep damnation of his taking-off;//
F D
And pity,// (like a naked newborn babe,//
D# E F
Striding the blast,// or heaven's cherubim,// horsed
Upon the sightless couriers of the air,)//
F#
Shall blow the horrid deed in every eye,//
G G F# F E
That tears shall drown the wind.// I have no spur
D# D C# C B
To prick the sides of my intent,// but only
A# A G# G F# F E D#
Vaulting ambition,// which o'erleaps itself
D C# C B A# A G# A A#
And falls on th' other side.//How now! What news?

as you can *easily* go! If you decide to make this line a modifier, drop your pitch.

This line begins the second of the two major builds in this speech. Macbeth begins a new thought pattern here as he shifts to a lower pitch of intensity. There is no place for a caesura in line 11, but the intensity of Macbeth's discovery justifies raising the pitch early in line 12 between "our" and "own."

Find your own natural pitch. If you can't hit C below middle C easily in your range, don't strain for it. Simply begin the exercise on a higher note, but try to follow the same general progression of accelerations and diminishing pitch levels.

Establish the pitch on "pity" firmly. Pick up the parenthetical modifiers at a pitch low enough to allow yourself to raise the intensity slowly until "Shall blow" is only a step above "And pity."

As Macbeth "releases," the pitch and intensity diminish. He ends with an intensity that is at almost the same pitch as the one with which he began.

decisions Were you distracted by the musical accompaniment at first? Did you eventually accept it and let it lead you, or did you fight to ignore the piano completely? The effect of the piano notes is similar to that of the musical crescendos typical of the background music in silent films. Once you can relax with the piano you will be less concerned with "how" you are doing the speech.

Did you breathe often enough to support each line? If you had an accompanist, ask him whether the ideas in your speech were logical and clear. Were you aware of the musical movement of the poetry in the speech? Did your acceleration in pitch seem to accompany the text and the objectives of the character you are playing?

Try to avoid breathing at obtrusive times. Ill-timed pauses can destroy the sound of the sense of the line and degenerate into a staccato rhythm. For example, if you allow yourself to take little pauses right after such words as "and" or "with" in order to breathe, you will leave your audience dangling in the middle of a phrase, which could lead to confusion. Remember that the intensity of your ideas should grow during your speech regardless of the rise or fall of your pitch.

extension Repeat the speech this time without the piano. Strive for naturalness, but maintain your build. Try to "orchestrate" a full scene between you and your partner. See if you can share rising and falling pitch changes, using the same musical notes. Repeat your scene, striving for naturalness within your builds.

WORD SHAPING

procedure Select one word from a text that you are working on, preferably a word you are having trouble with (possibly even a phrase). A word like "damnation" may seem cliché-ridden to a modern actor who does not believe in a religious hell. The phrase "horsed/Upon the sightless couriers of the air" may seem awfully obscure to any actor playing Macbeth. Most texts offer only "unseen messengers" as a reference for Macbeth's allusion.[4]

Lie down on your back or relax in a chair. Recall a moment in your recent past during which you felt similar to the way your character feels. Explore the moment sensorily. Now say the troublesome word or phrase from your line over and over again as you do the recall. Find another word that means the same thing to you as the word or phrase in question. If you have a strong association with your word, alternate it with the obscure word until you can color them both the same way.

If you are still stumped by a strange phrase, like the one above from *Macbeth,* try to put yourself in an imaginary situation. Imagine, for example, the Child Jesus driving a team of twenty black-and-white winged stallions above you. As they fly over your head, he shouts, "He is guilty—he is the murderer!" Imagine the horses coming closer and closer until they trample you. If you have claustrophobia or if you were ever caught in a crowd, you can use this feeling to color that nebulous phrase "horsed/ Upon the sightless couriers of the air." Use whatever works for you, but don't talk about it. Keep your personal images to yourself or you will exhaust them.

variation Accustom your breathing to your phrase. Let the rhythm of the phrase carry you into a physical movement. The more abstract the movement is, the better. Give in to the movement and let it grow.[5] Maintain it until you feel you are at your peak. Freeze! Now say your phrase without the movement. Give it all you've got in regard to the specific emotion you found for your word or phrase.

If your physical action was specific enough, you will be forced to color the word by using your voice alone. All your energy will go into describing the word vocally.

EXAMINING THE WORLD THROUGH SIXTEENTH-CENTURY EYES

explanation Read the following excerpt from the 1538 publication of *Batman upon Bartholemew, his book de proprietibus rerum.*[6] Remember that the Elizabethans printed the small letter "s" with an "f," and that occasionally a "v" appears as a "u," and a "j" as an "i."

> A humour is a fubstaunce actuallye moyft, by ioyning of elementall qualities, and is apt to nourifh and to feede the members, and to comfort the working thereof kindly, or cafually to let the workings thereof. For humour is the firft principall materiall of bodies that haue feeling, and chiefe helpe in theyr working, and that becaufe of nourifhing and feeding. Conftantinius faith, That the humours be called the children of the Elementes. For everye of the humours commeth of the qualitie of the Elementes. And ther be foure humours, Blood, Fleame, Cholar, and Melancholy; and are called fimple in comparifon to the members, though in refpect of the Elements, whofe children they bee, they be compofed. Thefe foure humours in quantitie and qualytie, obferuing evenneffe, with due proportion, make perfect and keepe in due ftate of health, all bodyes hauing blood: lyke as contrariwife, by their unequalneffe or infection they ingender and caufe fickneffe. Thefe humours be needful to the making of the bodye, and to the ruling and keeping thereof: and alfo to reftore what is loft in the body.[7]

The four humors that Batman refers to, namely, melancholy, phlegm, blood, and choler, correspond to the respective elements earth, water, air, and fire. The concept that the world was composed of these four elements, which became the humors in living bodies (bodies that have feeling), persisted from the time of the ancient Egyptian medical practices of Galen well into the seventeenth century. A harmonious balance of the elements was supposed to be necessary for the proper formation of the world, just as a harmonious balance of the humors was considered essential to the proper functioning of the human body, or any living body.[8]

Each of the four humors was thought to have a specific effect upon the body, and their dominance was held to determine not only the general health of a person but also his personality traits. By understanding the presumed cause and effect of the humors, an actor can more easily define the character he is playing, for he can decide how a humoral imbalance might affect that character emotionally. For example, in Shakespeare's *The Tempest,* Ariel's very name defines him as a spirit of the air, in contrast to Caliban's melancholy earthiness. Hamlet, being a Wittenberg graduate student and a brooder, calls attention to the elemental theory in relation to the Ghost of Old Hamlet:

> . . . The spirit that I have seen
> May be a devil; and the devil hath power
> T' assume a pleasing shape; yea, and perhaps
> Out of my weakness and my melancholy,
> As he is very potent with such spirits,
> Abuses me to damn me. . . . (*Hamlet,* II, ii, 626–631)

Ben Jonson went so far as to employ the elemental theory in the titles of two of his plays: *Every Man in His Humour* and *Every Man out of His Humour.*

Shakespeare's contemporary medical scientists had concluded that in bodies with feeling, earth became black bile (melancholy), with the qualities cold and dry; water became phlegm, with the qualities cold and moist; air became blood with the qualities hot and moist; and fire became yellow bile (choler) with the qualities hot and dry.

The four primary elements would enter your body through the food you would consume. Food was thought to travel from the stomach to the liver, where body heat would change the elements into humors. Some of these humors were then passed through the veins to the heart, where they became "vital spirits" that dominated the trunk and lower limbs of the body. Other humors traveled up the arteries to the brain, where they became "animal spirits" that dominated the thought process. The stomach and liver were the keys to personality traits, and a person was literally considered to *be* what he ate.

Eating too much hot, dry beef would cause you to become a choleric person, easy to excite into anger because you had been eating too much "fire." Overindulgence in hot, moist foods made you consume too much air (blood), and you would become overconfident and "sanguine," or uncontrollably cheerful. Overeating cold, moist foods caused you to take in too much water (phlegm), and you would become sluggish or phlegmatic. Overeating cold, dry foods made you consume too much earth (melancholy), and you would become too sober and thoughtful. Diet and bloodletting were the major cure-alls for any illness.

needs Select four male and four female volunteers from the study group. Place two chairs side by side in the middle of the work area.

procedure One man sits in one of the chairs and the rest of the men group around him; a woman sits in the other chair and the rest of the women gather around her. All four men are going to play components of one man; all four women are going to play components of one woman. The two seated performers will function as Water (Phlegm). They are the only man and woman who can relate to each other, and they are the choice-making representatives of their respective groups. They alone may converse with regular volume; the other six people will have to whisper.

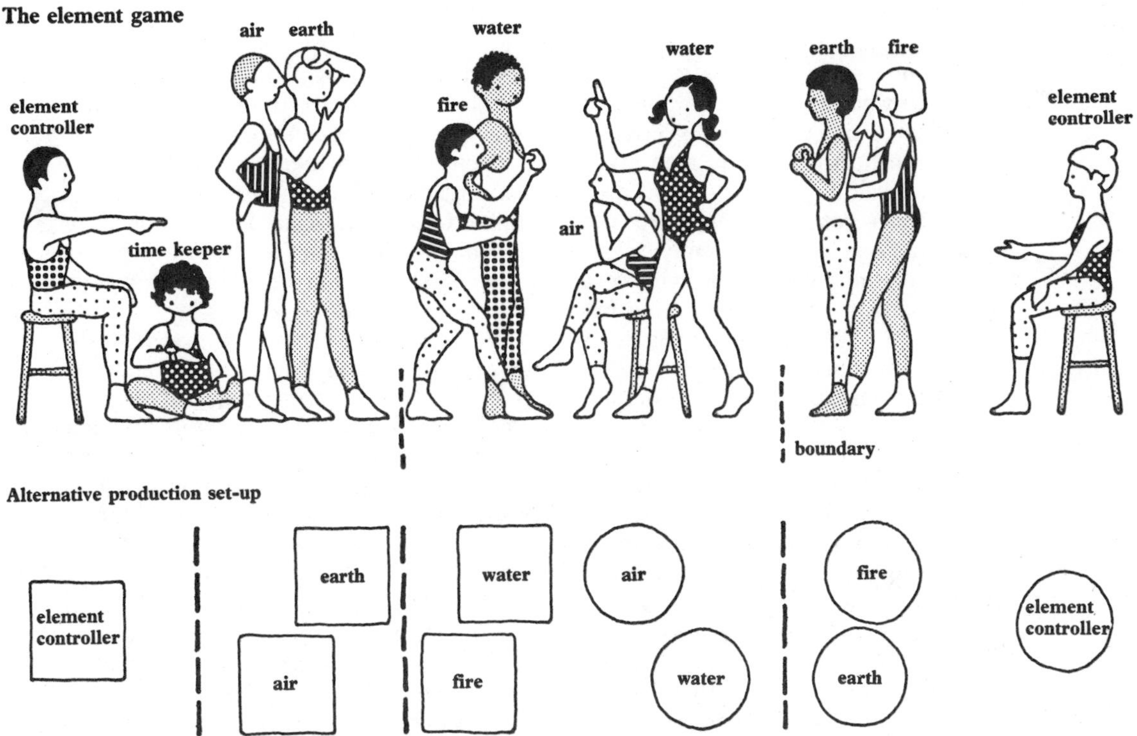

Water (Phlegm) is the logical vocal representative for each group for three reasons: the human body is basically water; water is changeable in form and will alter depending upon the other elements with which it is mixed; and a superabundance of water will cause you to be slow and phlegmatic at first, which is a good way to begin this exercise.

The Water spokesman for each group can be phlegmatic or emotionally erratic under the influence of his other elements. Just as the moon affects the sea, the moon, in the Elizabethan sense, can cause strange effects in a human being by exerting pressure on his water. The three performers behind each Water will play Earth, Air, and Fire, influencing Water to act according to what suits *their* individual Element-Humor's disposition. Earth (Melancholy) is a coolant, a mediator, and usually the most sober and thoughtful in his attempt to get Water to proceed along a sensible and cautious course of action in solving any dilemma. Air (Blood) cheerfully defines everything in terms of pain and pleasure for Water. Fire (Choler) is the speedy catalyst, defiant and quick to anger, who demands fast answers and solutions.

Each group of four actors will be assigned an objective to play; however, only Water in each group will actually be allowed to play against the other team vocally and physically. The three actors and three actresses playing Earth, Air, and Fire must remain solely within their own dispositions as they coach their respective Water. The actor and actress playing Water must conform to whatever their component elements tell them to do. In other words, they must pursue their objectives exactly as their components coach them. The Earth, Air, and Fire men must listen attentively to the woman playing Water as well as to their own Water representative. Each of the components must try to get his or her Water representative to act within the function of his or her own personal element. The Earth, Air, and Fire men take turns whispering to the male Water, who vocalizes their trains of thought. The female components carry on the same functions for their team.

The man and woman playing Water actually carry on the scene with each other for everyone else on their respective teams. They should maintain eye contact with each other and keep the flow of their scene going on between them as male and female Water. They should never pause to talk to their component elements. The component elements must stay behind the Waters and whisper in their ears. The man and woman playing Water should find themselves flowing from one tack to another, back and forth, as they pursue their objectives, all the while using different methods, depending upon which component element is influencing them at the time.

Any suggestions from the contrary-objectives list (see pp. 48–49) will work well for this exercise. After choosing a set of contrary objectives, the component elements should stand back and let the two Water spokesmen begin the exercise. After these two have set the stage, the Earth, Air, and Fire representatives should take very short turns working on Water in the center.

If your group chooses the situation in which the man wants to get the woman to agree to his immediate elopement plans and the woman wants to convince him that she would have a more meaningful life as a nun (see p. 48), the individual *male* arguments might sound like this:

male water: (whispering, because the two people playing Water must set the locale and the circumstances as a framework in which all eight people are to function) Honey, I got the car all packed outside. I have a couple hundred dollars in my wallet, and reservations at that wonderful little motel you suggested. Mass is just about over. Let's go and get married.

male fire: Tell her that this is the last day the license is good for.

male air: Put your arm around her; caress her shoulder.

male earth: Don't get too loud; you're in church. Nice people don't make scenes that attract attention.

female water: I'm sorry, John, I'm staying here in church. I've decided to be the bride of God instead. I'm going into a convent.

male water: A convent! (He is probably struck dumb by her statement. As Water, he will be phlegmatic until he decides how to approach her.) That doesn't make any sense!

male earth: Find out her motives. Prove to her that a heterosexual relationship—raising your children together—is the highest and most meaningful act which human beings are capable of.

male air: Remind her what a hot number she was at the drive-in movie last Friday night.

male fire: Tell her it was her idea to get married! You've paid for the reservation at the motel and the justice of the peace is waiting for you both right now!

Of course, the male Water must echo each of these ideas as well as respond to what the female Water replies. At first, you might encourage your study group to wade right into the exercise all at one time so that they each get the feeling of their specific function and the way their Element would play the objective. Remember that all four people on each team have the *same* objective, but each member uses different means to play this objective. After the exercise has proceeded for ten minutes or so, call a short halt and redefine the function of each Element. Elect a timekeeper and two Element controllers from the observers in the study group. From now on, every ninety seconds the Element controllers will decide whether Earth, Air, or Fire will move in to influence Water. The others must wait at least three feet away while, one at a time, each Element is allowed to work on Water for his team.

This adaptation operates much like a tag-team wrestling match. Each Element that moves in to compel Water to use his method of argument will be given one and a half minutes; then he must step back and allow another member of his elemental team to replace him. The timekeeper and the Element controllers should help you eliminate some of the frenetic quality of the exercise and allow the study group to zero in on each of the elemental components at work.

decisions

There are myriad ways to pursue an objective, rather than just hammer on one idea. The opposite methods represented by the different Element-Humors should demonstrate the variety of methods that you might use to play an objective.

Try to visualize the major roles in *Hamlet* as Element-Humors. Can you see Hamlet as Earth, Laertes as Fire, Horatio as Water, and Claudius as Air? Of course, each role contains the human possibility of going in any of four directions. For example, even the phlegmatic, cool Horatio becomes "rash as fire" in his last scene with Hamlet as he takes the poisoned cup to attempt suicide. The humors always cooperate, though they may seem to be functioning in opposite ways, and this creates a fully rounded characterization.

extension

Take the speech you performed to piano accompaniment and divide it into segments in which you feel that you are operating under the influence of a specific humor. Try performing the speech, concentrating on the humors that help you build intensity from one idea to the next. For example, while reading the following Macbeth speech, shift from one humor to another.

Suggestions for dominant humours

MACBETH
(I, vii, 1-28)

WATER
If it were done when 'tis done, then 'twere well
It were done quickly. If th' assassination
Could trammel up the consequence, and catch,
FIRE
With his surcease, success;// that but this blow
Might be the be-all and the end-all—here
But here, upon this bank and shoal of time,
EARTH
We'd jump the life to come.// But in these cases
We still have judgment here; that we but teach
Bloody instructions, which, being taught, return
AIR
To plague th' inventor;//this even-handed justice
Commends th' ingredients of our poison'd chalice
EARTH
To our own lips.// He's here in double trust:
First, as I am his kinsman and his subject—
Strong both against the deed; then, as his host,
Who should against his murderer shut the door,
Not bear the knife myself. Besides, this Duncan
Hath borne his faculties so meek, hath been
FIRE
So clear in his great office,// that his virtues
Will plead like angels, trumpet-tongu'd, against
The deep damnation of his taking-off;
And pity, like a naked newborn babe,
Striding the blast, or heaven's cherubim horsed
Upon the sightless couriers of the air,
Shall blow the horrid deed in every eye,
EARTH
That tears shall drown the wind.// I have no spur

Element-Humour shifts should be done at major transitions, almost always on the caesura in a line.

Macbeth sets the pace as Water-Phlegm, his basic self.

He becomes agitated, desirous of a fast answer under the dominance of the catalyst, Fire-Choler.

Macbeth shifts into considering his situation logically under the subduing influence of Earth-Melancholy.

Macbeth rapidly changes pace as he realizes how the murder will hurt his enjoyment of power by forcing him to stay alert to those who would do him harm. This preoccupation under the influence of Air-Blood triggers a whole new somber train of thought under the domination of Earth.

Macbeth compiles his list of reasons not to kill Duncan heatedly and emotionally; then Fire-Choler overcomes him again and he pushes for a quick decision, using erratic emotional imagery heavily laden with metaphors and similes. Such imagery is rare for Macbeth. Though he is slightly "flowery" with the murderers (III, i, 93-100) and extremely colorful in his lament for his wife (V, v, 17-28), he is usually terse and very direct. His final

To prick the sides of my intent, but only

Vaulting ambition, which o'erleaps itself

WATER
And falls on th' other side.// How now! What news?

decision as Earth in this speech does not mince words.

Macbeth returns to Water, his basic self, ready to interact with Lady Macbeth.

PHYSICALIZING A PERIOD WITH A POSE

needs Go to your library and check out some books that trace the development of the fine arts from the early Renaissance through Pieter Brueghel and El Greco. Examine slides or prints of the Sistine Chapel, "The Tower of Babel," "The View of Toledo," and "The Battle between Alexander and Darius."[9] Try to find a copy of Giacomo Arcimboldo's painting "The Allegory of Fire"; Arcimboldo depicted each of the element-humors in an almost expressionistic manner. Listen to some of music of the time; most college or public libraries have sets of records by the Bream Consort and madrigals from both the Jacobean and Elizabethan periods.[10]

discussion Separate the characters in each painting into representatives of earth, water, air, and fire. The later the painting is, the greater the fusion of Nature, God, and man should be. Notice the striving for individuality and the sense of something smoldering underneath a balanced view of the world.

Jacobean and Elizabethan costumes are generally tortured. They never flow *with* the line of the body as it moves; instead, they restrict your freedom of movement. If you hunch or bend over when you wear a costume with a boned corset you will find the bones poking your belly! It was not easy to be intimate casually during the Elizabethan and Jacobean periods.

procedure Choose a late Renaissance painting that reminds you of a scene you're rehearsing. Try to simulate the clothing as well as you can, using pieces from your own wardrobe or from your theatre costume shop. Adopt the same pose as the character in the painting. Motivate the pose. Decide why your character is comfortable in this position. Use the pose to create a secondary-characteristic exercise. Develop a pride in your new posture. Eliminate any tension you may feel. Walk around the work space with your new posture whenever you can motivate it as you rehearse your scene with your partner.

HANDLING A SOLILOQUY

procedure Choose a soliloquy from one of Shakespeare's seldom performed plays. For example, *Cymbeline, Timon of Athens, Coriolanus,* and *All's Well that Ends Well* contain excellent speeches for analysis, and they may also provide you with fresh classical audition material.

Gather the members of your study group and perform your soliloquy for them in three different ways: first, do it "naturalistically," purely for yourself; second, make contact by taking it completely *to* your audience; and finally, splash it a point directly over or between your observers' heads (or at an area in the *general* direction of several of them).

decisions

Did you change your objective to accommodate each new soliloquy method? In order to justify the first method, you must try to make a decision by yourself. To justify the second method, you need the audience's help in making your decision. Your third method also boils down to making a decision by yourself, but it is a much more theatrical method than the first, because you're sharing your ideas with the audience.

Ask your observers if they felt you were really pursuing an objective or if, instead, you seemed to be reciting the speech mechanically. When you delivered the soliloquy to a neutral point in the audience without making definite eye contact, did any of your observers feel the impulse to try to see what you were focusing on? If so, try shifting your neutral focus point several times during your speech, splashing different areas.

extension

Did you feel as though you were "reporting" an event, rather than experiencing it? This is the major difference between the craft of acting and the craft of oral interpretation. It is always more dramatic for an actor to make his decisions *onstage* during a soliloquy than to make them before he enters the stage.

If your soliloquy was designed to be funny or witty, you should probably make definite eye contact with your audience, especially if you're doing *Much Ado about Nothing* or *The Taming of the Shrew.* Repeat the soliloquy. Consciously attempt to make everything that you say a discovery that you can make onstage. All discoveries will lead you to a final decision that you will make during the speech. Try using the Inhalation Game (see p. 86) to give the impression of first-time illusion.

decisions

Shakespeare's actors performed on a thrust stage with an audience on three sides of them. The expensive seats were above the level of the stage, yet not too far from the action. This obliged the actors to lift their voices and maintain an erect posture as they performed emotionally and energetically in a presentation manner. Shakespeare's major competitive form of entertainment was bearbaiting. Obviously, a performer during the Jacobean period had to adapt his acting style to please such an audience, especially if he was all alone onstage performing a soliloquy.

suggestions

Decide what you need most in your soliloquy. Are you building up the nerve to convince yourself to do something? Do you need the audience's approval? Do you have an idea you can share with the audience as you make a decision? If your soliloquy is witty or funny, take it to the audience and share it. If the speech is serious, take it to yourself, but lift up your head so that the audience can see you make your decision.

Determine whether your character functions the way the other characters in the play do. Do any other characters have soliloquies? What are the decisions and objectives in their soliloquies? In *Richard III,* Richard is witty and seems to plan what is going to happen next, so he may use the audience; however, in the same play, Clarence would distract his audience if he took his speech about his nightmare (I, iv) directly to the house, especially since the jailer is also onstage at the time. Technically speaking, Richard is the only character in the play with a purely formal soliloquy.

Check the personal progression your character makes during his speech. What is his opinion at the beginning of the soliloquy and what is it at the end? How did he change his mind? What discoveries has he made during the speech? Can you create polarities in his position? Impose a total opposite for yourself to perform with the speech from beginning to end, even if there don't seem to be any real polarities there. If your character winds up loving at the end of a soliloquy, find a way to motivate trepidation or even anger at the beginning of the speech. Find the most divergent way of changing your mind onstage.

Decide how your speech relates to the rest of the play. Are the decisions you make here clear-cut? How far can you go vocally in relation to your personal "top"? How does this speech contribute to your progression within the entire play?

The following breakdown of Macbeth's soliloquy may help you employ these suggestions as you analyze your own choice of soliloquy material.

Paraphrasing your soliloquy in order to understand your progression

MACBETH
(I, vii, 1–28)

If it were done when 'tis done, then 'twere well
(I'll do it if it's over once I kill him.)
It were done quickly. If th' assassination
Could trammel up the consequence, and catch,
(I'll do it if I can be sure I'll get away with it.)
With his surcease, success; that but this blow
Might be the be-all and the end-all—here
But here, upon this bank and shoal of time,
(My wife and I would venture our souls for this power.)
We'd jump the life to come. But in these cases
(It might create a hell on earth for us.)
We still have judgment here; that we but teach
(He has so many friends, there are bound to be problems.)
Bloody instructions, which, being taught, return
(Someone may use my example and try to kill me.)
To plague th' inventor; this even-handed justice

Decisions about the soliloquy:

1. My objective is to decide if I have the nerve and the justification to kill Duncan.
2. I have little sense of humor about myself and certainly no sense of humor about what I intend to do to Duncan. I make my decisions independent of the audience.
3. Until line 7 I feel that speed and the hugeness of the crime will allow me

(I've always believed in an eye for an eye.)
Commends th' ingredients of our poison'd chalice
(Murdering me would be as justifiable as my killing Duncan.)
To our own lips. He's here in double trust:
(I know he believes in me.)
First, as I am his kinsman and his subject—
(He's related to me and I owe him fealty as my leader.)
Strong both against the deed; then, as his host,
Who should against his murderer shut the door,
(I would be violating natural law as well as man-made codes.)
Not bear the knife myself. Besides, this Duncan
Hath borne his faculties so meek, hath been
(He has been humble and just as a king.)
So clear in his great office, that his virtues
Will plead like angels, trumpet-tongu'd, against
(Everyone adores him as our sovereign.)
The deep damnation of his taking-off;
And pity, like a naked newborn babe,
Striding the blast, or heaven's cherubim, horsed
(Even God would be angry with me and punish me!)
Upon the sightless couriers of the air,
Shall blow the horrid deed in every eye,
(All Scotland would weep for Duncan!)
That tears shall drown the wind. I have no spur
To prick the sides of my intent, but only
(I have no real, justifiable reason to kill him.)
Vaulting ambition, which o'erleaps itself
(I'm ashamed of dishonorable aspirations.)
And falls on th' other side. How now! What news?

to get away with the murder. Then I begin to consider all the reasons why I shouldn't go through with it.

4. Lady Macbeth has a soliloquy when she reads the letter to herself (I, v, 13–28), and Banquo has a soliloquy when he remembers that the Witches told him that he will be the progenitor of kings (III, i, 1–10). Neither Banquo nor Lady Macbeth jokes with the audience. My soliloquy will be most effective if I lift my discoveries to a neutral point in the house so that the audience can see my transitions.

5. I discover that I cannot justify killing Duncan, but I would still like to be king if I could get away with the murder honorably.

chapter 13
STYLE ACTING 3—THE RESTORATION AND THE GEORGIAN PERIOD

FLIRTING IN THE PROMENADE

Restoration theatre was a coterie product of the aristocracy. Only the upper classes could afford such a luxury as attending a play. The aristocracy enjoyed its position of superiority and flaunted its wealth and its manners. Artificiality became the vogue and, naturally, the theatre reflected the spirit of its audience.

needs Because stylish manners and period gestures are so integral to the study of Restoration and eighteenth-century acting, you should begin your work by assembling props and costumes that will help you appreciate the external manifestations with which your character would be familiar. Go to your college or theatre costume shop for your paraphernalia. A man will need a three-quarter-length cape, a three-cornered hat, a sword and buckler, a cane or walking stick, and a pair of high-heeled shoes. A woman will need a wide collapsible fan (with about a ten-inch radius), and an adjustable rehearsal skirt equipped with metal underbracings. Feminine fashion moves from the horizontal farthingale and bum roll to a more circular type of hoop under the skirt, and the squared bodice changes to a "V" neckline as the Restoration shifts into the more modest Georgian period.

If prepared costume pieces are unavailable, try using your imagination to create satisfactory substitutes. To give the effect of wearing a cape, a man might either pin a twin-bed sheet around his shoulders or simply drape a raincoat over his shoulders and fasten it only at the neck. A man can easily reproduce the angle and effect of high-heeled shoes by taping wooden blocks to the heels of his own shoes or by putting rubber doorstops at the back of his heels inside his shoes. The block or doorstop will raise the back of his foot about one-and-a-half inches, giving him a forward tilt that he must learn to control by altering his posture. Men should roll their pants legs up to the knee so that they are cognizant of "making a leg" as they bow or greet a lady. A woman can fake a farthingale or a hoop by pinning a sheet to her waist and fastening either a hula hoop or an inflated inner tube around her hips underneath the sheet.

Handkerchiefs, which both men and women used frequently, should be carried by all the performers.

procedure All the members of the study group don their costume pieces and assemble for a promenade. The men form a large circle and walk clockwise around the periphery of the work space; the women form a smaller circle and walk counterclockwise inside the men's circle. Everyone takes three steps forward, then both circles halt. Each man and woman turns to the nearest person of the opposite sex and communicates the following objectives nonverbally: I want to impress her (him), to flirt with her (him), to invite her to go to dine with me (to get him to ask me out), and to assure myself of a sexual promise later on in the evening.

All the participants should insist upon economy from themselves and try to use their costume pieces, props, and posture creatively to accomplish their objectives. After three minutes, each performer regains any composure that may have been lost, bows or curtsies, and walks three more steps to find a new partner.

GOING TO BATH TO SOCIALIZE

needs Duplicate or post the following list:

Name	*Physical/emotional trait or problem*	*Objective*
Roger Backbite	harelip	To find a wealthy benefactor
Lillywhite Constant	clubfoot	
Manly Goodbody	gouty toe	To attract a lovely lady/handsome man
Thoughtful Holy	fallen arches	
Polly Pimpleflesh	knock-knees	To begin an exciting triangular affair
Frances Fidgetflesh	horrible acne	
Anxious Codpiece	pockmarks	To make husband/wife jealous
Sally Strumpet	warts or moles	
Pureheart Sobbing	bad breath	To pass myself off as a great lover
Witty Comment	crippled arm	
Constant Hornplugger	toothache	To pass myself off as an eunuch
Barry Bumpkin	gigantic nose	

Merry Mouthoff
Sir Lordover Littleguy
Smiling Thoughtless
Dr. Decibel Doubletalk
Miss Fanny Teaseley
Lord P. Elvis Thruster
Dr. Dustin Fuzzybrain
Rotter Noseful
Dafney Bifocal
Sir Perilous Pantsripper
Miss Fanciful Dangerbreast
Lady Begging-Wanton
Baron von Passionbreast
Limpest Handshake
Lord Boastful Rustysheath
Robroy Daggertongue
Sir Aimright O'Buckler
Miss Broadbeam-Stripwell
Lord Pecunious Slobberlip
Miss Fasting Neversmirtch
Lady Eaglebill-Grossbeak

trick knee
chafed thighs
continual sexual arousement
ulcers
asthmatic wind
lisp or baby-talk "R"
extreme myopia
stuffed nose and sinuses
deafness
cleft palate
stiff neck and spine
flinch or shoulder twitch
tobacco cough
dry lips, habitually moistened
constant laughter
constant sadness

To con money from the wealthy
To con money from the poor
To win compliments with my wit
To win compliments with my beauty without ever venturing anything
To consume as much good food and drink as is possible
To blackmail as many dupes as possible
To live by the honor code at all times
To spread the word of the Scriptures
To ascertain who are having affairs

procedure Each member of the study group chooses one item from each column on the list—a name, a physical/emotional aberration, and a basic objective. These items do not necessarily have to be combined in such a way that they produce a stereotype: for example, Mr. Rotter Noseful—stuffed nose and sinuses—To blackmail as many dupes as possible. Mixing up the categories is much more fun: for instance, Mr. Perilous Pantsripper—extreme myopia—To get women to fight for my favors. Each participant must digest his three items and create a characterization out of them, justifying his name, motivating his physical/emotional aberration, and selecting a need to substantiate his objective. And each should use all the necessary costume pieces and props, such as a fan (perhaps to hide a flaw) and a handkerchief for a woman, a walking stick, a tri-cornered hat, and a handkerchief for a man.

Set up two small circles of chairs at opposite ends of the work space. The men congregate at one end of the room, the women at the other. Use your imagination and motivate this exercise as seriously as you can. Both groups are to assume that they have gathered around a small, shallow pool of healing waters, rather like an indoor swimming pool of miniature size. The pool smells slightly of sulphur; the waters are warm. These are the restorative waters at Bath which date back to the Roman occupation of the British Isles. Each member of both groups is to bathe his or her afflicted area (the physical handicap) in a polite way, socializing and getting to know the other members of his or her group within their characterizations. Discuss your ailments; introduce one another by name. Relax into playing your character. Do not *try* to be theatrical.

discussion The bulk of the exercises in this chapter are an attempt to help you and your group relax into appropriate manners, gestures, and dress so that you will not be super-conscious of these problems when you play your scenes. Eventually, these externals will become second nature to you. You cannot play a scene with simplicity if you are constantly worried about externals. You must learn to find a way to *be* class rather than try to *act* class or you will succeed only in playing an attitude. Find the real human needs under the glossy artificial exterior.

suggestions Pick one or two partners and choose a scene from each of the following plays: William Congreve's *The Way of the World*, George Farquhar's *The Beaux Stratagem* (both Restoration); and Richard Brinsley Sheridan's *The Rivals* and Oliver Goldsmith's *She Stoops to Conquer* (both Georgian). These four plays have excellent twosome and threesome scenes for study.

Notice that there is a good deal of openness in sexual relations in the Restoration, as opposed to the more sedate and self-conscious handling of sex in the Georgian period. Most critics attribute this metamorphosis to the need to accommodate a new, mixed audience of both the exclusive Restoration aristocracy and the prudish middle class that rose to power during the Industrial Revolution of the Georgian period. However, you can't avoid the sexual undercurrent in Georgian plays, though sexual topics certainly are not handled as freely as such playwrights as Congreve and Farquhar handle them. The Georgian period, like the later Victorian period, shunned the public display of flagrant affairs. If you are working on a Restoration play, go ahead and flirt openly, but if it's a Georgian play, flirt secretly!

CREATING A VALENTINE

procedure After the men and women who participated in the two preceding exercises have grown accustomed to their new handicaps and their new character traits, they should again form two circles, as in Flirting in the Promenade Exercise. Proceed slowly! The objective, again, is to attract someone of the opposite sex and vie for her (his) affection within the scope of your character. After reading the suggested plays, you will have a better grasp of how to use the tortured, valentine-like language of a Faulkland from Sheridan's *The Rivals*, or the foppish, cutting remarks of a Witwould and the villainous insinuations of a Fainall from Congreve's *The Way of the World*.

Every ten minutes you must bow or curtsy and leave your current partner for another partner in the circle. Everyone in the group should make at least three changes of partners. After the third shift and adjustment, choose one of the first three partners with whom your character was compatible. Do the promenade together once again, conversing with each other as you arrange a tête-à-tête.

The gentleman escorts the lady to her seat on the periphery and sits beside her. If there is an odd number of people in your group, one person may have two lovers competing for his (her) affection. Relax and enjoy your partner with a spirit of serious fun. Discover your partner's name, aberration, and objective.

suggestion

Create a valentine for the lover you found during the promenade. Try to incorporate in your valentine all the character quirks that you have discovered about him (her).

Although giving valentines was particularly popular during the Victorian period, this custom certainly was not neglected during the Restoration, and was quite the vogue during the Georgian period. Valentines were minor works of art, often replete with cupids, classical allusions, Baroque settings, and occasionally religious symbols of undying love.

Very often anagrams were woven into a puzzle-like design that the recipient had to figure out in order to get the message. Occasionally a valentine was constructed like a crossword puzzle, but more often it featured a special way of opening so that the message was revealed slowly. In order to create a valentine with flair and individuality, you will have to consider your own traits as well as those of your partner. If you want to research your valentine, you might examine the book *Victoriana*, as well as the flowery style of speech in the plays you are reading.[1] Try to emulate the flow of the well-balanced prose of Congreve and Sheridan. If you prefer poetry, the simplest method is to pick out a

Example of valentine

fold-out flaps

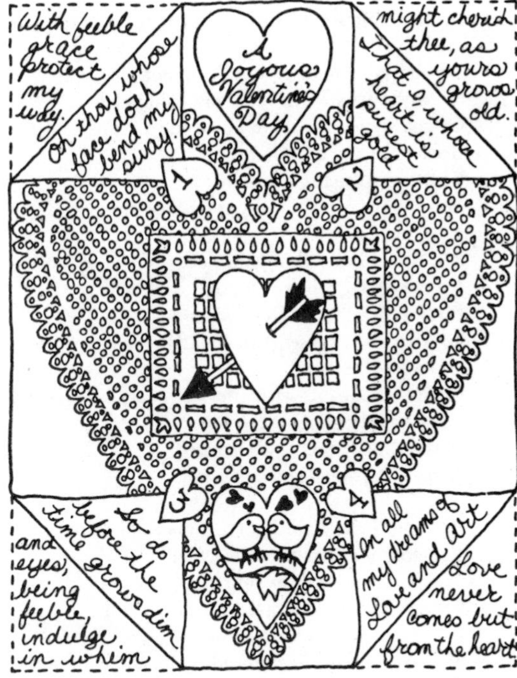

Shakespearean sonnet, retain the same last word in each line, and merely rewrite the first part of each line to suit your purposes, using the versification rules. The two valentines used as examples (on p. 179 and below) are not precise models to follow. Create what you need for your partner that satisfies your character objectives.

Valentine

Addressed in tender memory of past escapades to the Masters Felix Faultfinder, Manly Goodpants, Barry Bumpkin, Sir Roger Rightoff, the Baron von Passionbreast, Artful Sneerwell, and most particularly and confessionally to his most pure soul—Thoughtful Holy, from Miss Sally Strumpet.

Upon this day of red and white
I now announce and put in right
All the little rendez-vous
With each and every one of you.

You may think me crude and bold,
Ingrateful of the trust I hold
On your private little secrets
And your manly têtes-à-têtes.
Each of you will see the other
As each you are, in Lust, a brother.

To you my name is Sally Strumpet,
So forward I step to blow my trumpet
Of ghastly wrongs done all to me
Because of my deformity. . . .
Your use of me is très injust
When your eye is on my forty-inch bust.

Ah, Barry, Barry Bumpkin dear,
I was sleeping when you crept near
Playing Boucher's "Sheperdess"—
So what if I exposed two breasts?

Manly Goodpants with tricks to play,
I saw you weeping in the hay.
Manly Goodpants you I trusted
And my farthingale you dusted.

But you, Felix Faultfinder, round and sweet,
You told me that I had big feet,
And so to put you in your pips,
I showed you the proportion of my hips.

Sir Roger Rightoff, you said, "Oh, some showers!"
When we were yonder picking flowers;
And I believed you when you chucked my chin—
How nice to feel the rain with skin.

From across the hall I felt your stare
And from that moment I was bare—
Baron von Passionbreast was my all;
Too bad he was so shamefully small.

Artful Sneerwell had eyes like hounds
And all he wanted were my mounds,
And so I showed them to you all
And all you did was faint and fall.

Limpest Handshake, you were funny—
All your fumbling and your nose so runny,
No warrior you! You're not so bold!
You wouldn't even take a hold!

So to you all I say good-by
And none of you will pine and die.
You made me live up to my name
And I merit only half the blame.

Therefore I am renouncing all
And going to live in yonder hall.
There my purity I'll regain,
And all again will be the same.

Now through prayer and reverence
Thoughtful Holy will take my pence.
Whate'er he says, I'll do, I'll do—
And I will love him true, so true.

I'll play the Holy Mother and sigh
While yonder he ascends on high,
And I on billowing pillows lie;
He, to my breasts, will come and die.

I'll play the greatest part of all—
Why, I'll be Eve and cause the Fall!
I'll be the first Original Sin;
My self-respect again I'll win.

PERFORMING THE VALENTINE

needs If you have a phonograph handy, set a mood by playing Bach, Handel, Vivaldi, or Haydn softly in the background. Try to locate any music by Henry Purcell, the great English Restoration composer who wrote music for the elaborate, operatic restagings of Shakespeare's plays produced by Sir William Davenant.

The following quotation from Samuel Pepys' *Diary* clearly demonstrates the difference between Jacobean and Restoration dramaturgy. Pepys refers to Thomas Betterton's version of Shakespeare's *Macbeth* as it may have been conceived by Davenant: "Here [at the Duke's House where it was most frequently done] we saw 'Macbeth,' which, though I have seen it often, yet it is one of the best plays for a stage, and variety of dancing and music that I ever saw."[2] It is surely safe to assume that Betterton's *Macbeth* with "variety" and "dancing and music" was a far cry from Shakespeare's intention for the staging of the play.[3] Pepy's *Diary* may help you grasp the uniqueness of the Restoration spirit.

procedure Clear the center of the work area except for two chairs which should be placed side by side. The participants in the last exercise put on their costumes and sit next to their lovers on the periphery of the work space. Each pair of lovers (with the gentleman escorting the lady) will come to the center of the room, sit, and read their valentines to each other. The study group should choose one of two approaches: either each pair of lovers should pretend they are alone or all the participants should pretend to be at a gathering of their social circle so that they may enjoy the valentines together. Try to create a coffeehouse atmosphere similar to that in the first act of Congreve's *The Way of the World.*

decisions Did you pay attention to the typical posture and manners of the period? A gentleman should always try to pivot so that his lady takes the outward swing, showing off her gown. He should never sit when his lady stands! If you are playing the part of the gentleman, take your lady's hand at waist level so that neither of you needs to strain. Give her plenty of time to maneuver her gown. As you move between chairs, be careful to allow the lady enough room to handle the width of her skirt. Let her precede you. Be economical and gracious.

PHYSICALIZING RESTORATION AND GEORGIAN GESTURES

needs An accurate view of the extremes found in these two periods can be achieved only by comparing the relaxed and balanced loveliness typical of the paintings of Thomas Gainsborough and Sir Joshua Reynolds with the frenetic and caricaturish cartoons of William Hogarth. Hogarth's satiric engravings "The Harlot's Progress" and "The Rake's Progress" are graphic portrayals of the character traits listed in the second exercise in this chapter.[4] Hogarth chose to depict the ugliness and the disease of his times. He painted the hypocritical artificialities, the overdone makeup that was used to hide pimples, warts, the pockmarks of smallpox, and the lesions caused by the ravages of venereal disease. Read Samuel Pepys' *Diary* for a human portrait of the Restoration. Pepys fills his pages with a recital of his own physical ailments and those of his wife, along with their view of their world and their candid comments on the theatre of the time.[5] Anyone who finds himself enchanted with this general period will want to read in addition to Pepys' comments, the autobiography *An Apology for the Life of Mr. Colley Cibber, Comedian.*[6]

The Restoration aristocracy was extremely proud of its culture and very protective of its social position. Ballet lessons were quite popular as a further means to separate the rich from the "have-nots." As you put the finishing touches on your scene, remember that your choice of pose must have real human motivation, and that you should be alert to the effect your pose will have on your fellow performers. Always maintain your balance by keeping your weight evenly distributed between your feet. Take small, graceful steps, and make easy semicircular gestures. Any kind of overextension will call attention to itself. Of course, there are characters like Lady Wishfort in Congreve's *The Way of the World* whose comedy stems from their awkwardness; nevertheless, it is wise to learn how to do a movement correctly before you experiment with variations.

procedure

Set up two high-backed chairs at opposite ends of your work space and try the following balletic workout with your scene partner (the sequence of movements is the same for both of you).

Stand sideways to the back of your chair at an easy arm's distance and grip the top of the chair comfortably. Watch both your own movement and your partner's out of the corner of your eye. Flirt with each other as you do the next parts of the exercise.

If your right side is to the chair, extend your left leg directly out in front of you. Touch the floor with the tip of your toe. Point your toe, keeping your leg perfectly straight. Pivot your leg from the bowl of your hip, turning your knee and the top of your foot outward. Repeat this four times. Now about-face, and go through the whole procedure with your other leg. Check to see if your partner is admiring you.

Drop your arm gently and circle the work space and exchange chairs with your partner. Try to keep your toes pointed out and touching the ground at all times. You should be walking in a modified fourth position.

Grip the back of the chair just as you did before. Raise the opposite arm in front of you in a graceful curve (nothing in nature exists in a straight line), until your arm is even with your solar plexus. Sweep the arm gently down and out, drawing a quarter circle in the air, then gently back. About-face. Repeat the gesture with the other arm. All your gestures should appear to be effortless.

Promenade back to your original chair. Combine your leg gestures as described above with the arm gestures you performed first, and breathe relaxedly in time to the rhythm of the movement. Stand with your feet about a foot apart. Point your toes out, and you are in second position. Do a graceful, moderately deep knee-bend. Keep your torso erect. Rise. Repeat the knee-bend with the arm gesture four times. Wink at your partner each time you rise. For a lady, Restoration flirting is very different from twentieth-century flirting (Zsa Zsa and Eva Gabor are two of the most prominent Restoration-type flirters today). Twentieth-century clothing tends to hug a woman's hips and pelvis and to accentuate her legs. Restoration garments featured a tight, low bodice to plump up and expose as much of the breasts as possible without quite letting the nipples show. Cleavage and breasts were the major areas of sexual concentration. Concentrate your flirting in this area.

suggestions Try to find an external image for your role. For example, in Sheridan's *The Rivals*, Captain Absolute and Faulkland and their ladies, Lydia and Julia, are definitely Gainsborough people, whereas Acres, Sir Lucius, Lucy, Fag, and Mrs. Malaprop all spring from Hogarth's caricatures. Select a character from a period painting and move around the work space as you imagine that character would move. Create a psychological gesture from a Restoration dance step. Sir Lucius O'Trigger may discover that his everyday walking rhythm really adds up to a jig![7]

CREATING A PERIOD MAKE-UP

procedure After considering how your objectives and manners would affect your outward appearance, try to make yourself up to look like the character you have chosen. Motivate every shade, every line you apply. Use a Gainsborough, Reynolds, or Hogarth picture as your model. If you need suggestions for materials and how to apply them, pick up Richard Corson's thorough study, *Stage Makeup*.[8]

Begin with a regular corrective base and then launch into the camouflage that made the Restoration and Georgian eras unique and often outlandish. Overdone make-up and paste-on patches were fashionable for both men and women. If your character might have had pockmarks, a wart, a growth, flourishing pimples, draw any such disfigurements on your face first. Now experiment with ways to cover up whatever blemishes you've added.

Fag and Sir Lucius in Sheridan's *The Rivals*, and certainly Mrs. Malaprop, would try to conceal any facial flaws with patches. Goldsmith's *She Stoops to Conquer* takes place in the country rather than in the city, so there would not be such a heavy emphasis on make-up. However, Hastings is truly fashionable, a model of Georgian good taste (perhaps one patch). And while Tony Lumpkin's mother is *trying* to look as chic and citified as she possibly can, she might end up wearing what looks like a parody of stylish city make-up.

Just about all the characters in Congreve's *The Way of the World* might use make-up; even Mirabell and Millamant might apply one tiny patch or perhaps, high up on the cheekbone, a blue star to match a bit of eye shadow. Naturally, Lady Wishfort is hideously overdone. The maids in the three plays, particularly Lucy, Foible, and Kate Hardcastle (when she "stoops"), rarely use make-up. Tony Lumpkin wouldn't touch the stuff. However, Tony ought to have a ruddy, natural complexion and a red nose from boozing. Bumpkins like Sir Wilful, Sir Lucius, and Bob Acres might be a bit of sloppy with their patches—their true country flavor is their most dominant external trait.

If a man had had a really bad case of the pox, he might draw—in some detail—a carriage on one cheek, reins across the center of his face, and horses on his other cheek. His morning toilet might take him three hours or more! Stars were most commonly used for concealment or enhancement. Hogarth's work is full of them. A regular dime-store star of the grade-school variety and some spirit gum will do the trick. An "overdone" lady might have a tiny bird, perhaps even two doves, drawn as a patch. Try drawing some of the designs yourself, or cut them out of a magazine and paste them on your face. Naturally, the patch must be suitable for the character; and it should be recognizable and simple in its design, or an audience, seeing the character from a distance, might wonder what on earth seems to be "stuck to that actor's face."

Once a modern audience has recognized a role from a distance and has seen the performer under the role, it will accept nearly anything.[9] Lady Wishfort first appears in Congreve's *The Way of the World* when she begins the third act with a scene in which she is putting on her make-up to receive her suitor; Mrs. Malaprop's initial scene in Sheridan's *The Rivals* is a domestic scene in which she scolds Lydia in Lydia's boudoir; and Mrs. Hardcastle first turns up in Goldsmith's *She Stoops to Conquer* in an early-morning scene with her husband. In all three plays, the "overdone" lady may first appear partially made-up, so that the audience will see the actress under the make-up as a real human being. From this first appearance on, these three ladies may add more and more make-up as their day progresses throughout the action of the play.

If you are a male, you might feel odd putting on heavy facial grease or pancake to produce an artificiality the audience will accept as your conventional street make-up. Don't sacrifice your masculinity and begin to get campy. The Restoration and Georgian Englishman was the man who built an empire that stretched around the world. Try to find the proud peacock under the artificiality. Perhaps our New Orleans "fancy man" gambler is the closest American counterpart of the Restoration man.

During the eighteenth century, women's hair styles grew progressively more elaborate. Millamant in Congreve's *The Way of the World* would find ways of adorning her natural hair; however, Lydia and Julia in Sheridan's *The Rivals* would have to accustom themselves to wearing a headdress supported with wire and pads, powdered and pomaded into a coiffure that might reach a height of several feet! A Georgian lady would obviously have to maintain an erect posture. Lydia and Julia would most probably decorate their hair with strings of pearls, ribbons, and jewels, and perhaps an ostrich plume; however, Mrs. Hardcastle and Mrs. Malaprop might have gone in for stuffed birds, fake fruit and vegetables, and miniature portraits of their acquaintances as hair adornments. A woman might even use a ship in full sail as decoration for a coiffure.[10] Ladies' faces may appear strikingly white. You can get the right color by mixing some Clown White into your base or by using a white powder to finish the base. Abundant dry cheek rouge and strong red lip coloring are an absolute must in getting the proper doll-like effect.

decisions Does your make-up suit your character's objectives? Can you find a humanness under your make-up? Does your make-up help you feel expensive and special? Can you see yourself with a strong tendency toward hedonism and an absolute disrespect for conventional sacraments like marriage?

CREATING GAMES FOR REHEARSING RESTORATION AND GEORGIAN PLAYS

Exploring vulnerability

This game is tailored for Hastings and Neville in Goldsmith's *She Stoops to Conquer*, Faulkland and Julia in Sheridan's *The Rivals*, and possibly Petulant, Witwould, and Lady Wishfort in Congreve's *The Way of the World.* If your character seems to be in love; if he seems to be emotionally fragile; if he is easily hurt; if his objective is to test another's affection toward him; or if he simply seems to suffer from an inability to either give or accept love, try this exercise. A strong and willful performer who has a tendency to "show" the audience how hurt he is getting rather than letting himself "be" hurt, or who always feels that he must be "on top," may also find this method helpful.

procedure You and your partner stand at opposite sides of the work space (about fifteen feet apart) and say your lines to each other. Try to caress each other with each word: slowly reach out and caress each other's face and body across the distance.

Add the phrase "Please don't hurt me" to the end of every single line you speak. Couple piano notes with this exercise, tapping a slightly higher note every time either of you says, "Please don't hurt me."

decisions Try to continue saying "Please don't hurt me" with your eyes when you repeat the scene. Saying such a poignant phrase while raising your pitch should lead you into a theatrical romanticism.[11]

Exploring competition

This exercise is useful for both Mirabell and Millamant in Congreve's *The Way of the World* and young Absolute and Lydia in Sheridan's *The Rivals;* it may also help anyone who plays a scene with Tony Lumpkin in Goldsmith's *She Stoops to Conquer.*

procedure Both scene partners remove all rings and watches. Stand facing each other about a foot and a half apart. Stretch out your hands, palms up, toward your partner at about waist level. Your partner places his hands, palms down, directly *over* your hands without quite touching you. Disregard any blocking you may have established and begin your scene in this position. Play your scene with as much eye contact and involvement as possible, but whenever you feel that you can score a point, try to slap the backs of your partner's hands. The moment you miss his hands, change hand positions with him. Every time you hit even one of his hands, you score a point. Only the partner who has his hands on the bottom can slap; consequently, only he can score points.

decisions This game often causes a physical exasperation that can be transformed into a mental and emotional spark for the scene. Repeat the game whenever you feel your scene is losing its snap.[12]

Using beat objectives as asides

procedure Simply begin doing your scene together. Before each line you speak, turn toward the house and tell the audience what your beat objective is for your upcoming line, then play the line to your partner. Maintain your intensity with each other, even as you play your objectives out to the house.[13]

decisions Try to develop a mental attitude toward playing within a realistic convention with each other while using a theatrical convention for the audience. You don't need excessive volume to play asides. Restoration theatres were fairly small and the audience was usually composed of the intelligentsia. Maintain your clarity of direction. Look directly either at your partner or at your audience when using the aside technique.

Punctuating with a fan or a cane

explanation Try this exercise if your objective is to score points on your partner in an argument.

First the lady should practice snapping her fan. Hold one of the two supports on either side of your fan. Revolve your hand downward with a flick of the wrist so that the weight of the opposite support stick falls, opening the fan abruptly with a loud snap.

Sit down on a bench beside your partner. Choose a contrary-objective exercise and perform it, snapping your fan or tapping your cane immediately after you make a point. Never snap your fan before or during a line or the sound of the snap may obscure some of your words. Motivate each fan snap or each tap of the cane. Incorporate this trait into your objectives and into your character.

procedure Behave as though you were about to speak, and draw attention to yourself, either by snapping your fan or by tapping your cane. See how many different ways you can use this physical "gimmick" instead of speaking. As your partner turns to listen to what you have to say, shrug and pretend that you have changed your mind. Maintain a smile whenever you can. If you feel angry at your partner within the context of the scene, keep trying to smile, but let your fan or your cane snap and tap with your vexation. Either make points or let off steam, using your fan or your cane. Ask an observer to keep score for both of you when you try to incorporate this game into your structured scene for group criticism. Score a point for every *motivated* set of snaps or taps.

chapter 14
STYLE ACTING 4— SHAW, WILDE, AND COWARD

RAPID RATE OF UTTERANCE[1]

procedure

Gather your study group into a large circle in the center of the work area. (You can also do this exercise with just one partner.) Hand out copies of the "Grip-Top Sock" below and have everyone look it over. There are a few snags in it. Here are some pointers to help you perform the poem correctly: breathe only where there is a double slash at the end of a line; give "pukka" the long "u" sound, as in "pūke"; remember that here the word "super" is correctly pronounced "s-you-per"; watch the most difficult spots where the rhythm may falter—that is, at "trick" in the eighth line and "blotched" in the eleventh.

Chant the poem, carefully pronouncing every syllable so that each word is absolutely distinct. Your ultimate aim is to articulate at a rapid rate. Synchronize your breathing from person to person until the entire group has the sense of a Gestalt group rhythm. Once again, chant the poem in unison to your rhythm. After you have gone through the exercise twice, split up the lines. Everyone around the circle takes one line in succession as it becomes his turn. Try to maintain the Gestalt group rhythm. The minute one person fails by only a fraction of a beat or by a mispronunciation, the whole group must start over again from the beginning.

Grip-Top Sock

Give me the gift of a grip-top sock,//
A dip drape, ship-shape, tip-top sock://
Not your spiv-slick, slap-stick, slip-slop stock,
But a plastic elastic grip-top sock.//
None of your fantastic slack swap-slop
From a slapdash flash-cash haberdash shop//
Not a knick-knack, knit-lock, knock-kneed knickerbocker sock
With a mock-shot, blob-mottled trick tick-tocker clock.//
Not a super-sheer, seersucker pūkka sack-smock sock://
Not a spot-speckled, frog-freckled cheapshake's sock
Off a hotch-potch, moss-blotched botched scotch block.//
Nothing slip-slop, drip-drop,
Flip-flop or clip-clop://
Tip me to a tip-top
Grip-top sock.

extension Try taking two lines rather than one for each turn. If you are having trouble with the poem, try to relax into a smile when you say your line. The smile should help you place your words in the front of your mouth where you can control them.

Avoid counting ahead around the circle to figure out which line is coming your way. You'll only tighten yourself more if you try to plan ahead. Try this exercise with your scene partner every time you rehearse until you are capable of doing the poem very quickly without losing a single sound or beat.

variation Clap the underlying rhythm very lightly to establish a group metronome. Accelerate the clapping so that the rhythm is twice as fast and then four times as fast as it was originally. Now decelerate the rhythm, and as a group begin to speak the poem slowly, uttering every single sound in the entire poem, crawling from syllable to syllable in every word. Then speed up again, but this time try hard to hit every single sound. Once the group gets really good at the exercise, each person in the circle may take only one word at a time as he takes his turn. Maintain the basic poetic rhythm as well as you can.

decisions Were you counting ahead? Do you tend to do this in a play?—that is, do you rehearse your next line while someone else is speaking? This will trap you! You may be setting a pattern that will throw you if anything forces you to deviate from that pattern in any way. The character you are playing couldn't possibly think ahead before receiving the motivation for your next line. Take the time to go through your lines *well before* a performance. Never rehearse your lines in the wings while waiting for an entrance. Mouthing your lines at the last minute or as your partner says his lines defeats you mentally because you are admitting your fear of fumbling to yourself.

Try to avoid racing through your words because you feel inadequate to Shaw, Coward, or Wilde's intellectual verbosity. Slow your role down until you can master it, then speed it up. Remember that it will take some time for your audience to hear and digest what you have to say.

Your character must remain true to his own rhythm. That rhythm should complement the rhythms of the other characters onstage with you. If you are entering a scene which has already begun onstage, listen to the rhythm that your fellow actors have established so that you maintain the pace. Every new entrance onstage should cause a variation in the rhythm. Compare the intellectual rhythm of Henry Higgins, the logical and methodical rhythm of Pickering, the clever and materialistic rhythm of Doolittle, with the naive and emotional rhythm of Eliza in Shaw's *Pygmalion.* Each of Shaw's characters functions with a precise inner tempo.

suggestions Choose a new partner and select a scene from Shaw's *Pygmalion, Man and Superman,* or *Candida;* or from Wilde's *The Importance of Being Earnest;* or from Coward's *Blithe Spirit, Private Lives,* or *Fallen Angels.* Begin a character analysis and decide upon your character's rhythm as opposed to that of the other character(s) in your scene.

RECOGNIZING TONAL VARIATION[2]

procedure Begin a line run-through with your partner. Concentrate on your objectives and try to contact your partner as you look directly at him. Turn out all the lights and repeat the scene. Try even harder to contact your partner as you run through your scene in the dark. Put your feelings and energy exclusively into your voice. Concentrate on your *tones.*

decisions Where do you feel you are speaking from in your body? Once again, consider Shaw's *Pygmalion.* It seems that Higgins speaks from his head with intellectual head tones; Eliza from her heart with straightforward honesty; Doolittle from his materialistic "gut"; and Pickering from his chest or his throat with judicious tones. Though you can't change your body around, you can find a way to focus your tone into what Constantin Stanislavski and Michael Chekhov call your "imaginary center."[3]

Variation 1

Musically speaking, Higgins may be a clarinet or a flute; Eliza a violin; Pickering perhaps an oboe; and Doolittle a bassoon or maybe a bass violin (just to keep family ties with Eliza). Choose a musical instrument for your character. Relax your inhalation down into your breathing center, then yawn up a sound from your "imaginary center." Try to duplicate the sound of the instrument you have chosen.

extension Turn the lights off. Begin the scene again. Try to maintain your particular tone and your specific rhythm depending upon your instrument. Naturally, your character must sound like a human being, but you should find some fluctuation in tone by using your choice of a musical instrument as a model. It should be possible to orchestrate an entire play using every actor as a different instrument. Turn the lights back on and try the scene again. Try to stay true to your new tone and rhythm.

variation Ask everyone in your study group to create a character from a different musical instrument. Try reciting "Grip-Top Sock" again, with everyone remaining as true as he can to his individual musical tone and rhythm.

George Bernard Shaw was a music critic for many years. He was particularly fond of Mozart's skill with characterization. Shaw employed similar musical techniques to orchestrate many of his own plays.[4] Shaw's use of tone and rhythm in the *Don Juan in Hell* segment from the third act of *Man and Superman* is heavily reliant upon Mozart's *Don Giovanni.* If you are working on a scene from *Man and Superman* try listening to the Mozart opera before you lock into your character.

SPLITTING THE PERSONALITY

explanation This exercise is an updated version of the Elizabethan element-humor game (see pp. 165–171). The game works basically the same way, except that there are six players, three per team. The three performers on each side play the seperate functions of Id, Ego, and Superego. Avoid comparing the game with Freudian psychology at all costs! The exercise is designed only to help you explore the variety in your role by making you aware that your character contains polarities that provide you with myriad directions to follow in solving your character's dilemmas. All of these possibilities are open to you at the same time, and it is up to you while "in character" to make the dramatic decision onstage whether to solve your problem using your head, your heart, or your hands (respectively, your Superego, your Id, or your Ego).

procedure Select six volunteers, three males and three females, to play on each of the two opposing teams. Each team will have a Superego, an Id, and an Ego performer. The two Ego performers sit opposite each other in the center of the cleared work space. The two volunteers playing Id sit or kneel at their respective Ego's feet, and the two playing Superego stand behind their Ego partners. The only man and woman who can really interact are the two Ego performers.

The performer playing Id concentrates on physical gratification. Id's major arguments center around pain and pleasure, food, shelter, and sex (combining aspects of Blood and Choler or Air and Fire). The performer playing Superego concentrates on social etiquette and on the religious or political upbringing the character may have had. Superego's major arguments revolve around feelings of guilt and "what other people think" (somewhat like Earth-Melancholy). The performer playing Ego is responsible for the conscious decisions of the composite personality. The Ego must weigh what he wants erotically against what he needs intellectually (similar to Water-Phlegm). Either the Ego will appease his Id by fooling or ignoring his Superego or the

Ego will adopt the argument of the Superego, leaving his Id frustrated.[5]

The female Id and Superego watch the male Ego carefully. They advise their female Ego partner on how to play their team's objective, each offering her a different argument. The Ego makes her conscious decision between her partners' exhortations and plays her role to the male Ego, responding to that part of her personality that is dominating her at the moment. The Ids and Supergos may only whisper so that the Egos do not become confused.

The two Ego performers must carry on the scene with each other, maintaining eye contact and keeping the flow of their conversation going. The male Ego and the female Ego can never speak to their respective Id or Superego, nor can they speak to their opposite's Id or Superego. However, they *must* try to use the arguments that their respective Ego or Superego component whispers to them. The Id and Superego performers are allowed ninety-second shifts to coach their Ego representative. For example, if the Id has been influencing the Ego for the last minute and a half, the Superego takes over with a whole new set of directions to accomplish the objective. It is necessary that the members playing Id, Ego, and Superego on each team realize that they have one objective collectively; they must all try to accomplish their mutual objective in their own way.

If your study group is observing, elect a timekeeper. You don't need personality controllers because Id and Superego will simply alternate turns from their respective positions around the Ego. Ask the timekeeper to ring a little bell at every ninety-second shift. Use the old list of contrary objectives (see pp. 48–49) to get the game started.

decisions

Are the actors playing Ego really listening to their Id and Superego partners and shifting from physical to cerebral methods to accomplish the collective objective? A frustrated Id will probably act angry and childish. A conscience-stricken Superego may seem to be a bit parental. Since the Ego must take the responsibility for his actions, he may come across as fairly adult. There is generally a disproportionate relationship between the Id as Child and the Superego as Parent within every character you play.

Shaw's *Misalliance* deals with "parents and children" in a very direct manner. Notice the diverse ways the children handle themselves: Bentley as Id, Johnny as Ego, Joey as Superego, and Hypatia as a blend of the extremes of Id and Superego.

extension

Try using the split-personality game to realize the dramatic potential in your own scenes. Run through the entire scene once, employing the methods Id would use. Then repeat the scene, doing it as if you were totally under the dominion of Superego. Repeat it once more, this time with Ego in command. Then decide which direction offers the greatest dramatic potential.

If in-depth character analysis traps you into a stereotyped view of your role, use this method to help yourself break out. If you feel that your character usually performs as if he were under the influence of Superego, discover certain spots in your scene where you can jump into Id quickly.

Stretch the limits of your character while you are in early rehearsals. Try surprising your fellow performers with an "opposite," a piece of business that seems to be antithetical to the way your character might normally behave. You may have to apologize for your action "in character," but it is better to act dangerously than to take the safe, dull approach to an action or to a characterization. But remember that you must motivate whatever you do onstage in terms of your fellow performers.

Variation 1

After you and your partner have memorized the words in a scene you're doing for group criticism, ask two other actors and two other actresses to join you and your partner for a work session. These actors and actresses will perform the functions of Id and Superego for you (Ego) as you run through your scene. Your new Id and Superego will simply follow you around as you play the scene as Ego. Every time your cue comes, before saying your next line, listen to the whispered advice of your Id and Superego. Decide which approach to use. Then say your line and check your partner's response.

Variation 2

Try mixing males and females in the same split personality, but remain true to yourself within your sexual roles. In other words, a male Ego teamed with a female Id will have to operate with a female pleasure-pain drive, unless the female incorrectly tries to pretend to be a male. Try teaming the men with the women in mixed combinations as Id and Superego. Create multifaceted personalities.

Variation 3

Try using the split-personality game with an improvisation based on an unwritten scene in your play. For example, in Shaw's *Man and Superman* Tanner and Ann spend a good deal of Act I discussing their childhood together: how he bragged and bullied for her benefit and how she enjoyed his actions while feigning disinterest. An improvisation of their unwritten teenage skirmishes, using three actors as Tanner's Id, Ego, and Superego and three actresses as Ann's might sound like this:

Tanner's Id: Get Ann excited and jealous by telling her you went further with Rachel Rosetree than you did. Tighten your biceps and look sexy.

Tanner's Supergo: Tell Ann that you and Rachel have a deep mental understanding of each other's spirit and soul.

Tanner's Ego: (tightening his biceps) Rachel and I walked under the arbor the other day holding hands. We kissed twice. She looked into my eyes for an interminable length of time, then she began to cry, and I felt blood rushing through my lungs and into my diaphragm. I've never felt that way about anyone before in my life.

[Tanner's objective: I want to find a way to make Ann jealous of my feelings toward Rachel.]

Ann's Id: Make sure you keep him for yourself. Get him to compare you physically with Rachel. Purse your lips slightly and close your eyelids just a little.

Ann's Superego: Get him to make a secret pact with you so he will tell you everything that happens to him. Keep him a good boy. Ask him questions! Keep *him* doing all the talking!

Ann's Ego: (smiling and batting her eyes a trifle)
Oh, Jack, that's wonderful. I hope I can find such a romance. Do be true to your Ann and tell her everything that happens and I shall tell you of anything that may happen to me. Will you see her tomorrow? If so, will you tell me if she wears her hair the same way I do?

[Ann's objective: I want to lure Jack into telling me that I'm someone special to him.]

decisions All three personality components must play the objective as a group, concentrating on their specialized function within the whole personality. Physicalizing the way Jack and Ann may have talked with each other years before should certainly give you and your partner many insights into your characters, and help you tackle the scene at the end of Act I in *Man and Superman.*

CHOOSING A LOGICAL OPPOSITE

Phase 1

procedure Ask your partner or study group to help you create three lists. Compile a new set of contrary objectives for a male and a female to play together.

female: I want to convince him to buy a hot color television.
male: I want to force her to admit that crime does not pay.

female: I want to get him to propose marriage to me.
male: I want to convince her to abort our baby.

female: I want to prove to my employee that God is dead.
male: I want to force my boss to recognize the importance of religious holidays.

female: I want to make her agree to help me rob a gas station.
male: I want to convince him that all criminals are psychologically disturbed.

famale: I want to get her interested in me sexually.
male: I want to convince him of the purity of my mind and soul.

Compile a general list of relationships between people. For example:

Husband and wife for two months (for a year, six years, etc.)
Brother and sister.
Man and woman engaged for a year (for a month, etc.).
Total strangers.
Cousins (one wealthy, one poor).

Compile a list of actions that require physicalization. Try to select actions that differ widely in form and energy need. For example:

Humming an operatic song.
Cleaning your teeth.
Cleaning fish.
Shucking corn.
Eating candy.
Practicing vocal or speech exercises.
Doing push-ups and sit-ups.
Quoting the Bible.
Eating a greasy meal of spare ribs.
Washing your dog.
Combing your (his or her) hair.
Rearranging furniture.

Write the combinations of objectives that work together to produce conflict on separate slips of paper (one set of conflicting objectives per slip). Be sure to specify which objective is for the male (M) and which is for the female (F). Put the objectives into one paper bag. Write the varying human relationships on scraps of paper and put them into another paper bag. Lastly, write out the list of actions on separate pieces of paper, and put them into a third bag. Label the bags according to their contents. The longer the lists and the more slips of paper the better.

Phase 2

procedure Choose a partner. Reach into the first bag and select at random a set of objectives for yourself and your partner. Your partner reaches into the second bag and pulls out a slip that indicates your relationship. Each of you then select at random an individual action to do from the third bag. After you and your partner digest the ideas on the four slips of paper, go to the center of the cleared work space and improvise the scene. You must accept whatever your partner says as true, though you may modify it. Follow the usual rules for improvisations. Pantomime all necessary actions.

decisions Put all the papers back into their respective bags, mix them up, and continue the game until everyone in the study group has had a chance to play.

Did your objective get in the way of performing your action, or vice versa? The greater the opposition the better, as long as you remember to motivate your action as seriously as possible. For example, digging a grave as you sing a love song can be both funny and poignant. A seminude model posing for her artist-boyfriend while she hums something from *Die Walküre* and reads the classified want ads in order to find her boyfriend a paying job can be hysterical, especially if he is eating barbecued ribs or quoting the Bible as he paints.

Some of Shaw's and Wilde's characters have similar opposites built in. In Shaw's *Pygmalion,* Higgins teaches Eliza phonetics, rewarding her with candies as though she were a child (near the end of Act I in the film script).

Eliza may try to entice Higgins into being sexually interested in her as she practices her diction exercises. Higgins is probably a compulsive eater, especially when he's nervously making a series of discoveries or decisions. In Act IV, after returning from the ball, Higgins tries to quiet Eliza down by suggesting alternative plans for her future as he sips champagne and eats an apple! Higgins is capable of having only a clinical affair with Eliza's speech habits, and for all practical purposes he is deeply "involved" with her ears and her mouth.

Higgins has blocked off his Id in relation to women, so his Id takes the form of compulsive chocolate eating and champagne-drinking. In Act I Eliza has also submerged her Id to protect herself from the cockney low-lifes with whom she has had to associate. Later, because Higgins frustrates her Id, too, she succumbs to munching candy as a reward for learning to speak. Her opposition action, compulsive chocolate eating, is both logical and justified. By the end of *Pygmalion* Eliza has grown up emotionally. As an adult, she decides to marry Freddy and have babies. She frees her Id, so she no longer has a need for chocolates, but Higgins loses her as his mental playmate. Higgins may well end the play cramming his mouth with chocolates!

Experiment with various motivated actions as you rehearse your scene. Absorb your set! Check out the possibility of props to "play with" in the scene. The choice of one action may not be right; however, another action may illuminate your entire scene.

variation Return to the split-personality game, playing it exactly as before, except that this time the two volunteers playing the male Ego and the female Ego randomly select an action from the paper bag as in the choosing-opposites game. The Ego players must do this action as they try to pursue their objectives under the influence of their Id or Superego partners.

suggestions Compare Shaw's biases about acting, expressed in a letter to his friend McNulty and later published under the title "The Art of Rehearsal," with those of Wilde evidenced in his views on creativity in *De Profundis*.[6] Apply Philip Weissman's ideas in *Creativity in the Theatre* to the last two exercises.[7]

chapter 15
AUDITIONING AS A TECHNIQUE

If you are in a study course in which a final project of some sort is expected, an audition may well fill the bill. You and the other members of your study group can be of invaluable help to one another in the preparation of a professional audition, especially since any training program in acting should aim at helping the performer secure a job.

Set the same standards for your audition that you might expect to find in a professional situation. Try using as a model the requirements for the University Resident Theatre Association auditions or the Theatre Communications Group auditions. The U.R.T.A. auditions usually require three short pieces; the T.C.G. auditions, two. In both cases, one of the pieces should be from classical theatre (drama written before 1800). The total audition should not last more than five minutes. You must train yourself to be able to "produce" in a very short period of time something that is either emotionally moving or funny in order to be effective at auditioning.

Audition situations vary. You must be aware of the special requirements for the particular audition that you are attending. You should make every effort to adhere to the time limits and the techniques asked for by the auditioneers.

You will usually not have the chance to sing during a five-minute "herd call" (an audition in which a wide variety of actors are judged within a short time). You ought to mention as you leave the stage that you do sing; and you certainly make that fact obvious in your résumé. Occasionally, theatres will make arrangements to hear actors sing after a herd call. Types of auditions and the proper forms for résumés are amply covered in Robert Cohen's excellent book *Acting Professionally.*[1]

PRACTICAL RULES FOR AUDITIONING

Select *the best material that you possibly can—material that will sell you as you sell it.* The piece should be suited to your personality and capabilities. To the auditioneer, your choice of material reflects how you see yourself. An actor who chooses belligerent characters runs the risk of being thought of as hard to work with; however, the auditioneer often wants to see that possible "fire" of anger that an actor personally involved with a role can generate. Black actors should have at least one solid audition piece from Black Theatre. Remember that professional directors are directors because they want to direct, not because they want to alleviate ego problems. Be as pleasant and as warm as you can.

The best face you can show, especially when you introduce your material and yourself, features a smile that assures your auditioneer you are the kind of person that a director can mold and work with easily. An actor must show that he is capable of humility and flexibility.

Choosing the climax of a play is inadvisable. An actor needs the entire play behind him in order to work up to the emotional pitch requisite to performing the climax. Try to encourage your auditioneer to think, "If he can do this with a section in the first part of the second act, perhaps he can be magnificent in the last act!" Give your auditioneer a chance to envision more than what you do at the moment. Never show your top! To do so would only minimize your work. Realize that your dramatic "prowess" will not knock your auditioneers out; whether they be professionals in the theatre or in education, they will have seen pinnacles of emotion before you come along. Try to stimulate them gently.

Find good material from good playwrights without resorting to characters of the household-word type, such as Viola from Shakespeare's *Twelfth Night* or Richard from his *Richard III.* A young actor hunching up his left arm and sneering at an auditioneer is more likely to produce an unwanted guffaw than anything else, just as the fourteenth Viola on a long day will either put the auditioneer to sleep or drive him up the wall. Most directors have done such popular shows already. A director cannot help but compare you with his memory of an "untouchable" performance given by an actor with whom the director himself has worked in the past. Choose material from *plays* rather than from nondramatic fiction. Because of the way plays are constructed, their speeches have objectives and definite intent. Selecting material from nondramatic sources carries an undeniably educational atmosphere about it.

An audition is designed to present what you as a performer do best. Stretching should be done in a classroom or in rehearsal, not in an audition.

Choose roles within a ten-year range of your own age, depending upon your looks. Wild character roles or roles beyond your age level type you as the "catch-all" performer who did all the dirty work in high school or college but never got to play the central role. Maintain your artistic dignity and the elements of your work that are true to yourself. Be wary of the "brilliant new way" to do a speech! Remember that *you* are auditioning, not the person who helped you give form to your speech. Use what works for you!

Choose your pieces from a sensible variety of material. If the audition specifications call for two selections, perform one tragedy and one comedy piece. Within those genres one piece should be classical and one contemporary. One piece should be a character-type role within your range, and the other may be as straight a representation of yourself as possible. Theatre groups are usually interested in seeing if you can play yourself honestly, as well as perform small character changes with some degree of believability.

Be as succinct as possible. Too little said in introducing a new work can be baffling, but too much said runs the risk of "talking down" to a professional director. Your imaginary scenic location and the imaginary people on stage with you to whom you will refer through mimetic gesture are important. Plot outlines must be avoided like the plague.

Arrange the few pieces of furniture that you will need as early as possible; use only the props that are absolutely essential to the scene. Do not introduce yourself or begin until after you have set your stage, or you will have to fill your set-up time with interesting commentary. It is better to give the auditioneers a break from the last person, set your own stage quietly and quickly, then come forward with an expectant smile, and introduce your pieces all at one time. This will save you from stepping in and out of the role of narrator and actor-character too frequently. Thank your auditioneers for their time when you finish.

An actor should be warmed up before he enters the stage. *Try to confine all warm-ups and preparation to offstage areas. Prepare your warm-up half an hour before you perform.* Auditions ought to be done in shoes rather than in barefeet. After all, you usually don't act in a play barefooted. Wear good-quality clothing. However, any clothing that limits your performance of the piece or is so novel in style that it calls attention to its uniqueness is not a sound choice.

Self-contained segments from plays are excellent audition pieces. If a piece has a beginning, middle, and end within the short audition time allotted, the material will give you a feeling of completeness and solidity. Every good audition speech contains a progression from where you were before the speech began to where you are after the discoveries and decisions within your speech are realized. As you audition, ask yourself real questions and try to find real answers that require decisions in order to maintain the first-time illusion.

Pieces that require an imagined actor are often effective. The strongest objectives are found in scenes of mutual conflict. Remember to keep the imagined person downstage of yourself. Never walk downstage and deliver part of your speech upstage at nothing. Angling a downstage chair up toward you provides you with a point of focus and a good power position. Remember that your imagined person has dimension; the person's head should not sink below the level of the top of the chair if you decide to kneel down, or you will give the impression of talking to a midget. Picture the person you are talking to and maintain your concentration on your images.

Remember that there is a great difference between acting and auditioning. In an audition, you not only imagine your partner, but you must create the responses and motivations that he supplies as you speak to him. The chances of your being "in it" for an audition are almost nil; auditions must be *performed.* The images you set in rehearsal for an audition must be very strong and personal to keep their effect when you are nervewracked. Relax! Concentrate first on the amount of volume you need to fill the space. Relaxing with the image of your imaginary partner can be an immense security. Trust your preparation. Auditioneers will rarely stop you unless you exceed time limits badly. It is terribly deceptive to think, "If I only had another two minutes more I could show them." The longer you perform in front of your auditioneer, the more rope you unwind to hang yourself. Economy is best! Leave the auditioneers wanting more rather than wishing you had done less.

Eye contact with auditioneers can be dangerous. Many modern plays, particularly Thornton Wilder's, require audience contact. This does not mean direct, cognizant eye contact. Such contact robs the auditioneer of his aesthetic distance, makes him uncomfortable, suggests that the actor is asking for a direct response to his acting, and breaks the illusion of his theatrical aesthetic distance. Audience contact can very often be successfully achieved by splashing five seats at a time, or by looking slightly above the auditioneer's head.

Be as professional in your demands on yourself as possible. The only way to achieve results is to expect them.

suggestions

Bring several possible pieces to use for auditions the next time you meet with your study group. The group may help you select material that is best for your individual capabilities. After you have chosen your pieces, learn them and do them for group criticism, using the following check list:

a. Is the performer the right physical type for the role?
b. Can the performer fulfill the demands of the piece?
c. Will an auditioneer think the performer is a relaxed, flexible person?
d. Is the introduction to the piece too long? Is the introduction even necessary?
e. Is the performer playing his objective in the piece?
f. Is the performer trying to impress the auditioneer?
g. Does the piece reach an impossible emotional climax?
h. Is the speech of the household-word type?
i. Is there variety within the total audition?
j. Can the performer hold the audience's attention?
k. Has the performer arranged the furniture *before* beginning?

l. Is there dead space between the audition pieces?
m. Was the performer warmed up?
n. Does the audition have a logical beginning, middle, and end?
o. If the actor is imagining a second person, is he clear about the location of this person throughout the audition?
p. Has the performer sufficient voice to fill the audition room?
q. If the piece requires definite audience contact, is the actor allowing himself to make this contact?
r. Does the actor seem to have any special mannerisms that affect his work? Would an auditioneer mistake assumed character mannerisms for real acting problems with this actor?
s. Does the actor expect professional results from himself?
t. Are there sufficient differences between the roles the actor has chosen to use as audition pieces? Has the actor used the Character Quality Chart to be sure he is shaping space differently from one audition piece to the next?
u. Depending on the genre, is the piece moving or honestly funny? Might the piece be merely a product of in-group humor?

SUGGESTIONS FOR FRESH AUDITION PIECES

John Whiting, *The Devils:* Sister Jeanne

Leonard Melfi, *Times Square:* Bobo Society, Marigold Sobbing, or Butch

William Shakespeare, *Richard II* (I, ii): Duchess of Gloucester

William Shakespeare, *Henry VI*, Part II (III, i and ii); Part III (I, i and V, iv): the Queen

William Shakespeare, *All's Well That Ends Well:* Peyrolles

Oscar Wilde, *An Ideal Husband:* Mable Children

S. N. Behrman, *Biography:* Marion

Clare Boothe, *The Women:* Countess or Crystal

Arthur Wing Pinero, *The Second Mrs. Tanqueray:* Paula

David Rabe, *The Basic Training of Pavlo Hummel:* the Mother, Pavlo, Tower, or the Corporal

Alexandre Dumas fils, *The Demi-Monde:* Suzanne

Gotthold E. Lessing, *Miss Sara Sampson:* Marwood

Alexander Ostrovsky, *The Thunderstorm:* Katerina

Thomas Heywood, *A Woman Killed with Kindness:* Mistress Frankford

Edward Albee, *A Delicate Balance:* Claire

Arthur Kopit, *Oh Dad, Poor Dad, Mama's Hung You in the Closet and I'm Feelin' So Sad:* Madame Rosepettle

Arthur Kopit, *Indians:* Cody and John Grass
John Guare, *The House of Blue Leaves:* Bunny Flingus
Tennessee Williams, *The Eccentricities of a Nightingale:* Alma
Vittorio Alfieri, *Saul:* David or Saul
Clifford Odets, *Waiting for Lefty:* Sid or Fatt
William Saroyan, *The Time of Your Life:* Harry or Kit Carson
Niccolò Machiavelli, *La Mandragola:* The Friar
Thomas Middleton, *The Changeling:* De Flores
Molière, *The Would-Be Gentleman:* The Dancing Master
Peter Shaffer, *Five Finger Exercise:* Walter Langer
Victor Hugo, *Hernani:* Hernani
Johann Wolfgang von Goethe, *Egmont:* Brackenburg
Sophocles, *Antigone:* The Sentinel, Ismene and Antigone
Beaumont and Fletcher, *The Maid's Tragedy:* Amintor
Daniel Keyes, *Flowers for Algernon:* Charlie
Neil Simon, *The Last of the Red Hot Lovers:* Elaine or Bobby
Eugene O'Neill, *The Iceman Cometh:* Cora
Eugene O'Neill, *A Touch of the Poet:* Sarah
Eugene O'Neill, *The Great God Brown:* Dion
Eugene Ionesco, *Rhinoceros:* Beronger
Boris Vian, *The Empire Builders:* any of the family, especially the Father
Racine, *Andromache:* Hermione
Howard O. Sackler's *The Great White Hope:* several Black roles
Martin B. Duberman, *In White America:* the Little Rock segment
James Saunders, *The Next Time I'll Sing to You:* female roles
Anton Chekhov, *Uncle Vanya* (II): Sonya
Murray Shisgal, *Luv:* Ellen or Milt
Christopher Marlowe, *The Jew of Malta:* Barabas
Christopher Fry, *A Phoenix Too Frequent:* Dynamene
Federico García Lorca, *Blood Wedding:* the Bride
Menander, *The Bad-Tempered Man:* Cnemon
Menander, *The Arbitration:* Onesimes
Brendon Behan, The Quare Fellow: Dunlavin or any Prisoner
Jack Gelber, *The Connection:* Leach
Jean Genet, *The Balcony:* Irma or the Police Chief
Harold Pinter, *The Birthday Party:* Goldberg

NOTES

Introduction

1. George Santayana, "Art and Happiness," in *The Problems of Aesthetics: A Book of Readings*, ed. Eliseo Vivas and Murray Krieger (New York: Holt, Rinehart and Winston, 1963, pp. 526–529.
2. Viola Spolin, *Improvisation for the Theater* (Evanston, Ill.: Northwestern University, Press, 1963).
3. "Sympathetic magic" is defined by Oscar G. Brockett in his *History of the Theatre* (Boston: Allyn and Bacon, 1968), p. 3.
4. Stanislavski's use of improvisational techniques appears in all his books. See, for instance, *An Actor Prepares*, trans. Elizabeth Reynolds Hapgood (New York: Theatre Arts Books, 1956), passim, esp. "Concentration of Action," pp. 70–73; and *Building a Character*, trans. Elizabeth Reynolds Hapgood (New York: Theatre Arts Books, 1949), passim, esp. "Dressing a Character," pp. 9-19. See also *Stanislavski Produces Othello*, trans. Helen Nowak (London: G. Bles, 1948; New York: Theatre Arts Books, 1963), pp. 152-153, in which Stanislavski employs a simple improvisational technique with the actor playing Othello in the operatic version of *Othello*. He sets up a definite series of beat (unit) objectives—greet Desdemona, kiss her with some passion, amuse Iago, and so on (see pp. 149ff. of the present book). After performing five basic physical actions, the actor playing Othello begins to accept the circumstances in the structured scene of the opera.
5. Nikolai Gorchakov, *Stanislavski Directs* (New York: Grosset and Dunlap, 1962), p. 119.
6. Ibid., p. 299.

7. Richard Schechner, "The Bottomless Cup: An Interview with Geraldine Page," in *Stanislavski and America: An Anthology of Readings from the Tulane Drama Review,* ed. Erika Munk (Greenwich, Conn.: Fawcett Publications, 1967), pp. 239–240.
8. Richard Schechner, "Working with Live Material: An Interview with Lee Strasberg," in *Stanislavski and America,* p. 198.
9. *Tyrone Guthrie on Acting* (London: Studio Vista; New York: Viking Press, 1971), p. 32.
10. Paul Sills, "The Celebrated Occasion," *Tulane Drama Review* 9, No. 2 (Winter 1964), 167–168.
11. Michel St. Denis, *Theatre: The Rediscovery of Style* (New York: Theatre Arts Books, 1960), p. 102.
12. Richard Schechner, "'Would You Please Talk to Those People?' An Interview with Robert Lewis," in *Stanislavski and America,* p. 223.
13. Schechner, "The Bottomless Cup," pp. 239–240.
14. Michael Redgrave, *Mask or Face: Reflections in an Actor's Mirror* (New York: Theatre Arts Books, 1959), p. 52.
15. Spolin, *Improvisation,* p. 18. Part of the research in the Introduction was compiled with the aid of Ann Galvin Homan, a graduate student at the University of Minnesota during the spring of 1974.

Chapter 1

1. Douglas N. Morgan, "Psychology and Art Today: A Summary and Critique," in *Problems of Aesthetics,* pp. 34–37, gives an excellent application of Gestalt psychology to current trends in the arts.
2. Stretches and isolation exercises were typical of the stage-movement workout used by Cecil Kitkat at the Carnegie Institute of Technology when I studied there during 1960–1964. Professor Robert Moulton uses similar techniques at the University of Minnesota. The vocal exercises in this chapter were derived from many sources, though the originator of the general philosophy upon which these exercises are based is Kristin Linklater. Mark Zeller and Carol Pendergrast, both of whom studied directly with Kristin Linklater at the Tyrone Guthrie Theatre in Minneapolis, introduced several of these exercises to me at the American Conservatory Theatre (ACT) in San Francisco when we were colleagues in teaching there in 1968. Carol Pendergrast is an Assistant Professor in the Department of Theatre, University of Utah, Salt Lake City. Mark Zeller teaches with the Theatre Department in the Fine Arts College of New York University and operates his own studio in New York City. Associate Professor Mary Corrigan of Florida State University, Tallahassee and Sarasota, who also studied with Kristin Linklater, consulted with me when I constructed this warm-up at the University of Minnesota in 1972. The exercises for nasal resonance were introduced to me by Dr. Mel M. Slott, who led vocal workouts for the Hilberry Classic Theatre Company of Wayne State University, Michigan, in 1967 and 1968. Dr. Slott is an Associate Professor of Communicative Arts at Fayetteville State University, North Carolina. I have freely adapted many of these exercises to suit my own purposes.
3. This is an adaptation of the "Bacon and Eggs" exercise introduced by Maxine Klein when she was on the faculty of the Theatre Arts Department at the University of Minnesota. Ms. Klein is an Associate Professor of Theatre Arts at Boston University.
4. This exercise was developed by Mark Zeller.

5. These lip-and-tongue exercises were used by Carol Pendergrast and Jane Hill Mazzone Clementi at ACT in 1968. Jane Hill Mazzone-Clementi teaches at the College of the Redwoods in Eureka, California, and performs with the Grand Comedy Festival in Eureka and nearby Arcata.
6. Dr. Slott introduced this exercise at Wayne State University in 1967.
7. Professor Mary Corrigan also endorses this technique; however, she warns that rising up from the bent-over position utilizes a different set of muscles in supporting a tone. You should be careful to maintain a free and clear sound with little harshness and strain.
8. Perhaps you are not overly fond of touching or being touched. Having discussed this problem with Professor Corrigan, I have come to the conclusion that performers of this type must realize that such a psychological block will prevent them from going very far in the theatre, and that they had better learn to deal with touching. Even if an acting coach has had training in psychology, it is not a good idea for him or her to assume responsibility for group members with problems—that is not to the purpose of either acting or teaching an acting class. The coach may have a private talk with the student and suggest where the student might go for outside consultation, but within the classroom it is important that all students work and are treated in much the same way. Professor Corrigan also uses this back-rub technique to foster an aura of warmth and relaxation in the group as a means of eliminating the tensions resulting from self-imposed competition on the part of certain performers.
9. Pasqual Mario Marafioti, *Caruso's Method of Voice Production: The Scientific Culture of the Voice* (New York: D. Appleton and Co., 1922). Marafioti refers throughout the text to "back breathing" and to organic methods to promote relaxation.

Chapter 2

1. Mary Braaten coordinated and taught a group-oriented course in the Alexander Technique with me at the University of Minnesota in Continuing Education and Extension in 1973. The originator of the technique, F. Matthias Alexander, was an orator in Australia at the turn of the century. Alexander found that he was losing his voice owing to tensions and nervous constrictions caused by his anxiety about performing in public. He retired from public life and launched himself into a painfully arduous self-analysis until he found where he had placed unnecessary physical strain in his body. After resuming his lecturing, he organized a process of self-analysis and guided instruction in relaxation that has become known as the Alexander Technique.

   Ms. Braaten is currently finishing her graduate work and teaching this technique at Carnegie-Mellon University in Pittsburgh, Pennsylvania. For intensive training in Alexander Technique, Ms. Braaten recommends contacting Marjorie Barstow, 1445 South 20th Street, Lincoln, Nebraska 68502; Frank Pierce Jones, 33 Lexington Avenue, Cambridge, Massachusetts 02138; and the American Center for the Alexander Technique, 142 West Avenue, New York, New York 10023.

   Ms. Braaten pioneered a group Alexander experience at Minnesota based on the philosophy that students would learn to relax their bodies as they observed and in some cases actually guided other students in experiencing the technique. Ms. Braaten is primarily resonsible for the list of Body Metaphors, which she conceived as a means of getting students to relate their own bodies to expressions and type classifications they use in their daily lives.
2. Two texts that deal with similar tension problems are F. Matthias Alexander, *The Resurrection of the Body*, sel. and introd. Edward Maisel (New York: University Books, 1969; Dell, 1971); and Eugen Herrigel, *Zen in the Art of Archery*, trans. R. F. C. Hull (New York: Pantheon Books, 1953; Vintage, 1971). Professor Mary Corrigan required Herrigel's book for her

beginning voice sequence at the University of Minnesota. It is an excellent book to read if you are "results-conscious" and tend to work too hard at your acting instead of simply "letting things happen."

In his address to directors at the 1972 American Theatre Association Convention in San Francisco, William Ball, Artistic Director of the American Conservatory Theatre, urged teachers and students to explore Transcendental Meditation as a means of relaxing and centering their inward perspective. Plays, of course, are not written about perfectly centered people, but you may learn to find ways to center yourself so that you may better perceive why the characters you play are uncentered. Perhaps after exploring the process of centering yourself as a person you can find a way to reverse the process, that is, uncenter yourself to grasp your character's psychology; however, you must always be in control of your character onstage in performance.

Everyone who uses his emotions constantly in theatre should develop a daily relaxation plan. Edith Warman Skinner, who is a member of the drama faculty of the Juilliard School and who taught voice and diction when she was Professor of Drama at Carnegie-Mellon University, recommends the following text: Edmund Jacobson, *You Must Relax: A Practical Method of Reducing the Strains of Modern Living,* 3d ed., rev. and enl. (New York: Whittlesey House, 1948).

3. The technique introduced is rudimentary Alexander Technique. The methods of teaching Alexander are as diversified as the teachers working in it. The inquisitive student should write to Mary Braaten at Carnegie-Mellon University, Pittsburgh, Pennsylvania (see note 1 in this chapter). Alexander Technique is obviously extremely personal in nature. Ms. Braaten and I have used the technique with small groups (four students at a time) at the University of Minnesota. We found that the students learned by touching each other and watching each other progress. We accelerated their assignments from the performance of lyric poems to scene study and finally to singing a song from an operetta of their choice. For additional "self-help" exercises that feature a philosophy somewhat similar to the Alexander Technique, see Moshé Feldenkrais, *Awareness through Movement: Health Exercises for Personal Growth* (New York: Harper and Row, 1972).

4. This mimetic life cycle was defined by Carlo Mazzone-Clementi in his classes at the Carnegie Institute of Technology in 1962; I have freely adapted the system for the purpose of these exercises in relaxation and self-realization. Before coming to America, Mr. Mazzone-Clementi worked extensively with the Picolo di Milan, Vittorio Gassman, and Jacques Lecoq. In 1968 he was on the teaching staff at the American Conservatory Theatre. Recently he gave lecture demonstrations at the first International Festival of Mimes and Pantomimes, held at Viterbo College in Lacrosse, Wisconsin, and at the 1974 ATA Convention in Minneapolis. He is currently the Artistic Director of the Grand Comedy Festival in Eureka and Arcata, California, and operates his Commedia dell'Arte School during the winter season at Blue Lake, California.

5. "The seed" is a mime exercise of Mr. Mazzone-Clementi's that I also use in teaching mime at the University of Minnesota. In this instance, the exercise is used purely for expansion and relaxation, not necessarily for criticism. Exercises for relaxation are not meant to be structured for group criticism. Physical-mental disciplines such as Tai Ch'i might also be performed; they are truly meant for the personal self. Criticism often goes hand in hand with tension. During the 1972 ATA Convention, William Ball of ACT in San Francisco admonished directors to resist "negativism." Mr. Ball suggested avoiding words like "never," "no," "wrong," and in their place using phrases like "Try it this way" or "Find another value to try here." Such advice is definitely sound.

Chapter 3

1. Robert Benedetti introduced this exercise to the Master Class in Acting at the 1972 ATA Convention in San Francisco. At that time he was the Director of the Program in Theatre Arts at York University in Toronto, Canada. Dr. Benedetti is currently Dean of the School of the Theatre, California Institute of the Arts, Valencia. His excellent text, *The Actor at Work* (Englewood Cliffs, N.J.: Prentice-Hall, 1970), is highly recommended for all acting students.

   At first Dr. Benedetti used the word "Mama" instead of "Cookie," the word I use. He considers the former word too emotionally charged for a new group of people working together for the first time, and he also feels that the use of real blindfolds instead of simply closing your eyes can be dangerous.

2. This is an adaptation of an exercise introduced to me by Charles Werner Moore in 1961 when he was a member of the faculty at the Carnegie Institute of Technology. Dr. Moore is now an Associate Professor at Brandeis University in Waltham, Massachusetts, and he also teaches acting at Banff University in Alberta, Canada, during the summer season. He has directed on Broadway and at many regional theatres in America.

3. Mamako Yoneyama introduced this exercise while teaching at the 1968 summer congress of the American Conservatory Theatre. She gave lecture demonstrations at the first International Festival of Mimes and Pantomimes, held at Viterbo College in Lacrosse, Wisconsin, and at the 1974 ATA Convention in Minneapolis, doing a subsequent workshop session at the University of Minnesota. Ms. Yoneyama has now returned to her own studio at Casa de Taku, 5 Bancho 2 Banchi 4Go, Chiyoda-Ku, Tokyo, Japan.

4. Tony Sadlak is a creative free-lance professional photographer hired by ACT during the 1968 summer congress, during which he introduced this exercise.

5. Carlo Mazzone-Clementi introduced this exercise to his mime classes at the Carnegie Institute of Technology in 1962.

6. Tom Dennis introduced this exercise in 1964 when he was guest director for the West Virginia Historical Society's pageant, *Honey in the Rock,* in Beckley, and ran a workshop for the principals in the pageant, in which I played John Morgan. Mr. Dennis was at that time also resident director for Vanguard Productions, Inc., in Pittsburgh, having returned from training with the Berliner Ensemble under Karl Weber.

7. Robert Moulton introduced me to this technique in 1967 when he was guest choreographer working with Dr. Richard Spear at Wayne State University's Hilberry Theatre on a production of *Lysistrata.* Professor Moulton is the Head of the Acting Area in the Theatre Arts Department of the University of Minnesota.

8. Another exercise that Tony Sadlak introduced at ACT in 1968. As with impersonations, at first there seems to be a knack, until you discover that thinking ahead will trap you. It is interesting for observers to note at what point a group member ceases to be protective and begins to trust his intuition, and whether, during the performance of the exercise, he then starts to doubt his intuition midstream. Try using this exercise to help determine who the "loners" and who the "sharers" in the group are.

9. George Bernard Shaw, *The Collected Works of Bernard Shaw,* ed. Ayot St. Lawrence, 30 vols. (New York: W. H. Wise and Co., 1930–32). See especially Shaw's comments in Vol. 26 and 27, "Music in London." See also Cyril E. M. Joad, *Shaw* (London: Gollancz, 1949; Folcroft, Pa.: Folcroft Library Editions, 1971), pp. 54–59. It is not surprising for Joad to remark that Shaw "said little of Bach" (p. 54). Shaw was more interested in the "emotional" awakening in music, which is why he occasionally preferred the imprecision of second-rate composers to

the mathematical perfection of a technician like Bach. Shaw insisted that Shakespeare was really a musician, and he was highly critical of Sarah Bernhardt, who he felt spoke constantly in a monotone and needed to add a "full set of strings" to her lyre. The devotee of Shaw's attachment to music will want to analyze Jack Owen's "Beethovenish" criticism in Shaw's novel *Love among the Artists.*

10. This exercise is an adaptation of Viola Spolin's "The Silent Scream." See Spolin, *Improvisation,* p. 239.
11. Another of Tom Dennis' exercises from the 1964 workshop in Beckley, West Virginia. Mr. Dennis warned that this highly emotional exercise must be considered by the leader before proceeding. When Mr. Dennis introduced the exercise, an actress in the company became terribly upset; however, I have used the same exercise for over six years with no repercussions. Still, the leader must treat the exercise seriously, or there is simply no point in doing it at all.
12. Note that Stanislavski introduces objectives and conflict very late in *An Actor Prepares:* the chapter titled "The Super-Objective" is the fifteenth chapter in the book!
13. Alan Fletcher was the Artistic Director of the Seattle Repertory Theatre and the guest teacher of Advanced Acting on the staff of the American Conservatory Theatre in San Francisco when he introduced this exercise during the summer of 1968. He may be contacted through ACT, of which he is now the Director of the Conservatory.
14. See Spolin, *Improvisation,* p. 248, for her views on conflict. Professor Wesley Balk of the University of Minnesota has originated a technique that he calls "Shakespeare Games." The rules are still in the formative stages, since the game developed out of class work in the course "Acting for the Music Stage," but when formalized, the technique may become the model for extensive intercollegiate "competition"; for example, Minnesota played against Augustana College, Rock Island, Illinois, in a two-day arrangement in November 1972. Each college has a team comprised of students who have each memorized a scene from any Shakespearean play—a different scene per student. Each team is allowed no more than two players in the ring (the center of the work area) at one time. The participants are allowed to speak the consecutive lines from their own scene, and only their own scene, as they play, relating to one another and trying to justify their lines. The team that leads off may initiate a musical theme or even use properties; the opposing team sends in one or two of its members to begin an improvisation, using whatever methods or themes the first team has begun. Mime, tricks, emotion, ritual, tenderness, etc., may develop, purely improvisationally. Impartial score-keepers give points based sheerly on audience response. Nevertheless, the game has never been used to engender competition, but rather to create meaningful theatrical moments through skillful give-and-take in the comic, tragic, or romantic situations that develop. There is cooperation rather than conflict. In order to avoid conflict in the November 1972 games, the teams actually traded members during the four quarters.

Chapter 4

1. See Spolin, *Improvisation,* pp. 248–250, on conflict.
2. Mr. Lewis Palter introduced "Jump Exercises" to second-year acting students at Carnegie Institute of Technology in 1962. Mr. Palter is a professional actor working out of both New York and California and may be reached through the California Institute of the Arts at Valencia, where he is Co-director of the Theatre Program.
3. See Stanislavski, *An Actor Prepares,* pp. 105–119, for an explanation of objectives.
4. Jerome Rockwood, *The Craftsmen of Dionysus: An Approach to Acting* (Glenville, Ill.: Scott, Foresman, 1966), p. 48. Rockwood gives a fine synthesis of rules for doing improvisations.

5. See Stanislavski, *Stanislavski Produces Othello,* pp. 152–153, for an account of how Stanislavski helped the performers playing Othello and Desdemona to respond to each other romantically by encouraging them to use simple physical actions and objectives.
6. Edward Hastings is Executive Director and occasionally a Guest Director at ACT where he introduced "Contrary Objectives" in 1968 while working with the Master Class in Acting. Mr. Hastings also has a novel way of altering the children's game of "Mother, May I": the leader standing in front of the group defines the steps to be taken by the members of the group as "three pelvic-thrust Yul Brynner steps," etc. Then Mae West steps, and so on. The performer has to readjust to each new step given, using his imagination.
7. The "Detective Games" introduced by Alan Fletcher to the Master Class at ACT took two days to relax into comfortably, but they proved to be extremely popular with the class. Once the group has gotten the hang of the game, the exercise may be altered or used again and again in different ways. For example, they might do games in characterizations, using life studies, animal studies, or object studies. (see pp. 94–104).

Chapter 5

1. See Stanislavski, *Building a Character,* chap. 4, "Making the Body Expressive", and chap. 5, "Plasticity of Motion", for a fine analysis of anatomical structure and its relation to characterziation. See also Michael Chekhov, *To the Actor: On the Technique of Acting* (New York: Harper, 1953), chap. 5 "Psychological Gesture", which deals explicitly with movement as the experimental basis for playing a role.
2. The Adam and Eve exercise was introduced by Carlo Mazzone-Clementi in his mime class at the Carnegie Institute of Technology in 1962.

Chapter 6

1. Two excellent sources for stage jargon are Jerome Rockwood, *Craftsmen of Dionysus,* chap. 2, and Charles McGaw, *Acting Is Believing: A Basic Method,* 2d ed. (New York: Holt, Rinehart and Winston, 1966), chap. 11. See also Michael Green's spoof, *Downwind of Upstage: The Art of Coarse Acting* (New York: Hawthorn Books, 1966). Though this text is a parody, a good deal can be learned and digested from examining the allusions Green cites in so palatable a fashion.
2. See Stanislavski, *Building a Character,* p. 142, regarding Salvini

Chapter 7

1. Dr. Richard Brown formally presented this technique at the ATA Convention in San Francisco in 1972. Dr. Brown is Executive Director of the Institute for Acting Research and Chairman of the Theatre Department at the University of California, Riverside.

Chapter 8

1. This chart has been used effectively with both beginning undergraduates and advanced graduate students at the University of Minnesota.
2. Yiaprakia are lamb-stuffed grape leaves and moussaka is rather like a lasagne made with eggplant slices instead of noodles.
3. Item D on the character-analysis chart is purely personal, especially the choices of psychological gestures and sense-memory stimuli. Because of this, item D cannot be formalized, except in making the arbitrary choice of a study—that is, animal, life, secondary-characteristic, or object study.

4. See Chekhov, *To the Actor*, chap. 5, "Psychological Gesture."
5. The chart is based on Rudolf Laban, *The Mastery of Movement*, 3d ed., rev. and enl. by Lisa Ullmann (Boston: Plays, Inc., 1971). The star actors, animals, and much of the wording have been chosen by me to adapt the classifications for the purpose of the exercise. It must be stressed that Laban cites an infinite number of variations within the eight major classifications. Ullmann has translated certain terms on Laban's graph as "gentle," "firm," and "sudden" rather than "weak," "strong," and "quick," respectively. My preference of terms is guided by the instruction of Carol Mayo Jenkins, who introduced these classifications of effort-shape to the acting classes at the American Conservatory Theatre in 1968. Ms. Jenkins was an actress-instructor at ACT at the time and had trained under Laban's methods in Europe before joining that theatre.
6. Charles Werner Moore introduced similar animal and object studies to the second-year acting students at Carnegie Institute of Technology in 1962.
7. Stanislavski, *Building a Character*, chap. 2. Tortsov congratulates Kostya for his characterization of "the mildewed critic."

Chapter 10

1. *Tartuffe*, from Molière *The Misanthrope, and Other Plays*, trans. John Wood (Baltimore: Penguin Books, 1959) p. 135, translation C (John Wood, 1959).

Chapter 11

1. The following two sources are authentic and thorough: A. W. Pickard-Cambridge, *Dithyramb, Tragedy, and Comedy*, 2d ed., rev. T. B. L. Webster (Oxford: Clarendon Press, 1962); and H. D. F. Kitto, *Greek Tragedy: A Literary Study* (Garden City, N.Y.: Doubleday, 1954), in which Kitto debunks some of his own theories he offered in his earlier *The Greeks* (Baltimore: Penguin Books, 1951)—theories that are nevertheless worth tracing.
2. Lillian B. Lawler, *The Dance of the Ancient Greek Theatre* (Iowa City: University of Iowa Press, 1964).
3. Sophocles, Oedipus the King, in *A Treasury of the Theatre*, Vol. 1: *Aeschylus to Turgenev*, ed. John Gassner, rev. ed (New York: Simon and Schuster, 1963).
4. This exercise was introduced by Carlo Mazzone-Clementi to his mime classes at the Carnegie Institute of Technology in 1962.

   "The Departing Ship" is an excellent exercise in organic movement. The entire body should be excited, embarrassed, bored, sorrowful, etc., during the performance of the exercise.
5. Alan Fletcher introduced the "Three-Task" exercises to the advanced classes at ACT in 1968. Such exercises are a fine way of getting back to the basics in acting by reducing motivation to the lowest common denominator.
6. Nagle Jackson originated the system of Focus through Release and introduced it in 1968 at ACT. Mr. Jackson was Artistic Director at the Oregon Shakespeare Festival at that time; currently he runs the Milwaukee Repertory Theatre as Artistic Director for the company.
7. Alan H. Monroe and Douglas Ehninger, *Principles and Types of Speech* 6th ed. (Glenville, Ill.: Scott, Foresman, 1967), p. 265.
8. Over-detailed criticism generally results in cold analysis that will tighten an actor and often prevent him from "taking chances."

   The following works are recommended as additional source materials on the ancient Greeks: Peter D. Arnott, *An Introduction to Greek Theatre* (New York: St. Martin's Press, 1959); Margarete Bieber, *The History of the Greek and Roman Theater*, 2d ed., rev. and enl.

(Princeton: Princeton University Press, 1961); Iris Brooke, *Costume in Greek Classic Drama*, 2d ed. (New York: Theatre Arts Books, 1963); Gerald F. Else, *Aristotle's Poetics: The Argument* (Cambridge, Mass.: Harvard University Press, 1957); Gerald F. Else, "Aristotle and Satyr Play I," *Transactions of the American Philological Association* 70 (1939), 139–157; Philip Whaley Harsch, *A Handbook of Classical Drama* (Stanford: Stanford University Press, 1944); Roy C. Flickinger, *The Greek Theatre and Its Drama*, 4th ed. (Chicago: University of Chicago Press, 1936); C. T. Murphy, "A Survey of Recent Work on Aristophanes and Old Comedy," *Classical Weekly* 40 (1956), 201–211; and Friedrich Nietzsche, *The Birth of Tragedy*, trans. William A. Haussman, in *The Complete Works of Friedrich Nietzsche*, Vol. 1, ed. Oscar Levy (New York: Macmillan, 1924).

Chapter 12

1. Laban, *Mastery of Movement*, p. 136.
2. Benedetti, *Actor at Work*, pp. 110–116. Benedetti's entire Lesson 9, "Analyzing the Speech: Rhythm," is an invaluable guide to scansion and provides additional material, as well as another way of looking at versification for the somewhat bewildered student.
3. The techniques of underlining to denote stress are basically those of Edith Warman Skinner, who was Professor of Drama and a recognized specialist in Speech and Diction at the Carnegie Institute of Technology when I studied with her from 1960 to 1964. Instead of using an asterisk at the end of run-on lines, Dr. Skinner prefers to draw a line with an upward curve to denote a rising inflection, a line with a downward curve for a falling inflection, and a straight line for a level inflection or intonation on the fifth foot.
4. G. B. Harrison, ed., *Shakespeare, The Complete Works* (New York: Harcourt, Brace, 1952), p. 1195, note 28.
5. Teaching Sophomore Acting at the Carnegie Institute of Technology in 1962, Charles Werner Moore introduced an exercise in which the class members were to take only a few lines, either a couplet or a quatrain from any of Shakespeare's plays, and allow themselves to move freely to the sound, re-creating the sound with their bodies (for example, dragging a foot to simulate the hissing noise of sibilants). Like that exercise, the idea of the present one is to free your imagination so that definite associations with the actual sounds of the words will dominate you, though the mood of the play itself may influence your choice of movement pattern, rhythm, and vocalization.
6. Stephen Batman, *Batman upon Bartholemew, his book de proprietibus rerum* (1538; London: T. East, 1582), pp. 27–37. This book is available from University Microfilms, Ann Arbor, Michigan. The text was in extensive use in Shakespeare's time. It is a rich source of information concerning Elizabethan knowledge of medicine and the sociology of the period.
7. Ibid., p. 29. Batman also mentions Galen's theory of "the traveling uterus." It was thought that both men and women had a uterus that could travel throughout the body, particularly when a person became upset. For example, when Othello swoons in Act IV, a Jacobean audience might have thought that his uterus was moving up through his throat into his head! For centuries after Galen's death, hysteria was labeled "the disease of the mother." Such a physical imbalance would relate to the effect of heat upon water and blood. In ancient medicine the moon's cycle was often associated with women's menstrual cycle, because both cycles take generally the same amount of time and because menstrual agitation was allied with the emotionality that is often associated with periods of the full moon.
8. Louis John Dezseran, "Shakespeare's Usage of Witchcraft as a Dramatic Element in *Macbeth* and the Staging of the Witch Scenes in Subsequent Representative Productions" (Ph.D diss., Wayne State University, 1968), pp. 20–30.

9. See the following texts for Elizabethan and Jacobean materials on external movement, manners, and costumes: Roy C. Strong, *The Elizabethan Image: Painting in England, 1540–1620* (London: Tate Gallery, 1969), which has good photographs to lift with an opaque projector; Kurt Forster, *Mannerist Painting: The Sixteenth Century* (New York: McGraw-Hill, 1966); which comes with twenty-four two-by-two slides in pockets, as do the next two sources; Margaretta Salinger, *French Painting: The Seventeenth Century* (New York: McGraw-Hill, 1966); and Damie Stillman, *English Painting: The Great Masters 1730–1860* (New York: McGraw-Hill, 1966).

10. Here is a list of fairly authentic records to listen to: The Julian Bream Consort, *An Evening of Elizabethan Music* (RCA Victor, LDS2656); Harvard Summer School, Harold Schmidt, Conductor, *Choral Music of the Renaissance and Baroque* (HSS 1001/1002); The Ambrosian Singers, Denis Stevens, Conductor, *The Cries of London and Music in Honor of Queen Elizabeth I* (MHS 884); and The Purcell Consort, *English Madrigals from the Courts of Elizabeth I and James I* (Turnabout, TV34202).

    The following sources may be checked out at any college library, and often at a well-equipped public library. Ask the Reference Desk if the library carries microfilms of these documents. Actually poring over several of these works, which are generally short, will give you a firsthand picture of the social pressures operating during the Elizabethan-Jacobean era, especially since many texts on Shakespeare have simply reiterated the same misconceptions for years. See Henry Cornelius Agrippa, *Of the Vanitie and Uncertaintie of Arts and Sciences*, trans. Fa. San Gent. (London: Henry Wykes, 1569); Batman, *Batman upon Bartholemew*, (see note 6 to this chapter); Nicholas Breton, *Melancholike Humours* (London: Richard Braddock, 1600); Francis Coxe, *A Short Treatise Declaring the Detestable Wickednesse of Magicall Sciences* (London, 1561); Lambert Daneau, *A Dialogue of Witches* (London, 1575); Gifford, *A Discourse of the Subtill Practises of Devils by Witches and Sorcerers* (London: Toby Cooke, 1587); Henry Holland, *A Treatise against Witchcraft* (Cambridge, Eng.: John Legatt, 1590); James I, King of England, then James VI, King of Scotland, *Demonology in the Form of a Dialogue* (London, 1597); William Perkins, *A Discourse of the Damned Art of Witchcraft* (Finchingfield, Essex: Thomas Pickering, 1608) (Perkins died in 1602; the actual date of his sermon is uncertain); Rev. D. Urbanus Rhegius, *An Homely or Sermon of Good and Evil Angels*, trans. R. Robinson (1537; London: Charlwood, 1593); Edward White (his function uncertain), *A Detection of Damnable Driftes Practised by Three Witches at Chelmsford* (London, 1579); and William Wright (his function uncertain), "Declaring the Damnable Life and Death of Doctor Fian," in *Newes from Scotland* (London, 1591).

Chapter 13

1. James Laver, *Victoriana* (New York: Hawthorn Books, 1967), plates 18–28. The valentines used as examples were done by Deborah Noe, a graduate student in 1971, and Daniel West, an undergraduate in 1972, both at the University of Minnesota.
2. Samuel Pepys, *Diary*, ed. J. P. Kenyon, rev. ed. (New York: Macmillan, 1963), p. 165.
3. Dezseran, "Shakespeare's Usage of Witchcraft," p. 167.
4. Frederick Antal, *Hogarth and His Place in European Art* (New York: Basic Books, 1962). This book is filled with full-page plates from "The Rake's Progress" and "The Harlot's Progress," all of which are perfect for an opaque projector. See also Georg Cristoph Lichtenberg, *The World of Hogarth*, trans. Innes and Gustav Herdan (Boston: Houghton Mifflin, 1966).
5. Pepys, *Diary*, passim.
6. Colley Cibber, *An Apology for the Life of Colley Cibber, Comedian* . . . (London: J. Watts,

1740); a recent edition, edited by B. R. S. Fone, has the same text as the first edition (Ann Arbor: University of Michigan Press, 1968).

7. For an excellent compilation of Elizabethan and Restoration dance steps, see Louis Horst, *Pre-classic Dance Forms* (New York: Kamin Dance Publishers, 1960); and Jehan Tabourot (Thoinot Arbeau, pseud.), *Orchesography,* trans. Mary Stewart Evans (New York: Kamin Dance Publishers, 1948), which has been republished in an unabridged and corrected edition with a new introduction and rates by Julia Sutton and a new Labanotation Section by Mireille Backer and Julia Sutton (New York: Dover Publications, 1967).

8. Refer to the basic make-up kits suggested by Richard Corson in *Stage Makeup,* 4th ed. (New York: Appleton-Century-Crofts, 1967), p. 297.

9. I found that structuring aesthetic distance for the audience in this manner was especially effective in a production of *She Stoops to Conquer* that I directed at the Bucks County Playhouse in November 1969, with Margaret Mullen playing Mrs. Hardcastle. Ms. Mullen's first entrance was in a squabble scene between Mrs. Hardcastle and her husband in which she was seen trimming her wig; she later appeared in the same wig, flirting with William Grannel, who played Mr. Hastings. Having seen the human being under this wig, which was decorated with a multitude of tiny birds, pearls, and Christmas ornaments, the audience was quite willing to accept the comic use of the headdress later in the play.

10. Corson, *Stage Makeup,* p. 326.

11. The James-Lange theory, a psychological theory that has special implications for the performer, basically states that doing an external will motivate an internal involvement. See Konrad Lange, *Das Wesen der Kunst* . . . , 2 vols. (Berlin: G. Grote, 1901). See also Herbert Sidney Langfeld's article "Empathy" in *Problems in Aesthetics,* pp. 315–325. Langfeld often quotes Karl Grooz and Vernon K. Lipps' theories concerning art as an empathic re-creation of a piece of work by the beholder, who in his own fashion duplicates the artist's original inspiration. Langfeld makes a strong case for simplicity in art and capitalizes on the epigenetic theories of Carl Jung—that is, Jung's supposition that all peoples are capable of discerning what is essentially both truthful and beautiful in art. I feel that if art does not communicate, most of mankind will be robbed of the art of its own day. The performer's job is certainly more simplistic in this regard; if the performer plays a soporific energyless scene, the audience will re-create his work and nod off. Langfeld gives several good examples: for instance, the actor with the scratchy voice who causes the audience to cough empathically; the person reading an exciting novel who begins to mouth the words to make the novel "come alive." Merely smiling as you perform a comedy should help an audience laugh and appreciate your work, for the audience will find itself smiling right along with you. If *you* feel that something is "happening" onstage, the audience will share in that feeling.

12. In some instances, mental competition may be effective as long as the partners do not approach *acting* as a contest.

13. This exercise differs from telling the audience your *reaction* to what has been said, for it demands on-the-spot analytical thought. Aside technique does not require a complete physical move toward the audience, for that would totally violate the fourth-wall tradition. Often a simple step or merely a nod of the head, such as Jack Benny employs, will do. Whatever lets the audience know that you are contacting it *as the audience* for a specific purpose will suffice. The greater the physical separation that you create onstage between yourself and your fellow actors during an aside, the more "dead" time will elapse when you retrace your steps to resume the action with them. Properly used, asides will enhance and support the rhythm of your scene rather than retard it.

Chapter 14

1. This exercise for rapid rate of utterance was introduced by the actor Ken Ruta at ACT in 1968. Mr. Ruta was with the Tyrone Guthrie Theatre in Minneapolis for the 1974–75 season.
2. John Van Meter and Elvina Krause used this method of tonal and rhythmic cognizance with the cast of Shaw's *You Never Can Tell* at the Sponsors' Theatre in Flint, Michigan, during the summer of 1965.
3. For an elaboration of the "imaginary center," see Chekhov, *To the Actor,* Chap. 1, and Stanislavski, *An Actor Prepares,* chap. 10 on "Communion."
4. See Eric Bentley's comments on Shaw's musical ear, as well as his citations from W. H. Auden in reference to Shaw's love of Mozart's music, in *Bernard Shaw,* 2d ed. (London: Methuen, 1967), p. 90.
5. This game has tremendous faults in relation to Freudian psychology. It should not be wedged into Freudian terminology in any strict sense, for it simply will not fit.
6. Oscar Wilde, *De Profundis* (New York: Modern Library, 1926). Concentrate on Wilde's comments about the creative process, skimming pp. 36–52, but carefully reading pp. 64–72 and pp. 112–115. For Shaw's "The Art of Rehearsal," see George Bernard Shaw, *Shaw on Theatre,* ed. E. J. West (London: MacGibbon and Kee, 1958), p. 153.
7. Philip Weissman, *Creativity in the Theatre: A Psychoanalytic Study* (New York: Basic Books, 1965). Weissman's chap. 1, "The Actor," and chap. 14, "Crisis in Creative Acting," are particularly good.

Chapter 15

1. Robert Cohen, *Acting Professionally: Raw Facts about Acting and the Acting Industries* (Palo Alto, Calif.: National Press Books, 1972), passim. (In 1974 National Press Books changed its name to Mayfield Publishing Company.)